THE MAKEOVER

CRITICAL CULTURAL COMMUNICATION
General Editors: Sarah Banet-Weiser and Kent A. Ono

The Makeover

Reality Television and Reflexive Audiences

Katherine Sender

NEW YORK UNIVERSITY PRESS
New York and London

NEW YORK UNIVERSITY PRESS
New York and London
www.nyupress.org

References to Internet Websites (URLs) were accurate at the time of writing.
Neither the author nor New York University Press is responsible for URLs that
may have expired or changed since the manuscript was prepared.

LIBRARY OF CONGRESS CATALOGING-IN-PUBLICATION DATA
Sender, Katherine.
The makeover : reality television and reflexive audiences / Katherine Sender.
p. cm. — (Critical cultural communication)
Includes bibliographical references and index.
ISBN 978-0-8147-4069-9 (cl : alk. paper)
ISBN 978-0-8147-4070-5 (pb : alk. paper)
ISBN 978-0-8147-3897-9 (ebook)
ISBN 978-0-8147-7133-4 (ebook)
1. Reality television programs—History and criticism. 2. Makeover television programs—
History and criticism. I. Title.
PN1992.8.R43S47 2012
791.45'655—dc23
2012018748

New York University Press books are printed on acid-free paper,
and their binding materials are chosen for strength and durability.
We strive to use environmentally responsible suppliers and materials
to the greatest extent possible in publishing our books.

Manufactured in the United States of America
c 10 9 8 7 6 5 4 3 2 1
p 10 9 8 7 6 5 4 3 2 1

CONTENTS

ACKNOWLEDGMENTS

My sincere thanks go, first, to the generous people who completed the surveys and agreed to talk about makeover television for this project. They trusted me with their revealing perceptions of the shows and their engagements with them, even as they were aware of a general disparagement of the genre and its viewers.

The data collection and initial analysis would not have been possible without the skill and commitment of a team of research fellows at the Annenberg School for Communication at the University of Pennsylvania: Christopher Finlay, Nicole Rodgers, Adrienne Shaw, Riley Snorton, and Margaret Sullivan. Their rigor, enthusiasm, and sense of humor helped to produce an amazingly rich body of data.

This project has been supported by the unfailing dedication of the Annenberg staff, especially our librarian Sharon Black, whose shrewd eye kept a lookout for new work on the topic; and Rich Cardona, Lizz Cooper, and Cory Falk, without whose patient and timely computer support this project would have floundered.

Thanks also to my colleagues at Annenberg, with whom I have talked about various aspects of this project, especially Joe Cappella, Bob Hornik, Elihu Katz, Carolyn Marvin, Sharrona Pearl, and Barbie Zelizer. Diana Mutz generously shared her research participants with me. My special appreciation goes to the dean, Michael Delli Carpini, who was extraordinarily generous with research funds and time to complete this project.

Within the Penn community more broadly, my thanks and affection go to my colleagues in the Gender, Sexuality, and Women's Studies Program—Rita Barnard, Demie Kurz, and Shannon Lundeen—for their intellectual engagement with the project and for a summer fellowship in 2006. Other key Penn friends and colleagues have guided me along the way, including Peter Decherney, Kathy Peiss, and Peter Stallybrass.

Litty Paxton's friendship, humor, and insight during our walks with a certain little black dog have been immeasurably meaningful to me.

I was fortunate to spend my sabbatical year (2008–2009) at the Institute for Communication Studies at the University of Leeds. Here Stephen Coleman, John Corner, and David Hesmondhalgh gently pushed back on some of my most US-centric assumptions, as did Helen Wood during our visits while I was in residence there. Myria Georgiou's hilarious puncturing of gender and appearance norms during our weekly sleepovers provided light and important relief.

This project has also been sustained by enthusiastic exchanges with a broader community of scholars and friends, including Mark Andrejevic, Elizabeth Bird, Lynn Comella, Nick Couldry, Laura Grindstaff, Misha Kavka, Tania Lewis, Vicki Mayer, Toby Miller, Susan Murray, Radhika Parameswaran, Heather Thompson, Satoshi Tomioka, Clare Wardle, Brenda Weber, Emily West, and Louise Woodstock. Vincent Doyle and I have been traveling companions as we each completed our books for New York University Press—as always, our companionship makes it all seem possible.

The series editors Sarah Banet-Weiser and Kent Ono have been unflagging supporters of the project, even as the deadlines dragged out. Eric Zinner at New York University Press has been a model editor, coming through with a contract at the crucial moment and then steadfastly awaiting the book's completion. Thanks also go to two anonymous reviewers and to Graeme Turner (who generously offered to review the manuscript at a late but messy stage), all of whom gave such helpful feedback.

To these and the many people I have talked to along the way about makeover television, I give my sincere appreciation. This support has sustained me in my commitment to the genre as meaningful in the lives of the many people who watch it.

And, saving the best for last, my utmost thanks go to Valentina Cardo. We met discussing reality television, and this conversation has woven through our work and play since then. You have talked me down from a ledge or two, found me materials I didn't know existed, proofread my final manuscript, and kept me laughing. After five years of transatlantic love we are about to undergo our very own makeover. I can't wait to see the reveal.

1

Self-Projects

Makeover Shows and the Reflexive Imperative

The Biggest Loser's "wow" factor is mesmerizing—over a period of maybe twelve weeks to see someone completely change what they look like by their own hard work. I think that element could appeal to any people of any size. But what draws you in initially, for a thin person, might not be the same as a fat person. Where a fat person is drawn into the show with a "what if" concept, like "What if that was me?" or is approaching it as "Maybe I'll learn something from it." And I think that maybe that's the side of the show that is lacking in my opinion, is that there aren't many—it's very fleeting. It comes on, I watch it, I'm enthralled, I love the concept of it. When it's done, I don't really think about it until it's on again. It doesn't teach me anything; it doesn't give me life lessons; it's not an instruction book for how you at home could do it. It's portrayed as a contest to win money, and that's the primary objective. And so that's my one criticism is that I'm not learning anything. I'm just watching someone like me have the motivation and desire to do what I can't do, and then they achieve it and I wish I was them, and then the show's over, and then I just continue my life as a person who doesn't do that.
—Seth, *The Biggest Loser* interviewee

Midway through interviewing people who watch makeover television shows, I had a conversation with Seth,[1] a white, single, heterosexual man in his thirties. He was a fan of the United States version of the popular competitive weight loss show *The Biggest Loser* who wanted to lose about eighty pounds in weight. In the course of the interview, Seth articulated his complex and contradictory perceptions of this show that help to frame some of the central themes in this study. Above he notes the "wow" factor of seeing contestants going through dramatic physical transformation and the possibility of identifying with the contestants. He expresses his disappointment that the show is not more explicitly pedagogical, as well as his regret that he cannot convert these fleeting images of transformation into changes in his own life. He went on to note how body size and appearance are structured through gendered norms and modes of looking on *The Biggest Loser*:

> I think that it's a by-product of our society that success in life is tied to body image in some sense for both genders. As a guy who struggles with weight, I'm interested in that dynamic of a show, to see other guys. But it's fascinating to me to see how much, even though I am like that, that I also prescribe to the way we are as a culture, in that I see these women go on there and I'm like, "Oh, shit! Look at the size of her!" And the complete and utter disaster. My initial reaction is, "How could they do that to themselves?" It's kind of a selfish thing, kind of an arrogant thing, to be a guy who struggles with that and feels that [way] personally, to be able to look at someone else and be like, "You fat whale."

He was frankly aware of the double standards of appearance applied to women and men, and struggled between this awareness and his own contempt for the women contestants on the show. Makeover shows represent the transformation of ordinary people, most often women, through appropriate consumption, and in doing so reproduce norms of attractiveness and legitimize the audiences' scrutinizing gaze. But shows such as *The Biggest Loser* also bring men into these traditionally gendered modes of representation and inspection. The male turn in the makeover forces Seth to consider his own contradictory position in which he critically assesses the overweight women on the show at the same time as he must deal with his own heavy body within similar regimes of representation.

Seth considered how *The Biggest Loser* exposed the candidates as overweight and underdressed. As did many interviewees, he believed that however harsh, these routines of representation promoted shame that was functional for contestants on *The Biggest Loser*:

> I think that people that are as big as the people on that show are, it's like they have bottomed out, to want to be involved in a show on a major network, that's viewed by millions of people that are going to see them in awful shape in ill-fitting clothes, and a lot of skin. It's a pretty embarrassing thing, and I think that those people are at their breaking point for the most part.

Seth assumed that "bottoming out"—reaching a nadir of self-esteem—explained why candidates would expose themselves on broadcast television in a range of unflattering and revealing outfits. Bottoming out invokes a 12-step program ethos where the recognition and confession of shame is the first step toward personal transformation. As did other participants in this study, Seth saw such public shaming on *The Biggest Loser* as helpful in forcing candidates to change.

Seth went on to assume that a willingness to be represented this way was a guarantee of the candidates' authenticity. He said, "I really think that the people involved are genuine. I wouldn't have watched it a second season if I got the impression the first season that all the people there were motivated by the monetary aspect." He and other interviewees put a high premium on the authenticity of candidates, evidenced by having good reasons to go on a reality television show: to really work to change rather than to simply be in it for money, fame, or career reasons.

Seth was also aware that the show was constructed, despite all the claims to reality that the genre assumes. In his discussion of the genuineness of the candidates he continued, "[The producers] could be manufacturing or eliciting that response from me, but I really buy into it. I think [the candidates] are people who really want to improve their life and think that this show is going to do that." Even with his awareness that the production routines of the show could shape his responses, he nevertheless remained highly invested in the emotional realism of the show.[2] This was not only predicated on contestants taking part for the right reasons—"really want[ing] to improve their life"—but also evidenced by contestants' emotional expressivity.

Together, Seth's comments exemplify some of the tensions that structure audiences' discussions of makeover television that are the foundation of this project: tensions that involve learning, identification, gender, shame, authenticity, realism, and feeling. Seth acknowledged being inspired by candidates but unable to apply the show's techniques to himself. He recognized gendered standards of appearance, where women are judged unfairly according to their looks; at the same time, he saw the shame induced by being on a makeover show as a necessary part of its success. He was aware that the show is constructed, and how the producers and editors shaped his responses. He was nevertheless invested in the authenticity of the candidates, gauged by their motives for taking part and their emotional expressiveness. In order to hold these tensions in a productive relationship, I draw on contemporary theorizations of reflexivity across a number of fields. I do not mean reflexive as in reflex: an uncontrolled, unthought, instinctive reaction to a stimulus. On the contrary, Seth's quote reveals a sophisticated appraisal of himself and his engagements with *The Biggest Loser*, a reflexivity shared by many of the people we talked to about makeover shows. Instead, reflexivity describes how makeover shows rework ideas about the self through the particular demands of contemporary television programming. These shows mobilize audiences' reflexive engagements with the texts, their viewing habits, their social relations, and their ideas about themselves as projects to be worked on. I do not share the view of some of its celebrants that reflexivity is a natural attitude inherent to modernity, nor do I believe that reflexivity necessarily produces the freedom and insight that its most ardent advocates assume. Instead, I explore how audiences talk about the reflexive self as an accomplishment produced in part through their engagement with makeover television.

Makeover television shows offer a rich opportunity to consider contemporary anxieties about "the self," variously characterized as fragmented, performative, narcissistic, therapeutic, anxious, self-surveilling, and governmental. The genre also fuels a broader anxiety about reality television and its effects on audiences. Specific makeover programs will come and go; indeed, two of the shows I consider here, *Queer Eye for the Straight Guy* and *Starting Over*, have been cancelled since I started this project. The genre morphs into novel forms and themes, as we have seen with shows that have emerged more recently (*How to Look Good Naked* and *Bridalplasty*, for example). Makeover shows nevertheless articulate a particular set of concerns that mobilize contemporary ideas about the self within a much longer history of selfhood. The makeover genre draws on earlier, Romantic investments in interiority, expression, and authenticity. The reaffirmation of personal authenticity has been seen as especially important at a time when traditional frames of reference have been eroded. As Anita Biressi and Heather Nunn write, "Older forms of authority and security—the law, democratic government, judiciary, medical experts and so forth—have been critiqued and displaced by an increasing public political cynicism and a turn to the self as the only possible marker of integrity."[3] I consider analyses of modern, mediated selfhood and offer an intervention into the field of scholarly critiques of reality television that are based largely on textual analysis of television shows. To complement these, I draw on extensive conversations with audiences about their engagements with makeover television. As with earlier studies of media reception, I found that audiences' responses to these programs were far more nuanced and compelling than textual approaches alone could account for. These conversations with audiences about makeover television require a reconsideration of the meanings these shows have for the people who watch them, and illuminate their significance in the production of a reflexive self.

Makeover Television: Contexts and Characteristics

Makeover television shows can be a source of information, a point of identification, a guilty pleasure. They are also a densely articulated set of texts that encourage audiences to reflect on themselves and allow scholars, in turn, to reflect on the production of the self through contemporary media. Rather than taking for granted a self that is stable and preexisting, I draw from contemporary scholars to consider how media are used by audiences as a resource for constructing a reflexive self.[4] Like other reality television programs, makeover shows have proliferated rapidly as a product of particular economic, industrial, and technological circumstances in the first decade of the new century. These circumstances demand fast, cheap, and popular programming to counter the worst effects of audience fragmentation and the challenges this poses to advertising revenues. Makeover shows draw on already popular genres, including self-help literature, soap operas, and talk shows, that are attentive to intimacy, value emotional expression, and offer narrative frames within which audiences, especially women audiences, interpret their experiences.

The genre of makeover television, broadly defined, has rapidly expanded in the first decade of the twenty-first century. Brenda Weber, for example, studied hundreds of different shows among the 2,500 hours of makeover television she analyzed.[5] This burgeoning of makeover programming, and of reality television in general, has been met with significant scholarly attention.[6] Most of this attention has been directed toward reality texts, with some notable exceptions from the UK.[7] Suspicious of popular and scholarly critiques that dismiss the genre and disparage the people who enjoy it, I wanted to supplement this textual focus by turning attention to the people who watch makeover programs. A team of researchers at the University of Pennsylvania and I conducted extensive audience research on four US makeover shows. In addition to *The Biggest Loser*, we also looked at *Queer Eye*, where five gay men make over a hapless heterosexual guy; *Starting Over*, which features six women living together to get their lives in order; and *What Not to Wear*, in which mostly women are transformed from frumps and floozies into models of respectable upward mobility.[8] These typify distinct subgenres of makeovers: weight loss, male lifestyles, psychological change, and women's self-presentation, respectively, although each show contains some elements of the others. Even with these different emphases, all four shows exemplify the subgenre of reality television known as makeover shows. They feature "ordinary" people, even though, as Laura Grindstaff argues, there is little that is ordinary about the people who volunteer and are chosen to participate in reality shows.[9] The action is largely unscripted, with the work of constructing narratives taking place in the editing room. They focus on transformation precipitated by expert intervention and exemplified in the moment of "reveal" at the end of the episode or season. Each of these shows are unapologetically commercial; they are distributed on for-profit network and cable channels, and are thus dependent on revenue from advertising, ratings, product placements and tie-ins, multi-platform distribution, branded products, and so on. Finally, these shows focus on personal transformation—of the body, appearance, and psyche—rather than transformations of candidates' homes (*Trading Spaces*, *Hoarders*) or professional lives (*The Apprentice*, *Project Runway*).

For all the formulaic presentation of problems with their banal resolutions, this genre articulates a collection of attitudes and techniques that take the production of the self as their central, vexed concern. These shows represent a way of thinking about and working on the self that is historically and culturally specific to our contemporary economic, media, and social climate in the United States, although self-transformation is neither a new nor a specifically American phenomenon.[10]

How are narratives of the self articulated through this commercial form in our particular space and time? How do their shifting aesthetic, technological, and economic conditions frame these narratives? How do audiences engage with makeover shows as a resource to consider and express their selves? Among the group of highly invested viewers with whom we talked, makeover shows were part of an active project of self-making. This was not a playful, performative, poststructuralist, post-identity type of self-making, but was a sincere articulation of their inner, essential selves and the fraught problem of manifesting that real self in the world. The shows are a resource for this project, in which participants were reflexive about their selves, their media consumption, and their involvement in the academic project of research. However lowbrow, commercialized, feminized, and exploitative they may be, makeover shows offer a prism through which to consider the question, "How to live?"

All audience research must tread a treacherous path between textual determinism, which usually assumes that texts do terrible things to people (especially women and children), and the excesses of active audience theory, which celebrates people's freedom to make what they like of the texts they consume. In this book I hold in tension the ideological imperatives of the text with the need to do justice to audiences' investments in and negotiations with the texts. I offer a critique of makeovers shows' didactic instruction toward narrow versions of appropriate gender and race self-presentation, assumptions of upward mobility, and consumer appeals, as well as the demands on the shows to make enjoyable, profitable television. At the same time, I take seriously the ways in which makeover shows are made meaningful and important in the lives of the (mostly) women who watch them. As with other audience research studies, I have struggled to retain a critique of the shows without damning their viewers and fans, and to recognize the commercial, popular conventions of the shows without dismissing them as a hopelessly corrupted genre. By addressing audiences' engagements with the texts, their selves, and the research context as reflexive, I hope to avoid the impasse of earlier debates about media reception. This book explores how audience research enriches our understanding of reflexivity, and how thinking through reflexivity challenges audience research. Rather than uncritically celebrating reflexivity, I consider how audience research risks collaborating with an ideologically tempting but ultimately naive view of the modern reflexive self.

Queer Eye, Neoliberalism, and Governmentality

I began this project in 2005 as I was completing an analysis of the Bravo cable channel's show *Queer Eye for the Straight Guy*.[11] I was interested in this program because it appeared to be an inevitable outcome of the construction of gay taste and expertise that has become prevalent in mainstream consumer culture.[12] In this show, gay men were openly recognized for their labors in the style industries, and were particularly useful in the ongoing challenge of cultivating heterosexual men's domestic and intimate consumption. This analysis drew from scholarship that looked at reality television as a vehicle for neoliberal values of disciplined, self-monitoring, responsible citizenship. Scholars such as Laurie Ouellette and James Hay see the reality genre as doing important ideological work for the state that has reduced traditional forms of social support, for a labor economy that requires workers to be mobile and flexible, and for a media industry that needs cheap popular programming.[13] In this critique of reality television, the work of governing subjects moves from state apparatuses to the subjects themselves, in a process Michel Foucault termed "governmentality."[14] Reality shows propose "technologies of the self"—ways of appraising and caring for the self—that audiences are assumed to adopt.[15] These scholars argue that reality genres model a version of citizenship that demands that subjects take responsibility for the self, tolerate risk, and look to mediated experts for guidance on navigating modern life.

Surveillance is crucial to the production of this normative self. As Ouellette and Hay write, "Part of what reality TV teaches us in the early years of the new millennium is that in order to be good citizens we must allow ourselves to be watched as we watch those around us."[16] Referring to makeover shows specifically, Weber concludes that obtaining "love and empowerment requires writing normative gender, race, and class congruence on the body in ways that can be visually policed and affirmed by a collective body of like-minded citizens."[17] From this perspective, by representing examples of bad citizenship, makeover shows both encourage audiences to view candidates with contempt and to reform themselves in order to avoid such contempt from others. Bad citizenship can also be avoided by taking advice about appropriate consumption: "The makeover is . . . a vehicle through which experts communicate with the public directly as advocates of the power of consumer-based lifestyles to fulfill people's needs."[18]

The governmental approach helped me make sense of *Queer Eye's* project. Despite the apparent aim of making these straight male candidates better husbands and boyfriends, the show's parallel project exhorted them to be more mature, flexible, and willing professionals. Yet as I was finishing that research I was left with a sense of unease—I didn't trust how neatly this critique elided the show's contradictory elements, and I felt discomfort about what it implied about the audiences who watched the program. How could we make sense of *Queer Eye's* camp pleasures, especially insofar as they seemed to disrupt some of the text's most heteronormative assumptions? Did people who watched these shows willingly adopt the instruction, consumer appeals, and modes of self-monitoring modeled in the texts? And in the governmental emphasis on discipline and responsibility, where was the place for fun, frivolity, and mayhem that many of us enjoyed about this show? In the move to account for reality television as a relatively new media phenomenon, it seemed that scholars had forgotten a venerable history of especially feminist-grounded audience research that paid attention to pleasure and contradiction and that resisted a disparagement of lowbrow media audiences along with the lowbrow media themselves.[19] Wanting to explore the contradictions within *Queer Eye* in the context of this tradition of feminist audience research, I undertook a large-scale investigation of audiences' engagements with this and three other makeover shows.

Turning to Audiences

I situate this study of makeover audiences within a feminist cultural studies approach to media reception. This approach asserts that there is no single preferred meaning in texts which media scholars are privileged to discern. Even while there are textual factors at work (generic conventions, narrative closure, and so on), audiences are also active makers of meaning, and they experience pleasures in doing so. It is important and valuable to study lowbrow media forms such as romance novels, soap operas, and tabloid magazines from the perspective of their largely female, middle- and working-class audiences, in order to investigate how hierarchies of gender, class, and taste intersect with pleasure. Neither activity nor pleasure, however, guarantees political activity or resistance.[20]

As audience research has evolved, the idea of "the audience" has become increasingly complex and problematized. Consumers of media fragment across diverse platforms and genres, making the idea of a coherent entity, *the* audience, less relevant (if it ever was). Moreover, audience research scholars have argued that the very idea of "the audience" is more a product of market research and scholarly study than it actually describes a stable collectivity of viewers joined by a shared participation in media.[21] I use the term "audiences" and sometimes "viewers" here for want of better terms: by pluralizing them I hope to convey that there is not a coherent audience of makeover television, or even of each of the four shows. The data demonstrate that there are different meanings made of the shows, both between the shows and among the people who responded to each show. I do not assume that the people who participated in this study mirror "the audience" of makeover shows in general—as with makeover show candidates, the very fact of their participation marks them as distinct.

This project employs a number of approaches to understanding how makeover shows are meaningful to some of their most ardent viewers: an online survey for each of the four shows; follow-up interviews with volunteers from each of these surveys; interviews with a comparison group who were not regular viewers of the shows and were not recruited online; textual analysis of at least two seasons of each show; and textual analysis of press coverage of the shows and the makeover genre in general. Existing audience studies from Britain have taken reality television as a broad category or have focused on what is known there as "lifestyle television."[22] Yet the range of programs under the reality umbrella (from *Trading Spaces* to *Survivor*) and even within lifestyle programming (from *Wife Swap* to *What Not to Wear*) seemed so broad as to miss important differences between the shows. Audience research has moved from an initial focus on specific programs to genres and even, more ethnographically, to the use of media in everyday life.[23] I took the rather old-fashioned route of focusing on specific programs because I became interested in this project through my earlier textual analysis of *Queer Eye*. It seemed to me that this show was distinct in significant ways from other kinds of makeover shows—in its focus on heterosexual men, its casting of openly gay men as hosts, and in the gender and sexual contradictions in the show. I drew from this observation that within the makeover genre there would likely be specific elements of shows that addressed distinct aspects of self-transformation, and chose four shows that, I believed, would represent some important differences among them. This approach was borne out by finding that the people we talked to did, indeed, perceive and respond to the four shows with quite different emphases.

Our research team designed four online surveys, each tailored to one of the shows. The surveys were intended to probe such things as whether people who watched these shows learned things from them, followed their consumer advice, identified with candidates, assessed their emotional authenticity, critiqued the realism of the shows, and so on. We also asked about other shows they watched, and whether they avoided particular kinds of makeover shows. (See appendix I for research protocols, including a generic version of this survey.) We posted links to the survey on the official message boards for each show as well as on reality television blogs, all with the agreement of moderators. The response was overwhelming: within a week of posting the links, more than 1,800 people had completed one or more of the surveys (see appendix II for a breakdown of demographics on survey respondents). We considered the responses to the survey as we developed the protocols for the interviews to follow. Unsurprisingly, many respondents shared the view of a woman who wrote about *What Not to Wear*, "I like getting tips from the style experts and hair/makeup people. I, obviously, enjoy seeing the transformation of the 'guest,' and I like the personalities of the hosts." In response to whether she had picked up tips from the show, another wrote, "I can't think of anything specific, but I definitely have 'Oh, I learned that on *What Not to Wear*' moments when I'm shopping (as have my friends)." As critics of the genre have assumed, the shows' instruction, visible transformation, host–experts, and social sharing were common themes mentioned by respondents across all four shows.

However, the survey responses also complicated these themes. First, even those respondents who generally reported that they liked the shows "very much" criticized the instruction, consumer appeals, and representations of candidates they found in the programs. Another survey respondent said of *What Not to Wear*, "Subjects are encouraged to buy clothing that is often too expensive for the average person, e.g., a $200 pair of black pants or a $400 leather jacket. Although Stacey and Clinton consider this type of clothing 'classic' and 'timeless,' they don't account for the fashion industry deliberately changing pant leg widths, jacket styles, etc., every season." Another writer felt that *The Biggest Loser* "exploits the overweight people by putting them in skimpy outfits and having the men take off their shirts before being weighed." It was clear from the surveys that the model of the obliging viewer who willingly adopts the shows' pedagogic projects and participates in their shaming of "deviant" bodies was complicated by audiences' ambivalent reception of these programs.

The second striking feature of the surveys emerged from respondents' discussions of the candidates' transformation through each episode. A *Queer Eye* viewer contributed a widely shared opinion about the genre: "I love the whole total transformation experience that I see the candidates experience both in physical appearance and in psychological changes." Survey respondents across all four shows repeated that what they liked about the shows was the emphasis not only on changes in appearance but "inner" transformation as well. A woman wrote of *What Not to Wear*:

> I like that we get to see the whole transition of a person, starting from their reluctance to get out of their rut and how bad it is for them, to their final highly self-confident day when they feel they look great. I like that the physical transition tends to affect the person on the inside as well as how they look on the outside. Some of these people don't know how beautiful they are, or how professional they look. Sometimes they cry when they see themselves this way for the first time. It's very touching.

The investment in interiority was often connected with expressions of feeling, both by the candidates and by the people watching the shows. Interiority and expression, and their importance for authenticity, became a primary frame as we moved toward the interview phase of the project.

The survey responses were thus instructive as we developed questions for the follow-up interviews. Questions addressing the governmental critique, with its emphasis on self-discipline, rational adoption of advice, and a focus on self-surveillance needed to be complemented by questions that would probe people's emotional and pleasurable experiences with the shows, and with their intense investments in the inner self as a source of authenticity. We undertook 110 follow-up interviews with survey respondents who indicated that they would be willing to talk to us more about makeover shows. This group was roughly divided across the four shows, with some interviews about more than one of the shows.

I was concerned, however, that this approach to recruiting interviewees would mostly access people who were fans of the shows with easy access to the Internet. In order to get some sense of how people perceived the shows who were not regular viewers and who did not necessarily have online access, we also carried out interviews with twenty people who were recruited through a temp agency and local advertising and were not very familiar with the shows in this study (five people for each show—see appendix II for details). This comparison group furnished an illuminating range of responses to the shows that complements the data from the surveys and interviews with regular viewers.

As I began working with this material, what struck me most was participants' nuanced engagements with the shows. As did Seth, who opened this chapter, interviewees shared their enjoyment of the genre, sometimes in ways that conflicted with their own most humane principles. Others noted the contradictions between what they felt were the imperatives of the show and their own practices. One woman laughed as she told us that she and her husband watched *The Biggest Loser* together: "Well, this is going to sound really strange, based on what I told you, but [we have] kind of a competition to see who was right about who would win, while eating cake!" Further, there were many examples of interviewees who used the shows to make sense of their experiences, struggles, and social relationships. A fifty-one-year-old woman living with Crohn's disease poignantly discussed her application to be on *Starting Over*, which was rejected because the casting director perceived her to be too unwell:

I really wish I could have gone on [the show] because I think I could have been a positive role model instead of somebody who was all whiny and bitchy over their situation. But I've taken a lot of the things that they've done and just, whether it be writing down things, or sitting and reflecting on things that I've picked up, I do that an awful lot. In many different areas—I'm trying to think what areas I've done that. But it just doesn't seem like a day goes by where I don't learn something and think about it in correlation of myself. And see if I can't make that another useful tool in arsenal, because when you're sick it's not just all about drugs. It's about attitude and relaxation techniques and not getting all excited over nothing.

Of the four shows we looked at, *Starting Over* drew most explicitly on therapeutic and self-help techniques, making it especially available for this kind of relationship with the self. Across all the shows, however, it became increasingly clear that the regular viewers used the shows in an ongoing process of self-reflexivity. These programs offered a language for, a set of metaphors to describe, and a way of seeing the self.

In the production of a reflexive self, audiences did not merely parrot the norms of the shows; they negotiated with—even expressly refused—some of the texts' explicit themes. Sometimes this opposition was framed in terms of participants' awareness of the constructedness of media and its economic demands. One woman who watched both *The Biggest Loser* and *Queer Eye* considered how candidates on these shows were portrayed:

I'm sure a lot of the true personality comes through—but you're absolutely seeing what the editors want you to see. It's manipulated. I watch way too much reality TV, so I understand that it's almost never as it seems. I can recall when we first started watching—I was just discussing with a girlfriend—when we first started watching *Queer Eye*, we were sure that it [took] just two days, and that Thom was behind the scenes painting. And I think episodes one, two, and three, they did a ton of work and that maybe a lot of it was what we thought it was. But certainly now, none of it is what it appears. It's edited for content, just like the disclaimer at the end says in teeny, tiny lettering.

Even as this interviewee affirms that audiences see much of the "true personality" of the shows' candidates, she is also adept at pointing out the artifices of the show that elide the practical constraints on production. Further, her appraisal is partly worked out in conversation with another audience member; audiences developed often highly sophisticated critiques of the genre within their social relationships, both on- and offline. Audiences frequently observed the ways in which reality television isn't especially "real," noting its generic conventions, casting tropes, editing sleights of hand. They considered the economic contexts of the shows' production and the demand for high audience ratings, the influence of advertisers, and the necessity for product placement, much of which viewers disdained. In making sense of these data, it became clear that the governmental approach to reality television that emphasized audiences' acquiescence to the text and disciplined self-surveillance could not account for their astute critiques of the genre.

Reflexivity and Its Limits

I began to see that the mode of engagement many audiences took to the show was not obliging but *reflexive*. Audiences were reflexive about themselves, using the terms in which the shows addressed the self to make sense of their life trajectories. They were reflexive about the programs they watched, considering the effects of the economic, technological, and production contexts on the genre. And some were reflexive about the research process, recognizing that the surveys and interviews offered them a chance to construct a view of the shows and to critique the research process itself. These audiences used makeover television as a resource to articulate the self as a reflexive project, as something that must be critiqued, narrativized, transformed, and expressed within the mediated logics of late capitalism.

Charles Taylor situates the Western, modern self within a long historical trajectory of selfhood, vestiges of which remain in our contemporary version.[24] He describes this modern self as having an interiority that can—indeed must—be excavated, and is the source of the truth of a person. Even though the Greeks had a concept of interiority, it was not until Augustine in the fourth century that the idea of the self became an inner space one could enter to look up toward God.[25] This inner space was radically revised and somewhat secularized in eighteenth-century Romanticism, which posited the inner self as the essence of moral authority and truth, unencumbered by the alienating demands of industrializing societies. This interior self was the source of the inner voice, variously conceived by the Romantics as the voice of nature, creativity, and feeling. The exploration and articulation of the inner self produces a sense of endless depths of the soul: "The inescapable feeling of depth comes from the realization that whatever we bring up, there is always more down there. Depth lies in there being always, inescapably, something beyond our articulative power."[26]

Michel Foucault looks at the modern self in institutional terms, produced through religious confession.[27] He argues that the self is not a preexisting fact that must be expressed but is, instead, brought into being through the very act of articulation. Nikolas Rose draws on Foucault to consider how the idea of the self has been reworked in the twentieth century through the "psy disciplines": psychiatry, psychology, and psychoanalysis, as well as popularized forms of self-help.[28] Rose writes, "'The self' does not pre-exist the forms of its social recognition; it is a heterogeneous and shifting resultant of the social expectations targeted upon it, the social duties accorded it, the norms according to which it is judged, the pleasures and pains that entice and coerce it, the forms of self-inspection inculcated in it, the languages according to which it is spoken about and about which it learns to account for itself in thought and speech."[29] Both Foucault and Rose are attentive to the ways that discourses of the self serve institutional demands: for them, church and state. But Rose also mentions how the discourses of the psy disciplines have been reproduced through popular media: "A new genre of publishing has made rapid strides. Bookshops fill with paperbacks, each advocating a different therapeutic system and educating the reader in the procedures by which he or she can be transformed from dissatisfaction to fulfillment by systematically acting upon the psyche."[30]

Taylor also addresses how the modern self has been produced through mediated forms. He argues that the ideal of ordinariness, fundamental to the reality genre, emerged with the rise of the novel in the eighteenth century.[31] Moving away from archetypal plots and dramas, novels required that general principles be read from the particular and everyday. Novels also endorsed the values of sentiment and strategies of narrativization that affirmed the Romantic inner self, sentiments and narratives that transformed the ordinary into the uniquely individual. Graeme Turner argues that the contemporary media landscape, characterized in part by unprecedented opportunities for ordinary people to represent themselves, offers new possibilities of self-recognition, even construction: "Where the media might once have operated as a mediator or perhaps a broadcaster of cultural identities, its contemporary function is closer to that of a translator or even an author of identities."[32] Reality television doesn't fictionalize ordinariness, as in the novel, it represents ordinary people—or at least unusual groups of ordinary people willing to be represented in their ordinariness to potentially vast numbers of strangers.

Taylor sees the Romantic self as already reflexive, focused on exploring the inner depths, expressing the voice of truth discovered there, and drawing on mediated forms to articulate narratives of the self. Anthony Giddens builds on this to argue that modern identity has become increasingly self-reflexive; in contrast to the premodern self who was constrained by role and structural position, the modern self "has to be reflexively made . . . amid a puzzling diversity of options and possibilities."[33] Makeover television's raison d'être is to help people navigate this puzzling diversity of possibilities: What to wear? How to eat? Who to be? Makeover television is paradigmatically self-reflexive in Giddens's terms: its narratives and modes of representation posit identity, body, affect, and behavior as an intensely involving project of the self. The genre narrates that self as having a (traumatic) past and (idealized) future in a journey of self-discovery that requires constant self-scrutiny and revision. The shows reproduce and rework other narrativized and mediated modes of self-production, borrowing from the psy disciplines as well as women's magazines, talk shows, and self-help literature. Most seductively, makeover television shares with Romanticism the assumption that only through self reflexivity can subjects find their authentic, inner being: a self capable of being "true to oneself."[34] As Rachel Dubrofsky argues in her study of the series *The Bachelor* and *The Bachelorette*, the function of reality shows is less to effect personal transformation than it is to affirm "the constant (unchanged) self across disparate social spaces, verified by surveillance."[35]

Giddens and other advocates argue that reflexivity allows agency and choice, thereby affording individuals greater personal freedom. Ulrich Beck, for example, posits that reflexivity promotes autonomy from social structures and hierarchies: "The more societies are modernized, the more agents (subjects) acquire the ability to reflect on the social conditions of their existence and to change them accordingly."[36] Reflexivity encourages agency and allows for "detraditionalization": freeing oneself from structural determinations, norms, and expectations. Both Giddens and Beck hold an optimistic view of reflexivity, insofar as this allows subjects to critique the social and economic conditions of modernity. However, as Beverly Skeggs notes, historians and theorists of consumer and popular culture have traced the rise of introspection and self-expression to the formation of the professional classes.[37] In contrast, "the working-class have consistently been represented as incapable of acquiring the psychological depth needed for self-governance; hence their association with the 'mass.'"[38] Lifestyle television broadcasts beyond traditional class boundaries the expectation that learning to be self-reflexive is both therapeutically good and facilitating of upward class mobility.

Despite the troubling implications of self-introspection as a class project, the possibilities of reflexivity have been compelling for scholars who are interested in resisting some of the more top-down models of media effects. Media literacy aims to train audiences in a reflexive appraisal of the economic, industrial, technological, and aesthetic contexts of media production. This appraisal, it is hoped, protects audiences from an uncritical absorption of texts' most nefarious messages. Two British scholars, Annette Hill and John Corner, argue that the aesthetics of reality television encourage audiences' reflexive attitudes toward the genre.[39] As with other reality genres, makeover show routines prompt media reflexivity by showing candidates talking directly to camera and by allowing glimpses of production equipment such as microphones and cameras. In addition, the frictions between fact and fiction and between entertainment and education, which the give the reality metagenre its frisson, leave enough contradictions for audiences to appraise its truth claims. The ways in which the genre leaves its seams showing encourage viewers to consider the "reality" of reality television as constructed.

Reflexivity also has a long tradition in social science research and writing.[40] Pierre Bourdieu has advocated "epistemic reflexivity" through which sociology "continually turns back onto itself the scientific weapons it produces."[41] This is consistent with Bourdieu's analysis of habitus and field; within the field of intellectual inquiry, the scholar must rigorously investigate her own habitus and the routines of thought that shape this. Wacquant describes this approach: "What has to be constantly scrutinized and *neutralized, in the very act of construction of the object*, is the collective scientific unconscious embedded in theories, problems, and (especially national) categories of scholarly judgment."[42] For Bourdieu and Wacquant, this does not only mean that researchers must pay attention to their social position (gender, class, and so on) but also to the investments and limits of their intellectual field. These include the assumptions that underpin the intellectual enterprise itself and that radically separate thinking from the object of thought: "The subject of reflexivity must ultimately be the social scientific field *in toto*."[43] Importantly for Bourdieu, reflexivity must be a social commitment, not an individual one, and he derides what he sees as an American fashion in the social sciences for a solipsistic focus on scholars' personal feelings and biography. As with the other kinds of reflexivity, true epistemic reflexivity represents freedom, "the means of a potentially liberating awakening of consciousness."[44] Bourdieu's characteristically pessimistic view of social change is leavened here by an optimism of method.

Even with the different foci of these three types of reflexivity— towards the self, media, and method—they share some fundamental features. For Giddens, reflexivity means being able to reflect on one's life and history and to construct a coherent (if changing) narrative about the self. For Beck, reflexivity means being able to consider and possibly detach from the limits posed by one's class and gender. For Corner and Hill, reflexivity involves assessing reality television's generic conventions and aesthetics to critique its truth claims. For Bourdieu and others interested in methodological concerns, reflexivity is a responsibility for researchers to consider our own habitus and investments in shaping the assumptions and techniques of research. These three foci of reflexivity share fundamental features: the ability to see a phenomenon (the self, social structures, a text, a method) in context; to consider the possible influences this context has on the phenomenon; and to be attentive to processes, not only outcomes, because phenomena are always contingently situated in time and space. Further, these perspectives assume that reflexivity affords freedom from tradition, from the text, and from a partial worldview. Reflexivity is fundamentally illuminating.

Reflexivity proved a very productive concept in making sense of participants' engagements with the shows. It helped to situate the various ways they distanced from the texts even as they reinvested in them. It illuminated some of the pleasures of media critique, and ways to understand how these critiques were a form of knowing self-production within the research context. As I worked with this concept, however, I became suspicious of it. My critique of reflexivity was initially prompted by the data from interviewees and survey respondents. I noticed that even though people critiqued the advice offered by the shows' hosts, few people challenged the value placed on expertise in the shows. They hated product placement but didn't comment on consumption as a taken-for-granted method of self-transformation. They critiqued the realism of the shows' production processes but reinvested in the emotional realism reproduced through these processes. They reflected on their life trajectories and interior experiences, but not on the processes of narrativization and interiority themselves. If self-reflexivity facilitated a freedom from tradition, why did the outcomes of the makeovers seem so formulaic? If media reflexivity allowed a distance from the shows, why did people continue to watch and invest in them? Rather than presuming that reflexive audiences were freed from the texts, the reflexivity prompted by the shows seemed recursive, rerouting audiences back into the texts even as they felt mastery over them.

My suspicion was also aroused by the assumption that reflexivity is a value that we all, of course, uphold. It has entered the terminology of a wide range of activities—at the very least, documentary filmmaking, scholarly research, ethnographic writing, media literacy, and self-help. As the word becomes broadly adopted, it is both taken for granted and increasingly indistinct, what Gramsci called common sense.[45] We assume reflexivity to be such a natural good that its ideological work is overlooked. Part of this ideological work can be seen in its paradoxical reproduction of gendered and classed norms. Lisa Adkins, for example, argues that:

reflexivity should not be confused with (or understood to concern) a liberal freedom to question and critically deconstruct the rules and norms which previously governed gender. Indeed rather than detraditionalizing, it will be suggested that reflexivity is linked to a reworking or refashioning of gender, indeed that reflexivity is perhaps better conceived as a habit of gender in late modernity.[46]

I began to look at reflexivity within a discussion of "women's culture" that spans, for example, Janice Radway's research on readers of romance novels and Lauren Berlant's discussion of "cruel optimism" in relation to melodrama.[47] As do other forms of traditionally women-targeted media, makeover shows contain the promise of fulfillment, agency, and self-determination. But they are also "juxtapolitical," where "feminine realist-sentimentality thrives in *proximity* to the political" but never fully engages with a feminist critique, instead offering emotional succor and a sense of community.[48] Many of the women we talked to critiqued some of the shows' impossible demands to conform to unachievable (for most of us) standards of attractiveness, for example. They nevertheless situated happiness within consumer and domestic economies that are not invested in women's empowerment. The reflexive opportunities within makeover television did not prompt in audiences a stark appraisal of the workings of social structures, but reproduced these workings through their appeals to emotional authenticity.

I have also become interested in the ideological work reflexivity does in the area of audience research, which has traditionally been very attentive to the epistemological challenges of understanding the processes of reception. In their consideration of their research methods, Skeggs, Thumim, and Wood question the "finding" of reflexive subjects of lifestyle television. They argue that audiences' critical distance on reality shows did not display freedom from class structures but was a performance of cultural capital: "Self-reflexivity *itself* depends upon access to resources and concomitant forms of capital that are classed, raced, and gendered."[49] Similarly, my critique of self and media reflexivity as a contemporary common sense is complemented here by critical attention to the research process itself. Respondents were sometimes reflexive about their participation in research, and used the frame of the makeover to describe this experience. One woman, for example, compared the self-consciousness of being on reality television with her experience of being recorded in our interview. Another affirmed the value of authenticity in the interview setting, commenting that she was "trying to be as honest as I can be" in her conversation with us. Research reflexivity provided participants an opportunity to situate themselves and their media practices within their understanding of popular and scholarly critiques of lowbrow reality television. But as with their reflexive frames regarding the makeover shows themselves, this reflexivity remained recursive, where participants affirmed their position as having awareness and agency within the research context, but did not critique the research enterprise itself (at least to us). Audience studies that rely on self-reporting in surveys and interviews, as this one does, risk reproducing similar norms of reflexivity as do the makeover shows themselves. Both audience studies and makeover shows require that participants see themselves as if from outside, reflect on their contexts, narrate stories about themselves, and are authentic and expressive. Rather than seeing this as a paralyzing epistemological crisis, however, I argue that the processes of self-making inherent to both makeover television and audience research can productively inform a larger critique of reflexivity as contemporary common sense.

The Reveal: Coming Up Next

The chapters that follow take reflexivity and its limits as a primary lens through which to understand these highly invested audiences' engagement with makeover shows. The following chapter takes a brief detour away from audience data to contextualize makeover shows within a longer history of gendered self-improvement. I consider their highly normative values of femininity, upward mobility, discreet sexuality, and "ethnic anonymity."[50] Describing the four shows as an articulation of women's culture allows for a consideration of how this culture becomes democratized as a luxury that not only white, middle-class women must afford.

Chapters 3 through 5 consider the participants' responses in terms of the three central debates in makeover television scholarship: governmentality, surveillance, and realism. Chapter 3 complicates the critique that reality television produces obliging, rational, self-governing citizens. In contrast to this view, I found that many of the people we spoke to were highly reflexive about the instruction and consumer advice presented in the shows. Even when viewers discussed adopting guidance from the shows, this was far from a willing absorption and reproduction of the shows' rationalities. The degree to which audiences discussed adopting the shows' instructional and consumer imperatives was uneven, and audiences were as likely to critique the training and consumer messages they saw. I also consider how social uses of the shows—among viewers' intimate circle as well as online—temper our understanding of their didactic impact.

In chapter 4 I address audiences' perceptions of the makeover shows' representational routines. I embed viewers' responses at the intersection of two critiques of the shows' visual strategies: that makeover television promotes a distancing schadenfreude in audiences, on the one hand, and self-surveillance, on the other. Audiences distinguished what they saw as necessary social shaming from cruel humiliation, sometimes distancing from candidates, at other times identifying with them. Even as they critiqued the ways the shows represented candidates, however, there was some evidence that the audiences imagined how they would look if rendered through the scopic technologies of the shows (hidden cameras, mirrors, the eyes of the hosts). This suggests that the prophylactic assumptions of media reflexivity (being able to see and critique representational strategies) did not necessarily protect audiences from adopting these strategies in a process of self-reflexivity.

Chapter 5 engages with debates about reality shows and their realism. I found that the audiences we talked to were highly reflexive about the media they consume: the artifices of makeover shows, their editing conventions, the need to attract audiences, and so on. At the same time, they were highly invested in the narratives' emotional realism as a resource for self-reflexivity.[51] As with audiences' critiques of the shows' instructional and representational strategies, their skepticism about realism afforded a more invested engagement with the self-reflexive aspects of the shows.

Chapter 6 draws together threads from the preceding chapters to consider how audiences mobilized the shows' themes to produce a reflexive self. They drew self-reflexive themes from the episodes, employing mediated narratives to articulate selves that have interiority, seek congruence between an inner and outer self, and need to be expressed. I look at this as a reworking of Romantic ideas of the self within the neoliberal attention to self-production through a mediated, commercial gaze. I return to the suggestion that reflexivity is detraditionalizing to argue that makeover shows' dependence on rituals borrowed from Christianity, law enforcement, education, and elsewhere in fact reproduce highly institutionalized ideas about the self. This chapter argues that the reflexive self is not an inevitable manifestation of modernity but an accomplishment achieved by these audiences, in part through their engagement with makeover television.

Chapter 7 turns a skeptical gaze on reflexivity in the process of audience research itself. Here I consider the ways in which audiences are aware of their participation in the research process, explicitly shaping their narratives of their viewing pleasures and life stories and critiquing interviewers' techniques, and using the interview as an opportunity to display expertise. I conclude by considering the extent to which reflexivity may be a classed and gendered performance demanded by the research context, and the implications of this for audience research.

The concluding chapter revisits arguments about makeover television and audience research in light of reflexivity. I argue that by seeing how people work with makeover texts, we can move beyond a current textual emphasis on instruction and self-discipline. I also consider how thinking about reflexivity in makeover television aids a reconsideration of some of the central debates within audience research. These include what we mean by "the audience" and how we understand audiences as self- and institutionally aware participants in the research process itself. I conclude that reflexivity does not simply "free" audiences from the imperatives of makeover texts, or research participants from the academic enterprise. It does, however, require that we rethink reflexive selfhood as a negotiation between institutions and human qualities— longing, possibility, connectedness—that cannot be entirely encompassed by institutions or texts.

The Makeover: Reality Television and Reflexive Audiences is shaped by stories: the shows' stories of transformation, stories that our participants told us about watching the shows, stories that they told about themselves through their engagement with the shows, stories that I tell from the data. There are many paths through these stories; the route

I follow explores audiences' narratives in which the self has a highly reflexive attitude toward the self and its contexts. I do not see makeover shows as yet another example of how media dupe audiences into being ideologically docile. Far from being duped, audiences are well able to recognize and articulate the shows' constructions. Reflexivity, however, does not afford audiences unlimited agency or freedom to self-define, but can also be considered a new type of habitus that comes with demands and expectations. Makeover shows mobilize stories of the self that rework older, Romantic ideas about intimacy with the self, that provide a sense of postfeminist agency, and that manage the inevitable disappointments of making do in a world which fails to hold the interests of ordinary people as its central concern.

2

Gender and Genre

Making Over Women's Culture

On August 2, 2006, the US cable channel Bravo aired an exceptional episode of their makeover show *Queer Eye* that featured Miles, a female-to-male transgender person, with the project to "trans-form the trans-man." Since its debut in 2003, the show had featured five openly gay men, the Fab Five, who with camp ruthlessness took hapless heterosexual men to task for the state of their clothes, hair, skin, cooking, and apartments. By their fourth season, the Fab Five had broadened their scope of deserving candidates to include women, gay men, couples, and Miles. Miles is struggling to project himself as an adult man: his small stature and youthful appearance mean that he is often misread as a twelve-year-old boy. He is also suffering from a case of postadolescent acne brought on by testosterone shots. The Fab Five launch into their usual frenzied routine: advising Miles about outfits, giving him a haircut, offering a skin regimen, and redecorating his apartment. This makeover had a twist, however. This was not just about improving the guy, but teaching the guy how to be a guy. One host tells Miles, "Most guys don't learn grooming from their fathers, so you probably didn't get *anything*" by way of instruction when he was growing up. The episode doesn't stop at advice in male presentation, but is also expressly pedagogical about what it can mean to be female-to-male transgendered: we hear Miles's struggles to come out as a man at a women's college, watch him inject his thigh with testosterone, and accompany him to a self-defense class. In the episode's reveal, a freshly groomed and handsomely dressed Miles bounds into a party of his nears and dears, a very queer group that includes people who read—to me at least—as lesbian, gay, gender nonconforming, transgender, and heterosexual. The only photos Miles's Christian parents have of him up to this point is as a girl, and the most moving part of the episode is when he gives his family a photograph of himself as a man—evidence of both his gender transformation and his makeover. This episode comes with an unusual coda, in which the Fab Five offer "a word on tolerance: tolerance is okay, but acceptance is better." We hear about the importance of accepting people whatever their differences and life choices.

This *Queer Eye* episode featuring Miles is both routine and exceptional within the conventions of the makeover show. As in other examples of the makeover genre, we see the emphasis on dramatic physical transformation, the stress on appropriate gender presentation, the expressly didactic approach, the commercial frame, the use of surveillance, and the expression of feeling. The show exemplifies the overarching project of all makeover shows, in which the candidate's self-presentation must match his inner sense of himself. We watch the familiar sequences of the experts taking apart Miles's wardrobe and kitchen, finding embarrassing evidence under his bed, diagnosing the causes of his bad skin and hair. Like many of the other candidates, Miles is an obliging and appreciative student, and judging by the responses of his friends and family, the makeover is a success.

The Miles episode is exceptional, however, because it takes the production of masculinity as its explicit concern. *Queer Eye* is the only makeover show that has focused mainly on male makeovers, bringing men into the realms of intimate consumption and self-care that have proven such a challenge for marketers.[1] This episode emphasizes that, to paraphrase Simone de Beauvoir's famous assertion, one is not born a man, but becomes one.[2] Gender is produced through the cultivation of habitus: Bourdieu's expression that describes the lived, embodied knowledge we amass from growing up in specific bodies and environments.[3] Here Miles's history of being raised as a girl works against his sense of himself, so part of the Fab Five's work is to induct him into practices that allow him to create a new habitus aligned with his identity as a man.

However sympathetic we might feel to Miles's dilemmas of self-presentation, the normative projects of makeover shows have been the source of much critique: most makeover shows impose on their usually female candidates highly conventional versions of implicitly white, upwardly mobile, and sexually discreet femininity.[4] Yet as Miles's example suggests, gendered strategies of self-improvement have been democratized beyond women to include men and, if unusually, a transman. This chapter considers the four shows included in this study—*The Biggest Loser, Queer Eye, Starting Over,* and *What Not to Wear*—as examples of how reality television has reworked existing women's genres. As with other women's genres, these makeover shows are not exclusively about women or for women audiences alone. Rather, they prioritize historically feminine concerns, including self-presentation, consumerism, and an intimate relationship with the self produced through interiority, affect, authenticity, and the everyday. Like other cultural forms, the shows produce gendered norms and priorities through class assumptions, including the impetus toward upward social mobility, and implicitly raced norms, valuing white standards of appearance and behavior over others. In order to contextualize the audiences' responses to the shows that are the focus of the following chapters, here I briefly outline a historical trajectory whereby self-transformation has become feminized. I consider the normative elements of the shows that privilege discreetly sexy, implicitly white, professional modes of self-presentation. I discuss how women, and increasingly men, are required to be subject to scrutiny and to be emotionally expressive in light of that scrutiny. I also argue that within these highly gendered frames there is nevertheless some space for what Lauren Berlant calls "female complaint."[5]

This analysis provides the ground to make sense of audiences' reflexive engagements with the shows.

Feminizing Transformation

Makeover television sits squarely within what Berlant calls "women's culture."[6] This describes those cultural products through which women, especially, are organized as a market but experience themselves as part of an affective community. As with other examples of women's culture, makeover shows are concerned with "managing femininity," including the pleasures and ambivalences that come with this.[7] Women's culture "flourishes by circulating as an already felt need, a sense of emotional continuity among women who identify with the expectation that, as women, they will manage personal life and lubricate emotional worlds."[8] Focusing mainly (although not exclusively) on female concerns, and drawing a largely female audience, makeover shows perform the cultural operations that run through all women's genres: complaint without refusal, disappointment managed through hope, and a vaguely feminist sensibility accommodated by a feeling of collective suffering. Makeover television draws on themes and structures from existing women's genres, reworking these through the specific demands and conventions of reality television that are solidly located within a commercial context.

There is nothing inherently feminine about personal transformation. Makeover shows' emphasis on showing ordinary people undergoing change is a contemporary articulation of the quintessential characteristics of the American spirit: individualism and reinvention.[9] There is nothing inherently American about them either, as the import of *What Not to Wear* from the UK and the global franchising of *The Biggest Loser* attest. In the US context, however, personal transformation and self-improvement have historically been the prerogative of men, canonized in the writings of Benjamin Franklin and Horatio Alger. In the late nineteenth century, however, this career-oriented, bootstraps pragmatism joined another long-standing tradition of spiritual rebirth in quasi-religious approaches to self-improvement. Incorporating new spiritual themes in the form of "mind cure" philosophies of the late nineteenth century, the twentieth century saw an interweaving of spiritualism with pragmatism. Louise Woodstock writes, "The self-help books of the 1890s had argued that the individual must align himself with a divine order to achieve health and happiness. In the 1950s, the social world and its commercial imperatives became the realm to which individuals should accommodate. By the 1990s, however, individuals were directed to find answers within themselves."[10] This move toward interiority was also accompanied by a feminization of the field of self-help. Alongside the ongoing popularity of apparently gender-neutral titles such as Stephen Covey's *Seven Habits of Highly Effective People* exploded a market of self-help books for women. The confluence of the human potential movement with feminism in the 1970s laid the groundwork for women's self-help books such as Helen Gurley Brown's *Having It All* and Robin Norwood's *Women Who Love Too Much*.[11] This book market has proven highly popular and has spawned an industry of related revenue-generating products: magazines, DVDs, CDs, seminars, and so on. Market-data Enterprises, which tracks major market trends, estimated that the US self-help market was worth $10.5 billion in 2009.[12] Self-help themes imbue the makeover genre, including their emphasis on the need for personal transformation, the search for the authentic self, and the production of life narratives.

Makeover shows embed personal transformation in women's culture by repurposing themes and modes from existing women's and lowbrow television genres. As Wood, Skeggs, and Thumim write, "'Reality' television . . . continues the traditions associated with 'women's media'—soap operas, magazines, talk shows and melodramas—and their intense moralizing of domesticity and women's social worth."[13] Sonia Livingstone characterizes soap operas as a genre that attracts loyal viewers, mostly women, to televised narratives that unfold over sometimes very long periods, that are concerned with domestic and mundane issues, and that are both cheap to produce and relatively lowbrow. She also notes "the similarities between the genre of melodrama and that of soap opera; for example, the importance of such features as moral polarization, strong emotions, the personalization of ideological conflict, interiorization, female-orientation, and excess."[14] These themes have been increasingly brought into other prime time genres that involve "serial structure, multiple narratives involving a relatively large number of regular characters, and the deferral of closure."[15] These characteristics apply particularly to series-length makeovers like *The Biggest Loser* and *Starting Over*, in which narrative arcs associated with each participant, as well as their relationships, can play out over multiple episodes. All makeover shows draw on melodramatic narrative structures, however telegraphically: strong feeling, moral hierarchies, relational conflict, inner experience, and so on.

Makeover television also draws on talk show conventions, especially through the representation of "ordinary" people and their privileged place in the mobilization of feeling. As Grindstaff explains, nonexpert talk show guests are attributed with the authority of lived experience over training or professional credentials, and this gives weight to their emotional expression.[16] Their ordinariness gives them value, but they are also extraordinary insofar as they are selected from a range of people with similar characteristics and experience because of their ability to emote. According to Grindstaff, guests are "expected to deliver what I call, borrowing from film pornography, the 'money shot' of the talk-show text: joy, sorrow, rage, or remorse expressed in visible, bodily terms."[17] They are expected to be emotional (compared with the rational stance of experts) and, because they are relatively untrained in professional and media norms, their expressions appear highly authentic. The production of the money shot, the moment of raw feeling, is predicated both on the guests' ordinariness as the guarantee of genuineness, and their extraordinary ability to transcend cultural taboos on emotional expression. Further, as Joshua Gamson notes, daytime talk shows open a space for marginal discourses by giving a presence to classes and sexualities not usually represented in the artificial worlds of fictional television.[18] Similarly, makeover shows offer a space for ordinary people usually barred from the processes of media production.

Before the advent of hour-long makeover series, makeovers were already a staple of women's magazines. Kathy Peiss traces the first makeover in a US magazine to a *Mademoiselle* spread in 1936.[19] They have also made a regular appearance in segments on morning news programs and daytime talk shows such as *The Oprah Winfrey Show*. However, both in magazines and in televised segments, the focus is on the before-and-after comparison: hilariously unflattering shots of the woman before the makeover are compared with the flawless result. The entertainment here is the dramatic transformation, with little emphasis on the instruction offered. In episode- and series-length televised makeovers the emphasis is much more strongly on the processes of transformation: watching the candidate learn from experts how to conform to conventional norms of femininity and fashion. Further, in contemporary makeover shows, this transformation is emphatically not only in appearance but requires extensive attention to the inner self. Excavating the candidate's past, narrating her personal crisis that brought her so low, confessing her lack of self esteem, and so on, have become defining features of the genre.

We can thus see in contemporary makeover television a feminization of personal transformation through themes drawn from earlier women's genres. These are reworked through the specific demands and opportunities of reality television. Makeover shows are particularly well adapted to address the crisis of revenue experienced by network and cable television channels. Faced with increasingly fragmented audiences and diminished advertising revenues, broadcast and cable networks went in search of new iterations of cheap, revenue-generating, popular programming that could be easily franchised across the globe. Formats that had already proven popular abroad (such as *What Not to Wear*) could be adapted to a US context with relatively little risk. New styles of reality television programming—featuring nonactors in unscripted situations, using cheap locations and a shooting style that emphasizes "liveness"—were readily adaptable to makeover shows. Their transmission during peak evening hours (with the exception of *Starting Over*) represents the "daytiming" of primetime, where cheap, lowbrow, and feminized shows are programmed alongside expensive dramas.[20] The dispersal of audiences increasingly resistant to advertising has led programmers to look for alternative streams of revenue, in part through product placement. The insertion of domestic, quotidian products into the makeover seamlessly integrates these consumer appeals—at least, this is what advertisers hope. Themes from earlier women's genres such as soap operas, talk shows, and self-help literature are processed through the demands of commercial reality television to produce highly normative, intensified relations to the self in makeover television.

Gendered Projects

The Biggest Loser, Queer Eye, Starting Over, and *What Not to Wear* each present crises in gender as the candidate's defining problem. Cultural scholars have noted the particular stresses on gender relations at the beginning of the new millennium.[21] These include the increase of women workers, who now make up around 50 percent of the labor force, and the accompanying increase in women's economic independence. The global economy has precipitated a feminization of various types of work as the US economy moves from manufacture to service industries. High divorce rates challenge couples' sense of relationship security, and the increasing availability of gay, lesbian, bisexual, and transgender images in popular culture make nonnormative gender and sexual identifications seem more possible. As with other makeover shows, the four programs in this study respond to this destabilization of gender distinction by promoting largely conventional presentations of self, while also normalizing the increased demands on the labor force to be adaptable, flexible, and mobile.

Gendered crises are framed differently according to the premise of each show. *The Biggest Loser* represents fat as catastrophically erasing distinctions between women and men. Both in the shows and in the viewers' responses, people frequently refer to the male contestants' "man boobs" and "love handles," physical features usually associated with women's voluptuousness. Both women's and men's bodies are displayed weekly on the giant scale, when women contestants have to strip down to bike shorts and bras, and men to shorts without shirts. *The Biggest Loser* also represents being overweight as a crisis in sexuality. Contestants who are married or coupled are seen as loving, family-oriented people and not as sexually desirable; single contestants are portrayed as outside the dating pool while overweight. Losing weight restores masculine virility for men and feminine desirability for women. Matt and Suzy, the winner and third-place finalist, respectively, on season 2, became a romantic couple after the show, then married and had two children. Their family romance offered the ultimate success story of the show by apparently resolving the crisis of gender and sexuality that being overweight represents. Yet even as contestants are expected to restore gender integrity to their bodies, their inner transformation requires the development of both masculine and feminine skills. For both women and men contestants, the show is based on a competition, and themes of striving, hard work, and aggression dominate training sessions. On the other hand, the show requires of candidates a great deal of emotional work: talking about feelings and developing relationships with teammates in order to avoid being voted off. Winning the competition requires both physical (masculine) and emotional (feminine) labor.

The crisis of gender in *Queer Eye* is one of immaturity: young male candidates must find their way to adult masculinity. Looking at the candidate John Verdi's list of "Things to Do," one of the hosts, Thom, finds a series of goals: "Lose belly for summer," "Pay off debt," and, contradictorily, "Buy a motorcycle." Thom grabs the pen and writes at the top of the list "grow up." *Queer Eye*, however, is the least gender normative of the four shows. Focusing on male makeover candidates and featuring five openly gay men as experts disrupts the usual feminine cast of the genre. In one episode Kyan, the grooming host, discusses the art of the facial with Vincent, an African American man. Kyan suggests that Vincent do some male bonding with his friends by going for facials. Vincent replies that his friends would beat him up if he suggested such a thing. Cultivating practices usually associated with women and gay men prompts a vaguely submerged threat of male violence that the Fab Five gently but consistently work against. However, the hosts' induction of the straight guys into practices and relational styles usually associated with women does not make this show a model of gender subversion. Through adopting these practices, the straight guys are expected to mature into new kinds of adult men, who know how to be effective in the workplace, how to take care of their wives and girlfriends, and, most important, how to consume. Thus, while anomalously focusing on men, *Queer Eye* nevertheless invokes traditionally feminine concerns of the makeover: attention to the body, home, feelings, and related consumer practices.

Starting Over has the most explicit appeals to women's values, drawing on more or less feminist principles to frame the project. As a daytime show, *Starting Over* has both the latitude and the need to prioritize women's concerns. The all-women household and regular group therapy sessions invoke a feminist consciousness-raising model, even if the ideal of women's solidarity is frequently challenged by interactions within the house. The show includes some light critique of the struggles contemporary society poses for women. One episode shows the housemates considering domestic tasks as a form of labor that can be quantified and priced like other kinds of work. Another includes a frank discussion of women's sexuality, including masturbation and orgasms, in which one housemate describes herself as "a kinky kind of girl." In both group and individual sessions, the question of what it means to be women, mothers, and lovers is explicit and draws on self-help and women's empowerment themes. Arlie Hochschild observes that the absorption of feminist values into a new, intimate capitalism required a fusion of women's empowerment with masculine values of independence and self-reliance.[22] Accordingly, women are ready to graduate from the *Starting Over* house when they demonstrate that they are free of their unhealthy habits and relationships, have let go of the past, have made amends, and are ready to start a new life.

In *What Not to Wear* gender is worked through sexuality and upward professional mobility. The two main criticisms the hosts have of candidates is that they are too frumpy or too floozie, or in the case of women of color, too "hoochie." In the first, usually white, older women are judged as looking not sexy enough: they look older than they are, hide their bodies, and have low self-esteem. In the second, often younger women and women of color are criticized for being too sexy, dressing too young, showing off too much of their bodies, and having low self-esteem because they are giving themselves away for cheap. As the cohost Clinton tells the white, sexy-but-single Shireen, "When you look like trash, you don't attract jewels, you attract trash bags." Later he tells her that her outfits make her look like she's going to a "convenience store for a six-pack and some jerky"—stereotyped as white trash, in other words. Floozies cannot be taken seriously, either as love interests or as professional women. Makeovers seen as successful by the hosts feature those candidates who obligingly absorb consumer advice that enables them to present themselves as respectable, discreetly sexual, and as showing that they feel good about themselves.

The makeovers in all four shows thus address crises in gender, differently articulated through the body, attitude, and appearance. All shows offer highly normative, usually heterosexual solutions to these crises. Mimi White witnessed the appearance of 1980s proto-reality shows such as *The All New Dating Game*, *The New Newlywed Game*, and *Divorce Court* at a time of soaring divorce rates. She argues that these shows "can be seen as attempts to (re)instate the heterosexual couple as a stable social referent even as they endlessly rehearse the couple as a body constituted in unstable mobility."[23] Gender is rendered through an explicit and implicit heteronormativity, the accomplishment of which assures the candidates, hosts, and presumed audience that the makeover is a success.

Makeover shows fuse candidates' heteronormativity with the possibility of their upward professional mobility; in order to be credited with value in the world of work, women have to conform to narrow ideals of femininity. Considering UK makeover shows, Angela McRobbie and Gareth Palmer both note large class differences between the upper class, even aristocratic hosts and the usually working-class makeover candidates.[24] Beverly Skeggs argues that the reality genre's emphasis on "ordinary" people is a euphemism for focusing on working-class (usually) women, whose failings are revealed for the purposes of reform.[25]

In contrast, "ordinariness" in the US shows describes a vast middle class, represented in the shows by candidates whose jobs range from administrative assistants and paramedics to graphic designers and family doctors. Further, in the United States the distinction between candidates and hosts is less expressly one of class (at least class of origin as in the British series), but of expertise marked by a meritocratic accumulation of knowledge helped, in some cases, by the inherently good taste ascribed to gay men. The reproduction in the shows of a supposedly classless, meritocratic American society is then reproduced by the audiences we talked to, who suggested very few of the class affiliations in relation to the shows' candidates that Skeggs and her colleagues found in their study. This is not to say that makeover shows are not, in part, a class project, but that class difference is less obviously polarized and is replaced by the fantasy of the American Dream.

None of the hosts in these four shows comes from especially privileged backgrounds. The male hosts are either openly gay or can be read as gay, achieving the role of expert not because of being raised in an upper-class habitus but because of their professional experience and the magic of gay taste. The US shift from class-based cultural capital to expertise that can be learned is exemplified on *Starting Over*. Here a housemate from season 1, Andy Paige, became a makeover stylist in a later season of the show, suggesting that through a successful makeover you, too, may achieve a position of professional respect and affluence similar to that of the hosts.

Even though the US hosts aren't posh, they nevertheless cultivate the tastes of people more privileged than the candidates. Bourdieu's concept of habitus addresses the terms on which makeover shows make their appeals. Briefly, habitus describes how we create the lived environments of our upbringing: how one looks, one's tastes in popular entertainments and art, what one eats, and so on.[26] Significantly for makeover shows, habitus is embodied, written in the height, shape, and disposition of the body. Makeover shows offer instruction on how to embody the class presentations of a strata above one's own. They naturalize class privilege by representing the candidates' current habitus as wholly inadequate, rather than simply the habitus of a particular class. The routines of the shows—the ambush, the diagnoses of inadequacy, the use of surveillance—all contribute to a distancing from the candidates' origins and the insistence on adopting the appearance of privilege.

The effacement of class through gendered norms is particularly apparent in *The Biggest Loser*'s address of overweight bodies, both female and male. As with the other shows included in this project, *The Biggest Loser* makes no explicit reference to the socioeconomic status of the contestants, who are mostly lower middle class—police officers, stay-at-home-moms, hairdressers. However, the link between socioeconomic status and obesity is not addressed in the show, nor is being overweight considered in relation to the economics of food availability and affordability. Further, the show does not acknowledge the limits to upward mobility that being overweight represents. DeBeaumont, for example, found that although obese women in professional jobs earn only 4 percent less than their nonobese counterparts, large women in sales jobs earn 17 percent less than nonobese women.[27] Contestants on *The Biggest Loser* must trade their privacy for the opportunity to overcome barriers to their professional advancement. In order to get access to highly trained experts, special diets, and a twenty-four-hour gym, they volunteer to be exposed to constant surveillance. Meanwhile, the contestants are faulted for problems of the inner self: failures of will and crises of self-esteem.[28] They are cast as their own worst enemies, as lazy, passive, self-hating, and controlled by excessive appetites: the class contours of body size become displaced onto negative attributes usually ascribed to women.

An optimistic view of this class training might be that lower-middle- and working-class people now have televised access to the kinds of instruction that may help them in their upward professional mobility. Angela McRobbie warily describes this as a "redistribution of cultural capital."[29] This view sees reality television performing "a national/domestic/educative function by kindly providing instruction on areas of everyday life not covered in the school curriculum." McRobbie continues, "Bourdieu would, however, surely reply that by such means as these, deference and cultural goodwill to existing social hierarchies is inevitably confirmed."[30] By offering access to elevated tastes to a few, while audiences of limited means look on, makeover shows reaffirm the very social hierarchies written in and performed through classed bodies. Palmer's claims for British makeover shows hold true for American ones, too: "Class . . . *is* very much on the agenda of lifestyle television, but 'merely' as a question of taste."[31]

In the US context, class differences play out somewhat differently, and become intertwined with race and ethnic styles. Black and Latina women, in particular, are chastised for being too sexy and thus failing in the game of professional self-presentation. Yet explicit references to racial differences are effaced in the makeover shows included in this study. In *What Not to Wear*, Betty C., a Latina, was called "too hoochie" by her friends but was criticized by the hosts for dressing in an *age*-inappropriate way, without any reference to her distinctly ethnic style. The task for cohosts Stacy and Clinton was to take her teenage dance-club style and reform it into one appropriate for a professional woman in her thirties, suggesting outfits I would characterize as implicitly white. A very funny episode featuring another Latina, Cristina, came closest to blowing the lid off the raced norms of dress. Clinton and Stacy wanted to get her out of cleavage-emphasizing keyhole tops and into a brown tweed suit. Cristina was not impressed, and called the outfit "hilarious. . . . This makes me look like I'm going to have a cup of tea with the nuns from the local church: Too serious." Serious is old and white; hoochie is young and ethnic. Explicit recognition of racial difference in *What Not to Wear* is limited to suggesting different hair treatments for African American women (with uneven success, according to viewers) and celebrating darker skin tones. The show's makeup stylist, Carmindy, calls Cristina's complexion "mocha," which allows her to use "jewel-toned" makeup.

Queer Eye makes a greater effort than the other three shows to offer instruction that takes into consideration candidates' racial and ethnic background, especially in terms of cuisine and interior decorating. Rather than coming across as respectful, however, these attempts tend to promote an urbane cosmopolitanism, representing a privileged taste culture that can sample from ethnicities across the world but is not tied to any single one. In one episode the hosts admire the Jamaican American Rob Munroe's dreadlocks, but in matters of interior decor his taste is too specifically Jamaican. While buying furniture, Thom tells Rob, "A lot of this stuff [in the store], unlike your house, is from all over. There are things from Sri Lanka, the Philippines, Africa, all mixed in. . . . I want to bring together your photography, your love of ethnic furniture, and your respect for culture. I don't want you to get trapped in one area." Rob's racially distinctive style implies a retrograde identification with places and cultures past, hindering the progressive impulse toward sophisticated tastes based not on tradition but on a global marketplace.

Being unhealthily attached to one's cultural heritage also featured in *The Biggest Loser*, the most racially diverse of the four shows we looked at. African Americans are generally assumed to be more accepting of being overweight, although there is some contradictory evidence for this.[32] A rare mention of race in season 2 of *The Biggest Loser* reframed this cultural acceptance as a morbid tolerance for obesity in Black communities. Shannon, a Black woman contestant on season 2, recalled "being raised in a family that's always telling you that even though you're a Black woman, it's okay to be heavy. . . . It's very acceptable in my family to be this size. My whole family's this size. I got the opportunity to help everyone [by being on the show]—my daughter particularly." An acceptance of size among African Americans is described as an unhealthy, even lethal cultural heritage that Shannon must reject in order to save not only herself but also her daughter.

Starting Over also insists at moments that housemates, and especially women of color, break their ties with an unhealthy past. There is some bonding among the Black women in the house; one episode shows a housemate glad to see a new "sister" joining the show—a comment that offended some of the white participants in this study. Amid a vague feeling of racial solidarity, however, there are occasional references to how stereotypes and cultural norms hold the women back from starting over. In another episode one of the show's life coaches, Iyanla (an African American) tells a housemate that she is perpetuating the stereotype of Black women as angry. This frames racial stereotypes as the responsibility of Black people to fix. In another, Iyanla tells a Black housemate, Niambe, that "in the African American community it's taboo to criticize one's mother," but this is what Niambe must do in order to free herself from the tyranny of her mother's internalized voice.

Transformation for contestants in each of these shows requires a rupture with their unhealthy, limiting pasts, especially for people of color. In those rare instances where race is mentioned (and only ever regarding nonwhite candidates), candidates are advised to turn their back on their families and cultural heritage. What is presented as a much-needed restabilization of gender requires dissociating from one's racially embedded, classed past, in what Weber calls a condition of "ethnic anonymity."[33] Especially for less privileged groups, freedom from the past and from structural limitations becomes an obligation to break their emotional, relational, and aesthetic ties to their cultural heritage. This is nothing new, of course, but the promise of self-expression and improving one's self-esteem by doing so is particularly insidious.

Consuming Gender

These normative solutions to problems of the self are built on a bedrock of consumption. Makeover shows optimize reality television's commercial imperatives by inserting domestic, quotidian products into the narrative. In the makeover shows considered in this study, we see a reworking of the gendered features of consumption within the logic of late capitalism: by invoking postfeminist themes of empowerment through consumption; by drawing men into the historically female market of clothes, home, and grooming products; and by utilizing new technologies to maximize the cross-promotion of branded products.

The consumer ethic is most clearly expressed in *What Not to Wear*. Here the makeover is about not only buying, but also knowing the rules on how to buy apparel that is more "appropriate." Stores such as H&M and Lane Bryant have been featured on the show, as well as

Crest Whitestrips, a tooth whitening product, and the show's website is "brought to you by Macy's." The website offers extensive information on what products have been featured in any given episode, where to buy them, and how much they cost. *What Not to Wear* has a number of cross-promoted products, including DVDs of episodes and a book by the hosts, Clinton Kelly and Stacy London.[34] Martin Roberts argues that the British *What Not to Wear* routed feminist principles of women's empowerment through the domain of consumption, where "self-confidence and sexual attractiveness . . . depend on the services of the fashion and beauty industries—all of which . . . must be purchased."[35] A similar logic applies to the US version of *What Not to Wear*, which is even more focused on consumption through explicit product placement. A sequence at the end of each episode describes what the newly made-over candidate is wearing, where she purchased these items, and how much they cost. Rather than seeing this instruction as allowing women to express sexual empowerment through pleasurable consumption, as postfeminist celebrants might suggest, McRobbie warns that *What Not to Wear* expresses the anxieties of the privileged classes faced with a new group of financially independent women. No longer needing men, families, or communities, and "with money in their pockets, who knows what might happen?"[36] Makeover shows keep the engines of capital running on the backs of women's expenditure, while disciplining these women into demure, sexually discreet, family- and work-focused consumption.

Queer Eye attempts to foster male consumption by positing a crisis in masculinity based on inadequate consumption. The show uses gay men's expertise in a renewed attempt to solve the "problem" of the male consumer, which has plagued advertisers and media producers at least since the debut of *Esquire* magazine in 1933.[37] With few exceptions— classically electronics, cars, sporting goods, and pornography—white, heterosexual men have proven hard to train as consumers, especially of "intimate" goods usually associated with women: apparel, cosmetics, furniture and other decorating products, food and kitchen appliances. What is most striking about the show, however, is that the renewed attempt to cultivate male, heterosexual consumers comes through the welcomed expertise of openly gay men. As *Queer Eye* became a ratings hit (at least by cable standards) and a household name, the companies that vied to have their products featured on the show became increasingly well-known, and included the Tommy Hilfiger and Steven Allen men's clothing lines, as well as IKEA and Crest Whitestrips. Bravo also encouraged viewers to buy products associated with the show's brand, including books, DVDs, and T-shirts.[38] *Queer Eye* entices heterosexual men into a gay-inflected sphere of intimate consumption that nevertheless shores up their masculinity.

The Biggest Loser demonstrates less the cultivation of the new male market than the exploitation of new technologies to distribute the show's brand. Product placement here is relatively clumsy, featuring foods that manufacturers want to sell as "diet" items by building them into the structure of the show. For example, in one competition contestants had to run and find Jell-O in numerous refrigerators littered about a warehouse. In contrast, cross-promotion within the show and on the website of *Biggest Loser* products was extensive and sophisticated, including *The Biggest Loser* book, cookbook, calorie counter book, workout DVD, online weight loss club (subscribers pay "under $5 per week" for membership), and a phone text service offering diet and workout tips. The series cocreator Ben Silverman said, "When we created *The Biggest Loser*, we always envisioned it as a multiplatform lifestyle brand in and of itself, and this service will provide our audience with another opportunity to further interact with the show and make healthier lifestyle choices."[39] As *The Biggest Loser* has become franchised around the globe, with twenty-three local adaptations at the time of writing, the ethos of cross-platform promotion has similarly been exported.

Compared with the unapologetic consumerism of *The Biggest Loser*, *Queer Eye*, and *What Not to Wear*, the role of consumption on *Starting Over* is somewhat problematic within the therapeutic ethos of this show. The image makeovers that each graduating housemate undergoes feature little in the way of product placement, and there are relatively few sponsored products and services. Because of the emphasis in this show on inner change, the opportunities for relevant product placement are relatively few. In order to make space for sponsoring companies, the show includes a "Tips of the Week" advice section, paid for by Glade air freshener and Veet hair removal products. There are no cross-promoted brand media, but both life coaches on the show have numerous self-help books and CDs and run various workshops.[40] Not only is the rationale for product placement somewhat stretched on *Starting Over*, it is the only show among the four included in this research that had any critical approach to consumption. Late in the third season a young African American woman, Antonia, joined the house, wanting to start over in her financial life: compulsive shopping and no job had left her many thousands of dollars in credit card debt. Iyanla took her to expensive stores on Rodeo Drive in Beverly Hills and then told her she had to shop among the secondhand clothes at Buffalo Exchange. This message of frugality and financial responsibility is highly unusual, however, within a genre that normally assumes that the route to self-fulfillment is through shopping.

Starting Over aside, makeover shows in general epitomize the possibilities offered by reality television to provide alternative sources of revenue through sponsorship and product placement. The rationale for consumption is seamlessly written into *Queer Eye* and *What Not to Wear*, where the makeover is achieved through purchasing new products. In *The Biggest Loser*, the logic of instruction and support easily extends to other branded products—books, DVDs, and so on—as well as to paid subscription online support groups. The shows demonstrate the smooth integration of television programs with online content, drawing audiences to websites that include sponsored products, advertising, and brand products. With the exception of *Starting Over*, the makeover shows promote the consumption of goods as part of the larger project of self-making. Traditionally, consumption and personal authenticity have been seen as antithetical: women, considered inherently untrustworthy, used consumption to cover their real selves.[41] Contemporary makeover shows, in contrast, manage to hold in tension the paradox that the expression of a unique, authentic inner self is enabled by constructing a highly normative gender, race, and class presentation from the resources offered by mainstream consumer culture.

Female Complaint

Makeover shows offer viewers the pleasures of consumption, but they also promise other pleasures: like the daytime talk shows that preceded them, makeover shows provide a forum for marginalized, female concerns. For all their emphasis on being responsible for one's fate, makeover shows commonly draw on narratives of female complaint: bad luck and wrong men, ill health, overwork, overwhelm, and a lack of resources are familiar themes. Contemporary makeover shows thus share elements with the 1950s US proto-makeover show *Glamour Girl*, which pitted women against one another to compete for a makeover by sharing the most sympathy-inducing life story. Marsha Cassidy sees that show's success as evidence that the largely female audience wanted an expression of women's problems, to make "girl talk" public.[42] Cassidy sees the *Glamour Girl* makeover as "affirm[ing] for audiences the defects in Prince Charming's system"[43] because it makes explicit how postwar gender relations were not working for women. With their emphasis on the ordinary, contemporary makeover shows give participants a chance to voice female concerns and priorities, even as these are shaped within the commercial contexts of the shows' production and distribution.

Not only is there space in makeover shows for female complaint, these types of shows insert women's concerns into prime time programming. Makeover shows thus leverage space for a women's "intimate public," insisting on the significance of women's concerns, validating the importance of self-care, and encouraging male candidates and viewers to absorb some of these values. Berlant describes the "intimate public" as a "space of mediation in which the personal is refracted through the general," and where "emotional contact, of a sort, is made."[44] With its domestic location, use of the close-up shot, and emphasis on women's discourse and concerns, reality television is a "technology of intimacy," particularly well-placed to construct this sense of an intimate public in prime time.[45]

As part of this shift of intimate publics to prime time, men have become both the targets and a more likely audience for makeovers. Television instruction might helpfully make the men who watch it more likely to attend to their appearance, their emotional experience, and their relationships—all traditionally feminine preoccupations. Appeals to men, however, present another example of the reaches of consumer capitalism further into domestic life. As Susan Bordo notes, feminism didn't free women from scrutiny and objectification; instead, feminism has become reworked through the logics of consumer culture to subject men to similar demands for self-presentation and consumer behavior as women.[46]

For all the pleasures of feeling and assumed intimacy that makeover programs offer, Lauren Berlant, Misha Kavka, and Eva Illouz are interested in how affective relations are reworked through economic domains. Makeover shows are an articulation of what Illouz calls "emotional capitalism," describing "a culture in which emotional and economic discourses and practices mutually shape each other, . . . in which affect is made an essential aspect of economic behavior and in which emotional life—especially that of the middle classes—follows the logic of economic relations and exchange."[47] As with other women's genres, makeover shows increasingly demand from their candidates "emotional labor": work that women, traditionally, are required to perform.[48] "Women are not only expected to be compassionate and understanding," writes Berlant, "but to act both as teachers of compassion and surrogates for others' refusals or incapacities to feel appropriately and intelligently."[49] Hosts and below-the-line production staff work to elicit appropriate feelings from makeover candidates, as they have done in talk shows.[50] The candidates work on themselves to monitor the self, revise identity narratives, and produce appropriate affect. Candidates are also involved in the feeling work necessary to maintain relationships with their loved ones during the shows and, especially in the case of Queer Eye, afterward. Audiences engage emotionally with the shows, producing profits for the channel, advertisers, and sponsors. All these kinds of emotion work are examples of "immaterial labor" that Mark Andrejevic argues typifies the labor economies of reality television.[51] Andrejevic quotes from Maurizio Lazzarato's clarification of immaterial labor as involving "a series of activities that are not normally recognized as 'work'—in other words, the kinds of activities involved in defining and fixing cultural and artistic standards, fashions, tastes, consumer norms, and, more strategically, public opinion."[52] Not only are these activities not usually defined as work, they are often done by women, offering another example of uncompensated female labor.

Like the self-help books, soap operas, and talk shows that preceded the huge rise in popularity of reality television, makeover shows draw on the traditions of women's genres to produce an intimate public. This public offers pleasures to mostly women candidates and audiences, and also suggests a democratization of its themes to male audiences. For both women and men in the shows, contemporary makeovers intensify the relationship with the self already present in their precursors. They invoke themes of hope and possibility, the pleasure of being permitted to care for the self, and a sense of agency that a reflexive attitude promises. At the same time, these hopes and pleasures require work—shopping, self-monitoring, and emotional labor.

What I want to avoid here is a familiar undermining of women's genres through a simplistic formula: women watch shows in which they are represented as conforming to gender norms, and women audiences unthinkingly absorb and reproduce what they see on-screen. More than three decades of feminist-inspired research shows that women's engagements with both consumer culture and media texts are complex. How do audiences talk about makeover shows? How do they receive the instructional and commercial messages of the shows? What do they do with the appeals to emotion, authenticity, and intimacy? Do they discuss themselves according to the inner/outer split that dominates the shows' messages? How do they reflect on the genre in terms of their own experience? Important as critiques of gender-normative representations in makeover shows are, this book also considers how these densely invested texts operate in the gendered circuits of meaning between texts and audiences. This involves two shifts: to think beyond images to gendered forms of subjectivity, and to broaden from a focus on representation within texts to how people who watch the shows engage with these texts. The following chapters prioritize audiences' engagements with the shows to complicate the textual focus that appears here. Chapter 3 addresses the extent to which people who watch the show absorb, deploy, negotiate, and critique the shows' instruction, and how they reflexively situate the shows within their commercial contexts.

3

Not Like Paris Hilton

Instruction and Consumption in Makeover Shows

I watch [*What Not to Wear*] with my elementary-aged daughter. She is picking up cues about appropriate clothing and dressing to be attractive but not, as she says, like Paris Hilton.
—*What Not to Wear* survey respondent

The previous chapter offered a critique of makeover television that focused on how gender, class, and race norms are worked through contemporary demands to be more flexible workers and enthusiastic consumers. The rest of this book looks at how the audiences we talked to engaged with the project of self-making represented in these shows. People who watch the shows used them to guide their own and their loved ones' personal presentation within shared ideas of what it means to be attractive—but not like Paris Hilton. Yet their reflexive orientations to the texts, as well as to their own selves as projects that may be worked on through the messages of the texts, meant that these audiences negotiated the shows' instruction and consumer appeals. In this chapter I address the related themes of instruction and consumption. The shows all rest on the premise that experts offer advice about how to work on the self, and that much of that advice comes in the form of how to shop. There are two primary

frameworks for looking at how audiences engage with this advice. The
first, based on audience research, comes from the UK and is grounded in
a British tradition of public service broadcasting in which television must
"inform, educate, and entertain."[1] Annette Hill began her study of reality
television audiences believing that lifestyle programs had the potential
to teach viewers useful skills. However, she found that audiences valued the "idea of learning" more than they actually picked up information from the shows.[2] The second framework draws from Foucault's idea
of governmentality, outlined in chapter 1. This assumes that audiences
aspire to be good citizens by adopting the shows' guidelines for living as
a resource that they draw on to reform themselves in line with the values
of the neoliberal state.[3] These authors see makeovers as necessarily governmental, portraying transformations from wayward "before" bodies to
self-surveilling "after" bodies through the judicious application of "technologies of the self."[4] While doing this, they also promote consumption as
the primary means for self-transformation. In the public service model,
lifestyle television is a lost opportunity for helpful pedagogy. In the governmentality model, audiences reproduce worrying neoliberal values as a
result of watching makeover television. How did the people we talked to in
this study engage with the instruction offered by the makeover shows? To
what extent did the participants in the study situate themselves as willing
recipients of this instruction? Did they describe themselves as consum-
ing in ways recommended by the shows? And what were their perceptions of the advice, including consumer advice, offered by the shows? As
other scholars engaging in cultural studies–based audience research have
found, both the survey data and interviews here suggest much more complex engagements with the shows' instructional elements and commercial
appeals than critiques based on texts alone allow. Even as the participants
adopted some of the shows' advice in their reflexive self-presentations,
they critiqued this advice, drawing on media reflexivity cultivated, in part,
through their social interactions.

The Uses of Instruction

As the quote at the beginning of this book suggests, some viewers were
very invested in the advice makeover shows offer, and share this advice
with others. Indeed, the survey responses suggested that *What Not to*

Wear and *Starting Over* viewers were particularly invested in the expertise dispensed in these shows, if in somewhat different ways. *Starting Over* and *What Not to Wear* survey respondents and interviewees were not only more likely to say that they liked the instructional aspects of the show, but also were able to recall very specific, concrete advice they had gleaned from watching it. Viewers engaged with *The Biggest Loser* and *Queer Eye* in somewhat different ways, finding these motivating and entertaining, respectively.

What Not to Wear respondents were most likely to report picking up tips from the show. It was striking that in contrast to rather vague recollections from some other shows, *What Not to Wear* participants remembered very specific advice from the show's hosts, Stacy London and Clinton Kelly. A typical example were these guidelines picked up by a female survey respondent: "Pointy-toed shoes making the leg look longer, wearing straight cut jeans so as to not create an hourglass from the hip to the ankle, how much accessories can help an outfit, and to not buy so many separates without considering how they fit what you already have." Another woman wrote, "I have a pair of pointy boots and now they're out of fashion, but bought directly because of this show."

"Pointy shoes" was only one of a number of often-repeated phrases that people used to discuss specific advice from *What Not to Wear*. Among my favorite responses to our question "What tips have you picked up from the show?" was "lock and load." This refers to Stacy and Clinton's advice to large-breasted women that they wear jackets that button high enough to contain and conceal "the girls." Managing an unruly bosom is a regular feature of *What Not to Wear*. Another woman commented that she had "learned a lot from this show, because I've invested in a whole bunch of camis. That's all you can do. I'm not Lane Bryant size, but I'm like a 12. . . . You just have to wear the button open and a cami with a button-down shirt, which I wear all the time." Many people had also been instructed in the virtues of getting clothes altered to get a perfect fit, making me wonder if *What Not to Wear* has single-handedly revived the tailoring industry.

Women *What Not to Wear* respondents were most likely to say that they had bought products that were either featured on the show or similar to these products. Many paid attention to product placements during episodes and went to the *What Not to Wear* website to find additional information on the products featured during episodes, as Danica indicates in her discussion with he interviewer on product plbcement:

> DANICA: It's a little annoying, but it's cute. Yeah, they had the Zappos,
>   doing product placement on Zappos for a while. Now, it's changed
>   to DSW, at least this week it was. And I'm like, "Oh that was interest-
>   ing." And then, that was it—that's all I remember actually.
> INTERVIEWER: So have you ever bought anything or shopped anywhere
>   because you saw it on the show?
> D: No, but I did think of Zappos more often, I know that I did, because of
>   the show.
> I: It kind of became more of an option?
> D: Exactly; I know that I did. Plus, any time I ever get to New York, I will
>   be making sure I get to any of those stores.

Other viewers were annoyed by product placements on *What Not to Wear*, which I discuss more below. In general, however, women viewers of *What Not to Wear* were the most engaged with the advice and commercial appeals across all four shows. Male *What Not to Wear* survey respondents reported somewhat less engagement with the instruction on this show, unsurprisingly given how rarely the show makes over male candidates. In terms of *What Not to Wear*–branded products, only one interviewee said she had bought Stacy and Clinton's book spin-off from the show, *Dress Your Best*.

Many *What Not to Wear* respondents emphasized that they appreciated the learning aspects of the show, a theme that was repeated by many *Starting Over* participants. *Starting Over* interviewees contested the popular and scholarly dismissal of television programs in general—and feminine, daytime genres in particular—as having no educational value. One female viewer told us:

> It means a lot to me to actually say I can sit down and watch something
> on TV and learn from it. I can identify with how my father used to pick
> at us and say, "Why are you sitting there watching that boob tube?"
> Because a lot of stuff that's on TV right now doesn't need to be on there.
> But this was one show where I actually said, "I have got to watch this." If I
> missed it in the morning, I had to catch it in the afternoon.[5]

Starting Over respondents mentioned a series of very specific skills they had adopted from this show, and employed a specialized vocabulary to discuss these. A gay man who watched the show regularly said:

> I've definitely found mirrors in some of the characters on the show, like Jill and Alison. So I don't know if I've taken anything, but I've definitely done the mirroring thing, where I know I'm working on stuff for me. . . . And it's again an identification and empathy, and that's what I take from it, is the lessons that I learn from watching other people in a similar struggle. But basically it's about empathy.

Others mentioned recording advice and exercises in a journal for future use:

> I've written down several things in my journal: "Resentment means I'm resisting something. Resentment is a clear indication that you're resisting something that you're not assuming responsibility for." Every time you feel resentful say, "Thank you." It means someone else is assuming the responsibility for you. [A life] coach [said] about someone's mother [which] relates to mine: "She hasn't found that place of her own joy yet." "When you judge people, you make yourself the victim." "If it (the number on the scale) is just a number, than why have you placed so much importance on it?" Just recently when Christie accepted her mother for the woman she was, not blame her for the mother she wasn't.

Respondents frequently commented on how they used the show as a form of free psychotherapy. One female survey respondent liked the show for "therapy and all I pay is my cable bill! I take a little bit and try to apply it to my life." Another commented that "the life coaches help identify my issues and the houseguests show me the reality. I feel like I'm getting free therapy." The show's role of providing free therapy to people who might not otherwise get access to it was sometimes mentioned in pleas to help keep the show on the air. One full-time student wrote, "Please help in having the network bring back *Starting Over* for another season. . . . It really does help us who are not able to be on the show or that can't afford therapy like that on our own." Laurie Ouellette argues that court television shows like *Judge Judy* represent an "outsourcing of [the state's] governmental functions."[6] If neoliberalism involves a divestment of the state's responsibilities to care for the mental and physical health of its citizens, it is telling that women must look to a television show to provide inexpensive therapy otherwise unavailable to them.

Of the four shows, *Starting Over* had the least obtrusive product placement arrangements. Some viewers recalled seeing cleaning products prominently featured, and housemates' weight loss efforts were prominently supported by the Jenny Craig diet program and Curves gym. A few women commented that they already used the products featured, suggesting a successful marketing fit between the products and the anticipated audience. One woman recalled a few products that she'd seen on the show, including Curves, which she joined as a result of watching: "I went and joined Curves. . . . Watching Jill's story is what made me say, 'Okay, if she can do this, I can do this.'" More than for the other shows, *Starting Over* participants reported having bought products associated with the brand, primarily books by the shows' life coaches, Rhonda Britten and Iyanla Vanzant.[7]

The Biggest Loser offered quite a different example of engagement with the show's instructional content. A few survey respondents mentioned picking up tips from watching the show, such as "how to exercise and what to eat" from a male respondent, or this from a woman who wanted to lose more than one hundred pounds: "No eating after 6. Eating mini meals throughout the day to keep your metabolism up. Exercising (even though I don't do it). You can still have your carbs, but good ones." Yet more than the instructional value of the show, participants said they liked *The Biggest Loser* for its motivating potential. A woman wrote that she found the candidates "inspiring. [The show] helped me stay focused on my own weight loss goals, while usually during my evening television time I want to snack." Another survey respondent noted that "last season a couple of times [my husband and I] were on the treadmill when we watched it. We figured if they can work out, we can, too."

The Biggest Loser may be seen as more motivational than instructional because of particular elements of the show's format. Each episode is structured around a series of challenges within the overall competition to lose the most weight each week. The show offers very little in terms of detailed advice about diet and exercise, and if viewers remembered particular lessons it was because they were so unusual. One woman complained:

> I wish that they would focus more on the diet part of it, too, and they do somewhat. They show them—like when you go out to a restaurant, how to order off a menu, and how you can adjust menu items so that they're healthier, and they do show that to a certain degree, but I'm not sure why they moved off of it.

Most of the episodes portray contestants sweating profusely on a treadmill, or doing physically challenging tests, which offer viewers little in the way of actual instruction, but a great deal in terms of motivation. Yet even though they were often frustrated by the lack of explicit advice, very few of the respondents had purchased *The Biggest Loser* books or DVDs, where this material was available. One woman got the book from the library. Another regular viewer said:

> I'm hoping that Matt [winner of season 2] will have a book come out or something, or maybe like a wedding album of Matt and Suzy [who met on the show] and stuff like that. I think that would be kind of cool. And I know that the blue coach, he has a book out, but I didn't buy it. His name is Bob [Harper]. And I know that Jillian [Michaels] has a book out, but I didn't buy it either.

This interviewee's response suggests a very different engagement with the show that is more concerned with relational and celebrity elements associated with fandom than the more respectable, apparently rational search for weight loss advice books.

Queer Eye viewers framed the advice given by this shows' hosts within the context of gay expertise. Rachel, a heterosexual woman whose husband and home had been made over on *Queer Eye*, said:

> It's a long-standing thing that gay men know how to dress. You know, I'd marry a gay man tomorrow, except I'd never have sex. That's the only thing, I'd have to let him have a boyfriend. They know how to cook,

they know how to clean, they have culture, they have taste. And it's true, because any of my best gay men friends, they're just amazing people; they're cultured, they're well-traveled, they're well-spoken. They know how to dress, they know how to keep the house.

Another woman referenced the fine line the Fab Five had to tread between gay taste and being "too gay":

> DONNA: I love the way [Thom] decorates. I mean, he's not over the top. It's not what you would call gay. Like the one I was watching from last night where they were actually helping a gay guy out. And he said his roommates were expecting a big rainbow flag. And Thom said something like "I wish I would of done that," you know. But they wouldn't, because it is about being tasteful. I mean they can joke and be bawdy and risqué, but when it comes down to it, they're pretty tasteful guys, I think. God, I'm talking about them like they're my long lost friends!
>
> INTERVIEWER: Have you changed anything about your life through watching the show?
>
> D: Just, we dress a little better. And I'm a little cleaner actually. As far as, you know, cleaning out the bathtub more often. Things like that.

Discussing gay stereotypes, a young gay male interviewee experienced tensions with his family about watching the show because of Carson, one of the hosts:

> The only problem that I really have is *Queer Eye*, because Carson's really flamboyant and really eccentric. And I think he makes the show, because I know a lot of people always talk about him, and he adds more of the celebrity appeal to the show. It's hard because my family is very conservative, so I'm not really allowed to watch the show when anyone's home. I have to watch by myself. So I think just that part makes it hard, just that they are so stereotypical, and then my parents see that.

For all the appreciation of gay taste that *Queer Eye* relies on as a brand, these comments suggest a narrow frame within which this taste can be expressed on national television: the Fab Five must be gay, but not press a specifically gay style; they must be entertaining but not too flamboyant or eccentric.

Despite my earlier critique of the governmental thrust of *Queer Eye*, these audiences' responses demonstrate that this was the least instructional of the four shows, at least in terms of cultivating adult masculinity. Some participants noted that they used the show to educate young or homophobic men in their families about gay people, but mostly participants watched *Queer Eye* for its entertainment value. One woman compared the instructional potential of *The Biggest Loser* and *Queer Eye*: "I've learned some things on *Biggest Loser*—I've learned some things about body chemistry, or the physiology of exercise and weight loss. *Queer Eye*? Definitely not. I enjoy the boys. I enjoy their connection to each other." Hill notes an inverse relationship between entertainment and learning in her research on reality show audiences: the more entertaining viewers find a program, the less likely they are to see any educational value in it (this includes respondents' views of all reality shows, however, not just lifestyle television).[8] Because people find *Queer Eye* entertaining, this might mitigate against them also finding it educational.

An exception to this came from Rachel, whose husband had been featured on *Queer Eye*. Not only did she report avidly taking note of the show's advice, but told us that her husband had also borrowed recipes prior to being on the show, despite his initial antipathy toward it. During a cooking demonstration in which Ted was preparing prawns, her husband

> stopped dead in his tracks and he said, "We've got to do that for our next party." And this was before we even entertained notions of being on the show. And our next party, we made them, exactly the [same] way, and everybody was raving over it, and we're like, "Oh yeah, we got the recipe from *Queer Eye*." And it was so funny because a year later when we were on the show, people were saying, "God, getting the recipe from them wasn't enough—you had to go on the show?"

Yet Rachel was among very few respondents who talked about what they had learned from *Queer Eye*; most people deferred the question or equivocated about how much the show had actually influenced them.

When we probed them in interviews, people were at a loss to recall what they had learned, and were reluctant to attribute changes in behavior to the show alone. For example, a man in his forties was one of the few interviewees to acknowledge being influenced by *Queer Eye*'s advice, if ambivalently. He said, "I can't point to the show being the reason, but in the last couple of years, I'm balding. And I certainly didn't go the comb-over route or anything like that. My hair would be a little bit long—I wouldn't say long—but, bottom line, I get not a buzz cut every time I get a haircut, but it's much neater than it used to be." In terms of specific consumer advice, respondents very rarely said that they bought a product they had seen featured on *Queer Eye*. Their seeming lack of enthusiasm about purchasing specific products, however, contradicts the legendary success that being featured on *Queer Eye* apparently brought to brands.[9]

As with the other shows, *Queer Eye* audiences suggest that they do pick up some tips from the shows, although they also enjoy watching for other reasons. Interestingly, although there are similarities between *Queer Eye* and *What Not to Wear*, audiences of this latter show were much more likely to engage with the instruction and consumer information. *Starting Over* audiences also described applying the psychologically oriented techniques of the self to their own lives and relationships. In contrast with all these, *The Biggest Loser* was perceived as more motivational than instructional, in part because of the paucity of diet and exercise information on this show, which emphasized exertion and competitive factors more than the other shows. Rather than seeing makeover shows as uniformly governmental, or as promoting only the "idea of learning" over learning itself, these four shows suggest large differences in the forms of instruction and the absorption of these forms by even their most engaged audiences.

Social Uses of the Shows

Audiences across all four shows used the programs' instruction in highly social ways. Stewart Hoover and his colleagues address how families discussed media with intimates, friends, and colleagues as a way of affirming a social bond: "Interactions about the media function as a sort of social currency: Talking about the media gives people a way to talk about something they care about. Thus, such talk can be self-revelatory while also allowing a person to address issues of concern in the wider culture."[10] Similarly, the audiences in this study used the shows in their social contexts, both passing on and critiquing the instruction offered. They often acted as conduits for the shows' instruction, using their advice to pressure family and friends to conform to the shows' models of self-presentation. However, they didn't only transmit the shows' explicit instruction; they also drew on the shows to educate others beyond the routines of the makeover. Further, by bringing the shows into local and online social spaces, audiences also developed critical and reflexive attitudes to the instruction.

Heterosexual women participants in this study who watched *Queer Eye* talked quite frequently about using *Queer Eye* to browbeat their male partners. About two-thirds of heterosexual women survey respondents who were in a committed relationship reported passing on tips to men in their lives, generally about clothes, shaving, and other grooming tips. A few women interviewees mentioned using advice offered in the show in negotiations with their husbands about how to dress and entertain, for example: "My husband is usually [watching] right there with me, so I can just turn to him and say, 'Pay attention to this part!'" One of the most touching stories came from Donna, who recalled the effect of watching *Queer Eye* on her relationship with her husband:

> Well, actually, my husband had a mullet. For years! It got to be a source of contention.... Every time the *Queer Eye* guys would cut somebody's hair I would tell him about it: "See, your mullet is dead. Please, the eighties are over. The hair band is gone!" And a couple years ago on my birthday he came home with a haircut. Now, I don't know if it had anything to do with me saying all this stuff about *Queer Eye* changing him, but that was a great day.

INTERVIEWER: That's a great story.

D: That night he took me to a gay bar for my birthday.... He and I both thought there was going to be a drag show. Now, I live in a very small town in West Virginia. The gay bar isn't even here anymore. I mean, it was here for like six months. And we thought there was gonna be drag shows because they had had it. Well, it turned out they were having the show for the lesbians and they had real female strippers in there. So, we go to a gay bar and he gets to watch real women strip! But he had great hair! And he introduced me to the bartender, which he and I hit up . . . you know, started off the conversation. So I like to say he gave me a haircut and a gay man for my birthday. And that is love.

Even here, Donna deflects whether the show itself had anything to do with her husband's haircut and impulse to go to a gay bar, but it is interesting that she raised this in a conversation about whether she had changed anything in her life as a result of watching the show. Although people were rather reticent about attributing changes to *Queer Eye*, women were more likely to talk about how they used it to cajole their male partners.

Even with the shows as reinforcement, however, such persuasion is often a struggle. Danica told us about when her sister asked for a *What Not to Wear*–style makeover:

DANICA: She freaked out. I had it all ready, and said, "This is what you have to do." We have similar body types, but not really. And I was channeling my inner Stacy, and I'm like, "Here's what we can do, and let's look at your wardrobe," and I did the whole thing. I was like, this is what she needs, she's a stay-at-home mom, she didn't have a big budget. And she was a Mary Kay representative at the time. And I'm like, "You just have to look halfway decent, you need something that will go medium-casual to work." And I'm like, "Khakis are it for you, that's what you need, a few khakis." And she just lost it. I don't know what human being in the world doesn't own a pair of khakis, but my sister is that person. So that was the deal breaker, and we just stopped. And that was, what, two years ago? Yeah.

INTERVIEWEE: Do you think that maybe that's an example of where a stranger would have been more help?

D: Yes. And I tried so hard to be not a sister.

As with some women *Queer Eye* respondents who believed that advice from the Fab Five was more persuasive than advice from them, this woman also believed her sister would be somewhat more receptive to feedback from strangers. Although people do use the shows to advise others, such advice isn't necessarily easy to impart or receive.

Many *Starting Over* participants reported watching the show in conversation with other women. Some used it to connect with people across geographical distances: "I have thoroughly enjoyed it when my mom was able to get it. She lives in a small town in Kansas. We would watch it and we would talk about it before the next episode, or after, and that was a lot of fun." A bisexual woman respondent mentioned that she used the show's advice in her romantic relationship with another woman: "Well, it's so funny, because my partner, since we watch it together, we have our own little *Starting Over* house going. It opened this whole new line of communication and we use the same language." Because only 5 percent of *Starting Over* respondents identified as lesbian, bisexual, or queer women, such reports of using the show in women's sexual relationships with other women was very rare. The "homosociality" of the women-only household might make the show popular with lesbian viewers.[11] Yet the dearth of openly gay or bisexual women on the show (there was one bisexual woman in season 1) and the focus on heterosexual relationships and families suggest that lesbians need to do some conversion to make much of the show's content relevant to them.

Occasionally, participants talked about their social uses of the shows beyond the express instruction of the makeover. This was especially true of *Queer Eye* viewers. Women, in particular, welcomed the show's possibilities for improving their male family members' attitudes toward gay men. A female survey respondent wrote that she would like to nominate her ex-boyfriend because "he's a slob and a homophobe." Rachel testified to the actual benefits of being on the show in this regard:

> I have quite a few very close friends that are gay guys, and [my husband] was always intimidated, uncomfortable around them. And after spending a week with five gay men [while on *Queer Eye*], I mean he went short of having sex with them—I mean he just loves them. And it really broke the ice for him as far as the gay nation. It really made a big difference in him.

Her comment that her husband "went short of having sex with" the Fab Five reflects the anxiety many heterosexual people feel about affection between heterosexual and gay men. Rachel contained this anxiety by insisting that it wasn't a sexual connection, but it was nonetheless intimate and invested. In addition to all the other benefits of being on the show, Rachel gained a husband who learned from his contact with the Fab Five to be less homophobic and more accepting of her gay male friends.

Donna watched *Queer Eye* with her teen sons and used the show to talk to them about gay issues: "Being the show that it is, a lot of the times we talk about different gay issues. Because I'm definitely trying to raise the children to not be judgmental because of someone's sexuality." Talking about her twelve-year-old, she continued, "Sometimes he'll have questions like, you know, he'll say 'What do they mean?' because they have a lot of slang they'll throw out there." Yet when she described using tips from the show to persuade this son to dress a certain way, she joked, "He's just twelve. I can say, 'Please wear this,' and he'd fight. I can say, 'The sky is blue,' and he'll say, 'No mom, it's teal,' you know, because he's twelve." Both the research assistant who conducted this interview and I wondered whether her son would say the sky is teal not because he's twelve, but because he might be gay. We also wondered whether Donna was at least partially aware of this, and used the show to give him (as well as the rest of the family) access to images of gay people that she could contextualize through their discussions. The educational function of *Queer Eye* was not lost on the series producers; in fact, it was part of the show's original rationale. The hosts most explicitly adopted this educational function beyond the specifics of the makeover when they featured transman Miles, using the makeover to discuss the basics of female-to-male gender transition, as I discussed in the previous chapter.

Online Communities

Participants used the shows' instruction in their relationships with family and friends, even across geographical distances; they also discussed the makeover shows in their social engagements with others online. This extended their contact beyond their immediate family and friends to include people not previously known to them. Participants for all four shows discussed going to official websites to augment the instruction and shopping tips in the shows, and to see dramatic before and after pictures of makeover candidates. They also went to message boards to extend this instruction in their online interactions. There were large differences among the cohorts, however, regarding how much they went to show-specific sites and what they did there.

Some *What Not to Wear* respondents used the message board to get and share information about what looked attractive and how to find products that had been featured on the show (13 percent of *What Not to Wear* respondents were recruited from the show's official site). One woman who regularly watched the show and went online to post comments, said, "Sometimes people will discuss like, this is crazy but, clothing. Like some people will post, 'Do you think this is cute?' And sometimes people will post, 'I don't think that's becoming.' . . . And with the makeup and facial stuff, people will post, 'Do you know a product?' And I've posted about a product before." This was seen as especially important by those people who said that there was not enough information on the official *What Not to Wear* site to find featured products.

Respondents also described their interactions about *What Not to Wear* as a way of demonstrating their expertise. One said, "Usually I'll answer questions if someone has a specific question about fashion or about fit, or, I think because being petite, I tend to be like the expert shopper. Because we have to look harder for anything that fits us, so in looking around for our stuff we tend to find other people's stuff. So if someone writes in and says, 'I'm looking for a strapless black dress,' and I'll think, 'Oh, I saw that at Target.' So I'll write that in, answer their question." A male *What Not to Wear* participant, Robert, also discussed being a "very regular, very vocal contributor on the board." He told us:

I will post comments on the show. Quite often I answer other people's questions. And I will make comments about fashion, or I ask a lot of questions, too. There's been times when I'll say, "I don't really get this," and I'll post on the boards like, "Okay, ladies, here's my question: Am I just a dumb ignorant male chauvinist pig, or could someone clear this up for me?" And the boards are a pretty lively community . . . and there are friendships. And I would have never thought that such a thing was possible, but there are friendships there; there are rivalries there. Although I would say that most of the people who really insist on being dumb, just who are there to be offended, that are looking for a reason to be offended or just dumber than dirt usually weed themselves out quickly, basically because they can't hold their own in an argument. Yeah, I post typically once a day. And when I say I post once a day, I might spend a half hour there and put up five or six different posts. Sometimes it's not that often, but other times, yeah, I might put up five or six different posts a day.

Robert's performance of expertise includes an unapologetic acknowledgment of rivalries and of weeding out of people who can't hold their own in a feisty debate about fashion. This unusual perspective may be related to his gender. He was among the few men who were active posters on the *What Not to Wear* message boards; most of the female *What Not to Wear* respondents who spent some time online were more likely to describe getting and sharing information in a more collaborative way.

Starting Over participants described their social interactions online as offering a safe, supportive environment in which women could share exercises and explore the therapeutic themes from the show. Many of the *Starting Over* participants were recruited through an unofficial fan site, which I call here StartingOverSupport.com (SOS). One woman survey respondent wrote that even though there are "only about twenty people making changes on the TV, but there's like three hundred women [online] watching and doing the things that they're doing. A lot of people actually say that whenever Rhonda gives them an assignment, they actually do it at home, along with the people on the show." A *Starting Over* interviewee, Tori, compared the social but anonymous possibilities of SOS message boards with the automated features of the official *Starting Over* site. Tori did not like the official site's advice as "just being automated, I really wasn't getting any feedback, and I don't really know that many people, to offer feedback." She valued the anonymity of the online sites as allowing her to perform a more likeable version of herself:

> TORI: It's always good to get together with women that like the show, that you can share learning experiences with. It's still the distance of the Net, the anonymity.
>
> INTERVIEWER: In a good way or a bad way?

T: Probably a little of both. I'm a lot more likeable [online] than in person! [laughs].

These examples present an interesting contrast with the assumption that online interactions are inevitably diminished compared with those offline, and suggests possibilities for social connection online that are not possible or desirable offline. Rather than seeing mediated social interaction as a poor alternative to face-to-face contact, SOS users suggest that a particularly vivid kind of social bond is created precisely through the limits on personal intimacy that the Internet creates.

This personal anonymity did not mean, however, a lack of connection between the women on some of the message boards. One interviewee made the creator of SOS a quilt to thank her for her efforts. Others did a significant amount of labor to keep the sites up-to-date; one interviewee was a site administrator, and another interviewee posted synopses of episodes each week so that others who had missed episodes could follow along. The sites also gave members access to former housemates and Iyanla Vanzant's assistant, who regularly blogged and did live chats on the forum. A member described visits from former housemates and even, occasionally, one of the hosts:

> We have had special guest chats. And Meg has been there with us since before Christmas. She's a regular with us now, she's a nutball just like the rest of us! And we have had, who's been in there? . . . Kelly has been there. The Kim from season 3 has been there. Jill, all four of the couples from the boot camp, and I think it was about either two or three weeks ago we had Miss Iyanla there.

SOS thus offered a privileged mode of access to the participants in the show itself, reducing the social distance between them and the members. Among the four shows, *Starting Over*'s online communities expressed the most seamless continuity of the show's instruction, providing a somewhat anonymous context in which to develop and implement *Starting Over*'s women-oriented, self-help ethos. This is not to say that all *Starting Over* online groups are this supportive; we recruited mostly from SOS and the Yahoo group populated by viewers who had fled what were seen as the bitchy interactions on the official *Starting Over* boards.

A few *Starting Over* and *What Not to Wear* interviewees described their active engagement online as honing their expertise that they then intended to bring into their professional lives. Robert, the feisty *What Not to Wear* poster quoted above, had begun to employ *What Not to Wear*'s instruction to change his career from a salesman of hot water heaters to a job selling men's clothing:

> As I began watching this show, and through where I shop for my own menswear, I began developing an eye for what I like. It's gotten to the point I can walk into the shop and they don't ask me [if I need help]; basically I can walk up to what I want because I know what I'm looking for when I shop. And that's actually going to turn into a career for me, because if everything works out how it's supposed to, I'll be working in the men's suit business in the next month. . . . It came through watching the show and I found that I enjoyed men's fashion. It's not the end-all, be-all of everything—I know there are very serious issues in the world, but at the same time I found I enjoyed it.

Similarly, a woman *What Not to Wear* interviewee told us, "I love this show so much, and I'm so into this whole thing, I'm even considering doing image consulting as a career because I've just discovered I have a passion for this." Given how much emphasis *What Not to Wear*, in particular, puts on the value of looking more professional in order to get a better job, it seems fitting that some viewers take this one stage further: adopting the training of the show as a skill for their own professional advancement.

Starting Over viewers also used professional advice from the show, in two ways: first, by identifying with the candidates as they went through the starting over process and were inspired to become more ambitious and self-directed in their career choices; and second, by identifying with the hosts and adopting their professional expertise. One interviewee told us that as a result of watching the show, "there were many things that I've changed, now that I'm in the career that I like and I'm looking the way that I want to look and I'm projecting myself the way that I want to. I don't think that I would have done it as effectively had I not seen it in other women [on the show]." This woman was also inspired by the show to consider a change in career, telling us, "I'm actually interested in becoming a certified life coach."

Perhaps the most intensely engaged of all the *Starting Over* participants was Jackie, who identified herself as a "social worker/community activist," a member of a UN committee on posttraumatic stress disorder, and a resident of rural, coastal Canada. Very involved in her local community, Jackie told us about bringing skills from the show to local women:

> I'm getting asked by women, "Could you do a workshop on women and spirituality?" "Could you do a workshop on women and sexual abuse?" "Could you do . . . " whatever, and the community is starting to open up. Now is that because of *Starting Over*? I don't know, maybe . . . There's no psychologists or psychiatrists or anything like that in the mental health field up here. And people who are trained to do counseling are undertrained, and inaccurately trained. So there's not a lot of mental health up here, and yet I'm seeing major mental health changes. And when I go out, I'm hearing women starting to talk to each other differently. So I think that that's because of the show—that and *Oprah*! That's the other show I always recommend, is watch *Oprah*.

Jackie was also very involved in the SOS online community, having become a moderator for the discussion board, and then using discussions from there in her own professional writing:

> I'm a columnist, so I use a lot of that stuff for my columns, too, which is cool. I just did a column on spanking, but it came out of that website because somebody said, "Should you spank or not?" And when I wrote my response, I realized what I'd done was written a column, and so I just lifted it—it's mine, and it became a column. And then I got paid for it!

Jackie used expertise gleaned from the show to supplement her training as a social worker. By encouraging community members to watch *Starting Over* and *Oprah* for therapeutic guidance, she turned a dearth of health services into an audience for commercial media companies. But this is not only a case of Jackie using popular culture in order to work, partly voluntarily, to perform the welfare role of the state. There was a strong sense of personal pride and agency in Jackie's interview, which suggested that the adoption of *Starting Over*'s instruction enhanced her standing in her community's eyes and her own.

Both Robert and Jackie could be considered a version of the "fan–scholar": those invested viewers who, according to Matt Hills, "seek to explain their fan culture to and for itself, and who also criticise and analyse the media industry."[12] Robert and Jackie were "fan–experts" who engaged intensely with *What Not to Wear* and *Starting Over*, respectively, folding the instruction they gained from the shows into their own professional expertise. Robert and Jackie both used the message boards as an intermediate realm in which they offer advice, hone their skills as "experts," and, in Jackie's case, criticize the show's representatives. Both participated in the message boards to convert their subcultural capital—specialized knowledge accumulated from watching the shows—to economic capital: a job at Men's Wearhouse for Robert, a paid column for Jackie.[13]

In contrast to the more active engagement of this study's participants in the *What Not to Wear* and *Starting Over* message boards, *The Biggest Loser* and *Queer Eye* participants tended to go online mostly for information about what was happening on the show: for before-and-after photographs, information about upcoming episodes, and news about candidates and hosts. A *Biggest Loser* viewer said that she goes online to "check to see what Matt is doing and what Suzy is doing because they're my favorites. And then I heard they got engaged so I've seen their proposal, like, over twenty times. It always makes me cry; I'm such a sap." A *Queer Eye* viewer used the official site to learn more about the Fab Five: "I went [to the Bravo *Queer Eye* site] because I wanted to read about everybody and get to know them because they're now my friends. I know, I'm so sad!" Both these participants expressed shame about their online activity that was focused on people in the shows with whom they closely identify.

In general though, few of the *Queer Eye* and *Biggest Loser* respondents discussed online activity much at all. Some *Queer Eye* respondents noted that the show's official site wasn't especially active anymore (less than 10 percent of survey respondents were recruited from *Queer Eye*-specific sites). *The Biggest Loser* is more complicated: During the interview period, there were very active message threads on the official

The Biggest Loser site, including many offering posters' tips for weight loss and exercise. Yet *The Biggest Loser* participants in this study did not talk about using online resources such as message boards as a social context to get information or motivate them to lose weight. The lower rates of online social interaction among *The Biggest Loser* viewers in this study may be an artifact of the recruitment process, given that the majority of respondents for *The Biggest Loser* were recruited from non–*Biggest Loser* specific sites such as RealityBlurred.com (less than 6 percent of *The Biggest Loser* survey respondents heard about the survey from *The Biggest Loser*–specific sites).

The Limits of Instruction

Even though participants discussed using the instruction the shows offered, they nevertheless articulated critiques of the shows. Many of these critiques were cultivated within social contexts of watching the shows. A woman interviewee mentioned watching *What Not to Wear* with her husband: "Usually we talk about Stacy and Clinton, how funny they are. And then my husband doesn't really think that [makeup expert] Carmindy should be on the show. It's kind of a running joke now, he's like, 'She looks like a porn star.'" Many participants mentioned enjoying highly reflexive engagements with the shows in the contexts of their social relationships, both embodied and online.

Critique falls into two categories: In the first, participants criticized the shows and their hosts in terms of the amount and quality of the instruction. In the second, participants engaged reflexively with the instruction, seeing it in the context of a commercial media enterprise. The *What Not to Wear* hosts were criticized mostly for having bad taste: "The hosts have no sense of style," one survey respondent wrote. Many people commented that Stacy and Clinton didn't consider the candidates' lives enough. One woman wrote, "You can wear $800 jeans to play with your kid at the park, but chances are you probably want to wear some easygoing good pants, a T-shirt, and some tennis shoes to play with your kid at the park. And they make it seem as though you need to dress up even to go to the park to play with the kids." Promoting clothes that were too expensive for a candidate's lifestyle or budget was a common complaint.

Respondents also criticized *What Not to Wear* for "trying to make everyone look the same." For example, "Some of the advice can be repetitive: they recommend a lot of the same things (structured jacket, certain types of skirts, etc.)." Another woman complained, "They keep pushing pointy-toed high heels on this show, and while I can understand what they are saying, I cannot ever envision a time when I would try them on, much less wear them." Some *What Not to Wear* interviewees also mentioned that the experts were not skilled at working with Black women's hair and complexions. An African American respondent said, "I think Carmindy might not know how to do their makeup with their darker skin. And I think that Nick [the show's hair stylist] had some problems with hair, but that's normal, and we expect that, and they all expect that when they get on the show. People don't know how to do our hair." A white woman concurred: "Nick, the hairstylist, doesn't really have a lot of experience with African American hair. So I think at times when they've had women on there that have wanted to go with natural hair rather than trying to make their hair look like white women's, that he hasn't known what to do with it." This woman thought the show should do a better job: "Maybe if that wasn't his area of expertise, they could have someone else to help him." The critique that *What Not to Wear*'s advice is too generic, including pressing implicitly white norms of beauty on candidates, seems at odds with the show's emphasis on "dressing the body you have." Although the show's hosts emphasize that candidates must boost their best features and minimize their flaws, some respondent perceived this advice as both generic and racially homogenizing.

When respondents criticized *The Biggest Loser*'s instruction it was most commonly for health reasons. One woman commented:

> I think that because of that whole aspect of it, if you lose fifteen pounds, you're the Biggest Loser that week, so it really champions losing that much at a time. I'd much prefer to see a show that watches people lose weight in a moderate way, losing a few pounds a week or something like that. I think that would be a much better show to teach people about how to live a healthy life.

Here the demands of television to offer the dramatic "money shot," those moments of surprise at the weekly weigh-ins, clashed with viewers' own knowledge of healthy ways to lose weight and their interest in watching a weight loss show that is more realistic and sustainable.[14] *The Biggest Loser*'s emphasis on the value of losing weight for health reasons is thus contradicted by its televised methods, in which the political economy of television production and audiences demand quick and simplistic solutions to complex problems of the self.

Starting Over also came under much criticism for its dangerous methods, though here the damage was more likely to be emotional and psychological than physical. A survey respondent who made a point of watching the show every day was nevertheless quite critical of it. She wrote:

> The life coaches are not qualified mental health professionals and push people into very emotional issues they are not qualified to deal with. They could do psychological harm and I'm not confident that [the resident psychologist] Stan Katz can prevent this because he can be pretty quacky himself. Example: It was downright professionally irresponsible of Katz to stand by while Rhonda humiliated Lisa by making her dress up as a three-year-old. This is nothing more than an outdated quack regression therapy that has done harm to numerous people in the 1970s and '80s. In my opinion, Rhonda is a sadistic, power-hungry person who gets off on humiliating the houseguests.

The assignments given to women in the *Starting Over* house frequently came under criticism: another woman disliked the "cage exercises, psycho mumbo jumbo, [and] humiliating houseguests by having them dress as children [and] sit in boxes." Even though this was usually expressed with sympathy for the candidate, this man expressed a rare example of schadenfreude:

> [*Starting Over*] offers ridiculous unregulated "psychological advice" to grown women who should know better. I do suppose it's inspirational for some people with real problems but let's face it—this season they dressed a forty-year-old woman in a baby doll dress for three days because she was told she was acting childish. Then they sent her out in public. This is reality TV at its best.

Lisa's stint as a three-year-old had produced controversial—and memorable—television.

Viewers also took the shows to task not for offering bad advice, but for not giving enough instruction. *What Not to Wear* respondents expressed frustration with a lack of information on the show in a number of ways. Danielle was among those who complained that the show made over only a narrow range of women, ignoring larger women and women over forty:

> DANIELLE: My mom was visiting and I took her shopping and we got all these new clothes. I totally helped my mom with information I got from the show, as well as helping myself and my husband and things like that. And my mom's in her sixties, so it was useful. And she's a plus size, and it was really challenging to help my mom find clothes in plus sizes. And they do have people who are a little heavier on the show, but I don't think they've ever had anyone who was like *plus*.
>
> INTERVIEWER: Like someone over a 16?
>
> D: Yeah, somebody that's a size 20 or more, something like that. Because there really are unique challenges, and it really is difficult.

A plus-sized interviewee said that she knew more about how to shop for large women than the *What Not to Wear* hosts did: "I think that it's something that's out of their particular expertise. I mean certainly the rules that they set for these people are helpful, but they all seem to end up at Lane Bryant." Ending up at Lane Bryant probably reflects the show's sponsorship deals more than it betrays the hosts' lack of knowledge, however, reflecting the impact of product placement on the kind of instruction the shows offer.

Both women and men viewers also noted that they have very few male makeovers on *What Not to Wear*: at its most gender representative, season 2 featured men in only 20 percent of the episodes. When the show does make over men, respondents commented that the instruction is less skilled. A woman told us in an interview:

> They don't have as many men [on the show]. . . . A lot of times they really just aren't tailoring to the person's lifestyle. And a few times they haven't even really tailored to their body types. There was one guy on

there [whose] sleeves were always too long, and Clinton told him, "Well, just tuck under the sleeves at the bottom." And it's like, "What?! No, you take it to a tailor and you have the sleeves shortened."

What Not to Wear viewers also at times expressed frustration that the show did not offer more explicit instructions about where to buy the featured products: "Have I shopped because of the show? Definitely. But not specific places. And I think that's one of the things about the show is that it really doesn't do a good job of, saying where the items are from." As did other interviewees, this woman mentioned that she went to the *What Not to Wear* official website in order to try to get more information on products featured on the show. Yet some people criticized the website for similar reasons as the show, for not offering enough advice to men, larger women, and older people.

The Biggest Loser participants also complained that there was "not enough emphasis on the diet component—the show focuses too much on exercise," especially in later seasons. Another respondent wanted to learn more about "nutrition and portion control," someone else about "more cooking kind of stuff, because I don't know my way around the kitchen." One respondent specified that she would like to see more advice for vegetarians who wanted to lose weight. The emphasis on exercise over explicit instruction about how to follow a particular diet may have a great deal to do with the televised aspects of the show: it is much more gratifying to see contestants' sweat and tears produced by exceeding what they imagined was physically possible than it is to see a lesson in how to gauge the number of calories in a burger.

Interviewees commented that the lack of information in the television show might be intended to force people to buy books and DVDs associated with the brand. One woman said, "I think they should focus more on the education so that people like me who really want to [can] learn in addition to watching the show. I mean watching the show could substitute for having to go out and buy these books and get the knowledge that way." Another observed that in order to get the most valuable information, motivated viewers had to purchase more TLC/ *What Not to Wear*–related products, generating income for the company. Asked whether she had learned things about weight loss from *The Biggest Loser*, Sandra said, "No, and I think that's deliberate, because you can get all that if you purchase it online. . . . Again, it's marketing and I'm mindful of that." How much information a show contains about details of a makeover depends on a number of constraints: time, televisual interest, integration into the narrative, and so on. But in a media economy where less revenue comes from advertising, media companies have to generate profits through other, brand-related products. Withholding some information to entice viewers to purchase a range of branded products and visit ad-supported websites is a marketing model designed to supplement increasingly meager advertising revenues.

Although some *What Not to Wear* interviewees were frustrated about the lack of specific information about products on that show, respondents were also very critical of product placements in this and the other shows. *The Biggest Loser* interviewees commented on the "shameless plugging" of some products: Seth remembered a dessert that had been featured on the show, chanting, "Jell-O! Jell-O! Jell-O! Jell-O!" When we asked if he had bought the dessert because of the show, he responded, "Hell no." Robert recalled a discussion on the *What Not to Wear* message boards about Crest Whitestrips, a teeth-bleaching product:

Last season the production company had Carmindy pushing the Crest Whitestrips. She would get done at the end of each makeup makeover and say, "You know? The best thing that would work for you is a really big smile." And Carmindy could just never pull it off looking natural. And so it was just clumsily done, and everybody on the boards was just like, "Ooh, the way she presents it, I've got no interest in buying the product!"

Queer Eye viewers were also occasionally disappointed at the obvious product placement in that show, even as they were aware of this as a feature of reality television. Keith said:

Some of the gifts they give are great—the TVs and computers, all that stuff. But it just seems like it's to give to get sponsors' attention and product placement and all that. That's the way of the world within reality TV and everyone does it. They probably do it not as poorly as a lot of other shows, but if there's one thing that you kind of shake your head at every week, it's usually that.

Participants also sometimes worried that paid plugs for products swayed the hosts' judgment. Although, for example, the *Queer Eye* hosts asserted that they only chose products they thought were genuinely right for the candidate, for many viewers the taint of commercialism was at odds with what they saw as the informational aspects of the show. This puts *Queer Eye* and *What Not to Wear* in a particularly difficult position. Many of the people we talked to wanted more information on where to get products, and yet they also don't want to see "shameless plugs." When the product information was seen to be for the benefit of people watching the show, our participants tended to see this as valuable information; when it was seen as for the benefit of advertisers, it was treated with hostility. The shows' producers must tread a fine line between the demands for information and the risk of discrediting that information by linking it too explicitly with the economic conditions of production.

Only one respondent critiqued product placement for expressly political reasons. Discussing products that had been featured on *Starting Over*, one viewer said, "I hate Curves. The guy who started it also funded protests at abortion clinics." This same woman, however, mentioned paying attention to products sponsored by this show "in the same way I would with *Ms.* magazine, if they were taking that kind of financial support because I really do see that they're supporting something that's very unique on TV, and that is a woman-centered show, which I find very unique on the TV schedule." Other *Starting Over* participants bought sponsored products as a sign of support for a show under threat, making this cohort the only group that talked about the leverage potential of consumption. I was surprised that *Queer Eye* viewers showed no similar impulses toward the strategic consumption of placed products as a sign of support for such an openly gay program. Neither gay nor straight participants in this study mentioned the politics of gay consumption or showed the legendary loyalty of gay consumers that mainstream companies relied on when entering the gay market.[15]

Obvious product placement prompted a reflexive critique about the commercial contexts of the makeover shows and how these contexts shaped the kind of information offered. One woman identified product placement as an alternative to or supplement for advertising in an age where technologies allow viewers to zip through commercials: "Most of the girls I know that watch [*Starting Over*], they either TiVo it or they DVR so they can zip through all of the commercials, but [the company] found a way to get past that! [laughing]." Only one *What Not to Wear* viewer was sympathetic to the financial demands of television production:

> Well, you need to have money to put the show on, so if you get money from Crest Whitestrips you get money from Crest Whitestrips. And if that's where you're getting the money you shouldn't feel any shame about saying Crest Whitestrips, you know? And I know if you read the forums, some people get a little bit upset, they think it's overdone. But I'm like, "Hey, the show's got to get on the air. Are you willing to send them a million dollars a season?"

This was an unusually sympathetic approach to product placement, compared with most people who saw commercial sponsorship as distorting, corrupting, or distracting attention from the "real" instruction of the shows.

Participants in this study frequently commented that they shared with others online critiques and information about the shows' production processes that afforded them a critical distance from the shows' advice and commercialism. Sometimes this critique may have fed back to the show's producers. Robert, for example, thought that the discussion board's lampooning of the clumsy Crest Whitestrips product placement in *What Not to Wear* had resulted in a lessening of Whitestrips mentions. He mused, "I don't know if it was just focus groups, or maybe they actually paid attention to the boards for once, but enough people on the boards were just saying, 'Stop.'" Participants in this study were thus able to consider the role of audiences, including online posters, in the circuits of production of the shows, especially as far as product placement was concerned.

Audiences' reflexivity regarding the shows' instruction complicates the governmental model of reality television, which presumes an individual viewer in a private conversation with television content. As other audience research scholars have found, makeover show reception occurs in often highly social contexts, whether online or with local intimates. The Whitestrips example also suggests that online message boards were quite active in cultivating critiques of the shows' advice and consumer plugs. As viewers shared information about the shows, the television production process, and the business aspects of reality television production, this prompted (in some respondents at least) media reflexivity about the shows and their commercial context.

Comparing Meanings and Critiques

The interviews with twenty people who were not regular viewers of the shows and were not recruited online offers a useful point of comparison. Would people not familiar with the shows adopt or critique their instruction? Interviewees in the comparison group expressed more divergent opinions on all four shows. As did the regular viewers, some *Biggest Loser* comparison group interviewees found the episode they watched motivating to begin exercising and losing weight: "Because everybody could go to the gym and talk to the trainer and do what they gotta do." But others expressed vociferous rejection of the show as offensive. One woman's response to the episode was "outrage . . . I mean it was interesting to see how they—the structure of the show, how they created it and manipulated [the contestants]. . . . But I guess it was informative in a sociological way or something." All the male comparison group *Queer Eye* viewers said they picked up tips from the episode. One heterosexual man said, "When I first heard about the show, I thought they were trying to convert straight guys." Once he'd seen the sample episode, not only did he say he'd start watching it and recommend it to friends, but wanted to be on the show. The *Starting Over* viewers expressed the most polarized responses to the show. One male viewer used elements from the episode to talk at length about his own narrative of self-discovery; another saw the show as "contrived" and the solutions as "all too simple. As if to think that you go to this house and you walk away fine. What the hell is a life coach anyway? It sounds like a big scam." When asked if he had found anything useful about watching the episode he said, "It makes me want to watch less TV. It makes me want to read a book."

The comparison group viewers were generally unimpressed by *What Not to Wear*: the men found it hard to relate to the advice given to a woman candidate, and a Latino man commented that he wanted to see makeover programs that feature men of color. He would like the show more

> if I watched it and there were men on there, and if there were like other men of color. Because you know, I can't wear Abercrombie & Fitch; it's made for like skinny guys. And I'm not skinny, so I couldn't really watch that show. But if there was something pertaining to like—and not necessarily ethnic clothing—but something that pertained to just my body type . . .

This man addressed style issues for men of color not as "ethnic clothing" but a question of fit: most shows feature clothes for skinny white men, like the preppy apparel from Abercrombie. He was one of the few interviewees who linked the clothing recommendations made by makeover show hosts to implicitly white norms of style.

Some of the most vociferous criticisms of the consumer features of the shows also came from the comparison group. Most interviewees in this cohort could remember numerous product placements in the episodes they had just seen, except for Genevieve, who watched a *Starting Over* episode and ironically referenced theories of media effects. She couldn't remember any featured products, "which means that I'm probably gonna go out and buy whatever was on the show [and ask myself,] 'Why do I want this?'" She did go on to consider that the "product" promoted by *Starting Over* was less cleaning fluids or steaks than a racially specific attitude to the self embodied by psychotherapy: "I think there's a very sort of like white pedagogy of introspection happening in it. And I think that's appealing. I mean certainly I found myself sort of like, 'Oh yeah, maybe you should go to therapy.' Like maybe that was the product that was featured." Of all our interviewees (regular and comparison group viewers), Genevieve was the only one who saw the therapeutic aspects of *Starting Over* as a product, linked to an industry and a consumer economy; she was also the only one who saw *Starting Over's* therapeutic orientation as racially framed, as a "white pedagogy of introspection." Genevieve described herself as a white, queer-identified woman with a master's degree; both her education and distance from hegemonic norms of sexuality might have enabled a more reflexive perspective on the show.

A couple of *What Not to Wear* comparison group viewers were highly critical of the commercial aspects of that show. They muttered quite often during the screening of the test episode about the wisdom of spending $430 on a pair of shoes as extravagant and unrealistic for most viewers. An African American man voiced the most articulate critique of consumer society that *What Not to Wear* typified: "I think that in the Western culture we live in a materialistic society where we're trained to be consumers. And I think that all the change basically amounts to spending money and making somebody else rich. So I think that shopping doesn't change our thoughts or change our minds." The comparison group, then, reflected far more divergent and somewhat more critical views of the four shows. This is to be expected from the method of their recruitment: these were people who were not regular viewers of the shows (though some of them were regular viewers of other reality and makeover shows); and they were not recruited from online sites that may have already built some consensus around the virtues and faults of the shows.

Media Reflexivity and Its Contradictions

Popular and scholarly writers may be overly anxious about makeover shows' influence on audiences' behaviors and consumer habits. The governmental critique worries about an insidious adoption of the models of normative citizenship offered through makeover shows' instruction. In contrast, the public service broadcasting approach taken by Hill worries that the useful elements of lifestyle television's instruction are reduced to merely an *idea* of learning as valuable. The participants' responses here suggest that neither view adequately addresses the complexities of how they engaged with the expressly instructional and commercial elements of these shows. The participants' discussions of the instructional elements of the four shows suggest that highly motivated viewers, as most of our respondents were, did watch the shows in part for the advice they offer, and did pick up tips from them. Women, in particular, used this advice in their social relationships, employing it to browbeat (usually male) family members into better behavior, and integrated the shows' advice in their relationships with female family members and friends. Some of the shows' instruction might be seen as having a social benefit, for example with viewers' discussions of their use of *Queer Eye* to rehabilitate homophobic men in their lives to be more gay-friendly. The instructional aspects of the shows were also a central point of their online sociability, as viewers discussed among themselves advice from the shows and how to integrate this into their own lives. Further, some of the most dedicated viewers, the fan–experts, used information from the shows for their own professional advancement.

This is not to suggest, however, that these participants simply absorbed each show's instruction wholesale. There was a great deal of variability among the shows in terms of how invested audiences were in their instructional elements. Many regular viewers across the four shows were highly media-reflexive about the instruction offered by the shows, their consumer advice, and how both of these were framed by the shows' commercial imperatives. The shows' most didactic elements were mitigated by audiences' social contexts: these viewers shared information about production and industrial contexts among themselves, especially online, enabling a degree of critical distance from the shows.

Media reflexivity alone, however, did not necessarily protect regular viewers from makeover shows' overarching assumption of progress toward a better version of the self, achieved largely through more adequate consumption. Indeed, the sense of agency that many participants brought to the shows' appeals might paradoxically strengthen the shows' underlying assumptions; audiences negotiated the details of the texts, and did so in social collaboration with other fans, but nevertheless overlooked the pervasive, intimate workings of capital. Although many participants critiqued specific advice and consumer appeals, what Roland Barthes would call the shows' *parole*, they found little purchase on their *langue*.[16] Borrowing from Saussurean linguistics, Barthes argued that whereas parole refers to particular utterances and local dialects, langue describes the underlying structure of a language. Audiences identified and critiqued the makeover shows' instruction and consumer plugs—their parole. Yet there was little comment on the project of the makeover; regular viewers took it for granted that the overweight contestants on *The Biggest Loser* should lose weight, or that the scruffy candidates on *What Not to Wear* should look more professional. Further, there was no critique from regular viewers of the underlying premise that consumption is the appropriate way of solving the problems of self-presentation. The shows' assumptions about gender, professionalism, upward mobility, and implicitly middle-class, feminine forms of self-presentation—their langue—were almost never addressed by regular viewers, although some comparison group viewers did take the shows to task for these. Like Schudson's review of the impact of advertising, it is not the effects of specific instructions we should worry about, but the ethos of consumption that underpins makeovers as a genre.[17] Media reflexivity offers no guarantees about leveraging these deep, structural and structuring elements of the text: their common sense.

I continue a discussion of the promise and limits of media reflexivity in the next chapter, where I consider participants' discussions of the representational routines of the four shows. Popular and scholarly critiques assume that, on one hand, audiences watch the show to laugh and point at people less fortunate than themselves; on the other, the Foucault-inspired critique presumes that people willingly adopt a self-monitoring gaze as a result of watching the shows. I found some of each of these orientations, negotiated through a complex moral hierarchy of personal responsibility and social normativeness. But I also found that audiences were reflexive about how wayward bodies were represented, drawing on their knowledge of the workings of a highly commercial media industry.

4

Shame on You

Schadenfreude and Surveillance

Even as viewers sitting at home on their butts are lured in by tear-jerking
teasers that promise inspiration from these dieters, smokers and slobs, they
are also manipulated into snickering, "Hee, hee, hee, they have fat asses."
—Sarah Rodman, *Boston Herald*

INTERVIEWER: How does the show convince the people on it that they
need to make changes?
DANICA: That secret footage. I think that's the biggest eye-opener because
people have body image issues, positive or negative, about themselves. I
know, I might think I look cute in something, and my husband will be like,
"What are you thinking?" And he will send me back. And it's sort of a joke,
because I sort of know it doesn't look good, but I feel good, and that's what
matters. . . . And when they see that secret footage, when they see themselves as some random person on television, that's when they lose it, that's
when they know that they have to give in.
—*What Not to Wear* interview

Like many journalists, Sarah Rodman assumes that exposure and
humiliation are makeover shows' stock-in-trade. Of *The Biggest Loser*'s home channel, she worries that "NBC" now stood for the "Nothing But Cruelty network" and that "survival and talent are out, and
self-improvement by way of self-abasement is in."[1] Danica's quote suggests, however, that some audiences find value in seeing themselves
through the eyes of another, whether this is through the footage secretly
recorded and later watched by millions of strangers, or through the
scrutiny of a loved one. Some observers of the representational routines of makeover television are concerned that audiences enjoy feeling
contempt or schadenfreude toward the shows' participants, where they
laugh and point at the candidates' failings and falls from grace. Graeme
Turner writes, "It is not surprising that criticism of reality TV programs

which involve humiliation of some kind or another should provoke the question: what do these programs say about the society that chooses to watch them for entertainment?"[2] Others worry that audiences obligingly adopt the self-monitoring gaze cultivated by the shows. Brenda Weber argues that makeover shows teach "subjects through unspoken means how to conduct themselves, so that if I, as a viewer at home, see someone ridiculed in a Plexiglas box due to her wrinkles and sun spots, I fully understand that I must work to enact a makeover of myself so as to avert the censorious gaze I've seen demonstrated on television."[3] This chapter considers audiences' responses to how makeover candidates are represented on the shows according to these axes of contemptuous distancing and self-adjusting identification. What do audiences make of surveillance and shame in the process of the candidate's makeover? To what extent do they adopt the shows' surveillance techniques to see themselves as if through the gaze of another? As with the previous chapter, media and self-reflexivity work in a complex and contradictory way. On one hand, audiences draw on their understanding of the routines of television to critique how candidates are exposed and manipulated on the shows. On the other, they formulate complex hierarchies of moral value, assessing whether a scene is useful or exploitative according to normative standards of self-presentation. Our participants did sometimes talk about adopting a show's monitoring gaze, but this tended to be very program-specific, rather than a property of the genre.

Makeover shows have democratized gendered structures of looking and being looked at, where traditionally feminine modes of being represented—what Laura Mulvey famously called "to-be-looked-at-ness"—have become increasingly applied to ordinary women and men.[4] New mobile cameras and wireless microphones enable producers to gather footage from many of the most intimate moments in reality show participants' lives—even the shower in *The Real World* is partially available for viewing. Makeover shows use surveillance in the process of the makeover itself, as a (usually punitive) device to promote transformation. Most obviously, producers select footage from continuously recorded action, some of which the candidate is unaware of (*What Not to Wear*'s hidden camera footage) and others of which candidates willingly or contractually engage in (*The Biggest Loser*'s "confessional pantry" and *What Not to Wear*'s video diary). This continuous technical monitoring is supplemented by other visual techniques. Candidates' bodies, clothes, and homes are subjected to visual scrutiny by hosts. Friends and family weigh in on their perceptions of the candidates' failings. The shows use specific visualizing techniques, such as the 360-degree mirror in *What Not to Wear* and the giant scale in *The Biggest Loser*, as evidence of the candidates' need to change. Beyond the production context, the real and imagined audience watches as the scenes of exposure and reform unfold, culminating in the dramatic moment of the reveal. The gaze may no longer be male, but it is certainly omniscient.

Both cultural and psychological approaches suggest a fundamental relationship between being seen and the sense that one exists, that one matters. George Gerbner and Larry Gross wrote in the 1970s that the underrepresentation of minority groups on television constituted "symbolic annihilation."[5] To have social and political power requires being acknowledged at all. More recently, Mark Andrejevic argues that reality show participants submit to constant surveillance in part to have their authenticity affirmed as self-knowing and expressive subjects.[6] If self-respect is the ability to look oneself in the eye, reality TV naturalizes and intensifies this by displacing the gaze on potentially millions of watchers. In Wood and Skeggs's words, "The desire to watch and be watched can be seen as part of the endless pursuit of the confirmation of selfhood among the loss of other more certain life trajectories: I see/ am seen, therefore I am."[7] Audiences' perception that they are witnessing the surveillance of ordinary people, rather than actors, intensifies their engagements with the techniques of representation. A regular *What Not to Wear* viewer recalled the show's "hidden camera thing, where you didn't know [you were being filmed]. It's a bizarre, loss of privacy, American thing. We'll take pictures of you and that will be amusing. But you do do that and you see that it is real, and you see their real reaction to that, so that seems real." Even if this is seen as slightly creepy, surveillance offers evidence of "the real," facilitated both by the cooperation of intimate others and by the technologies and processes of reality television formats.

But the power of these surveillance techniques to render candidates authentic comes with costs. Existing in the eyes of the other is also central to the experience of shame. Gershen Kaufman writes that "to feel shame is to feel *seen* in a painfully diminished sense. Shame reveals the inner self, exposing it to view."[8] Sarah Ahmed draws from Jean-Paul Sartre to develop the relationship between being seen and the experience of self: "In shame, I expose to myself that I am a failure through the gaze of an ideal other."[9] Eve Sedgwick and Adam Frank discuss the psychologist Silvan Tomkins, who found that shame was provoked in infants by a disruption of the parental gaze, a looking away, having been seen and found wanting.[10] Through this need to see oneself as if from the outside, shame can be contrasted with guilt: whereas guilt is the result of being caught transgressing a norm, shame requires a revision of one's self-concept, of the view of the self by the self. Guilt demands apology, shame a self-reflexive reevaluation.

Makeover shows represent shame as intimate and interior, experienced through the body, about the body, as an estrangement from the social body. But because shame is felt in and about the body it is experienced as natural, and is therefore hard to see as a product of shared social and political conditions. Walter Benjamin observed that shame is "no more personal than the life and thought that [govern] it."[11] Shame is physically and intimately experienced; in that moment of flooding, it isolates its sufferer from her milieu. Yet because we are likely to feel shame about disruptions in relationships in which we are invested, this feeling connects the intimate self with the social body. This social body is not a universal, neutral body, nor even a familial body, but is morphed according to hierarchies of visibility, structured through gender, race, and class. Shame is differentially applied, for example, to raced bodies, where Black people are subject to heightened degrees of scrutiny and critique. Riley Snorton argues that white anxieties about Black people's sexuality are constantly projected onto the bodies of Black people in order to maintain and legitimate racial hierarchies.[12] Shame is also invoked when bodies are out of place: according to Rita Felski, class mobility is especially likely to produce shame as an outcome of feeling in an unfamiliar habitus.[13] On the one hand, upward mobility is a social expectation that is the raison d'être of the makeover; on the other, candidates are humiliated for stepping out of their given position. Further, shame can be mobilized on the bodies of usually privileged people who are perceived to be behaving badly. Judith Halberstam suggests that shame feminizes its sufferers because it is "a gendered form of sexual abjection: it belongs to the feminine, and when men find themselves 'flooded' with shame, chances are they are being feminized in some way and against their will."[14] As men become makeover candidates, they are subjected to similarly feminizing modes of scrutiny and punishment that women, people of color, GLBT people, and other marginalized groups have long had to suffer. Unself-consciousness is a mark of privilege, a freedom to be unconcerned about the good opinion of others. In contrast, less privileged people are all too familiar with the need to "watch yourself."

Given the centrality of surveillance in all reality television, it is no surprise that shame is a fundamental affect in this metagenre. But it is particularly mobilized in makeover shows that take the transformation of the person as its central project. Candidates are shamed into reform through being made to see themselves through the eyes of another. Popular wisdom would suggest that witnessing the public exposure of another's failings would prompt schadenfreude in audiences: an "'emotional manifestation of beliefs about justice,' an almost puritanical pleasure in seeing punishment meted out to those who deserve it, without having to mete it out oneself."[15] Others have argued that shame is not only distancing but peculiarly vicarious: we are shamed by others' shame. Eve Sedgwick writes, "Someone else's embarrassment, stigma, debility, bad smell, or strange behavior, seemingly nothing to do with me, can so readily flood me. . . . This is the double movement shame makes: toward painful individuation, toward uncontrollable relationality."[16] Even talking about shame can be shaming, as I found when I blushed to my roots describing this chapter to a colleague.

The deployment of surveillance and shame has been seen as central in contemporary citizenship, facilitated by new cultural modes such as reality television. From this view, reality television draws on surveillance techniques that swap the monolithic, controlling gaze of Big Brother for the micro and localized technologies of watching in *Big Brother*. In the introduction to their anthology about reality television, for example, Murray and Ouellette write, "Part of what reality TV teaches us in the early years of the new millennium is that in order to be good citizens we must allow ourselves to be watched as we watch those around us."[17] In makeover television, the willing subjection to external surveillance is assumed to be supplanted by self-surveillance and monitoring. There is a little research on how audiences look at reality show participants, but less on the extent to which they adopt the self-surveillance techniques that characterize makeover shows in particular. A couple of tantalizing suggestions come from audience research in the United States and Britain. In her research with American reality show viewers, Alice Hall found some evidence of laughing at others' expense, including at terrible singers who audition for shows such as *American Idol*. She writes that an "element of enjoyment seemed . . . to include a strong element of schadenfreude, of taking pleasure in another's misfortune."[18] Other scholars who have looked at audience perceptions of lifestyle shows argue that surveillance and shaming techniques are met with profound ambivalence by audiences. Wood, Skeggs, and Thumim found that the women in their study of lifestyle television both judged the women on-screen who were represented as failing in the norms of conventionally respectable femininity, and critiqued the standards by which they were being assessed.[19]

The responses from audiences in this study suggest their more complex engagement with the shows' representations of wayward pre-makeover candidates than the spectrum between schadenfreude and a willing submission to self-surveillance suggests. Moments of shame in the shows were assessed according to their usefulness in promoting normative gender, class, and race performances by candidates in the shows. Yet these audiences were concerned to distinguish a functional shaming of candidates from a gratuitous humiliation brought on by exploitative producers. Their reception of what they perceived as the humiliating aspects of the shows were marked more by intense ambivalence and sometimes identification than by the contempt and schadenfreude that critics assume.

Saving Face

Some viewers discussed techniques within the show that made the candidates look at themselves and their habits. A woman described some of these processes on *The Biggest Loser*:

> One episode, they had all kinds of desserts and fried foods and all kinds of fast foods and some people act like, "Wow, I actually eat most of this

stuff." I mean you don't think about it, but when it's all there in front of you, you start thinking. And then some of the stuff they make them do, they realize, "Wow, if I wasn't so big, maybe I could climb these stairs without gagging for air," or "Maybe I could fit in this ride at the amusement park with my kids. I'm missing out on so many things with my family," and especially with children, with younger children, you realize how much you're missing out because you can't really participate. It just forces them to look at how they've been living.

Others described the role of the hosts in pointing out to candidates that they needed to reappraise their lifestyles. One woman described the role of the Fab Five in *Queer Eye*:

When they go into their house and they're like, "My God, look at you. Look at things you own! Here are some examples of why you should never ever wear this. And how disgusting is your refrigerator—you can't live like this anymore." Really just pointing out the things that are visible to everybody that they probably miss in their day-to-day lives.

Many people we talked to saw the publicness of makeovers as a necessary and beneficial element for the makeover candidates. A *Biggest Loser* viewer developed this theme:

Because you are in the public eye, that was the biggest push for [the candidates] to continue. That was my feeling, because I know that if other people are following you, you have a tendency to continue, not just in weight loss, this is with anything, but mostly we're talking about that. And I do believe that when you're following through that, you don't want to feel like a quitter in front of a million people, as compared to just a few people that may know you [laughing]. But it was just so intense. It didn't stop me from looking.

This interviewee affirmed the value for *The Biggest Loser* contestants of being accountable to the million people watching the show. At the same time, she recognized somewhat sheepishly that she was part of a mass disciplining gaze.

Queer Eye similarly capitalized not only on the gay male hosts but also on the audience to convince sloppy straight guys that they needed to transform themselves. One heterosexual male viewer argued for the power of the television audience to do what women in the straight guys' lives couldn't accomplish: "Being on television, and being exposed to such a wide audience: I think it might drive home the point to people a little bit better than your wife saying for thirty years that you need to change something." Rachel, married to a man who was made over on *Queer Eye*, found that the most compelling part of the process was "the reality of seeing yourself on television. Because people go to counseling, people go to Weight Watchers, all that kind of stuff, and it's not until you actually see yourself on TV that you go, 'Oh, I really have to do this.' And you realize that other people besides your immediate family are seeing whatever the situation is." Many of the people we spoke to imagined what it was like for candidates to be exposed to millions of television viewers and what the impact of this internalized gaze might be; Rachel actually had this experience.

Shame connects the intimate body with the social body, and is also used to indicate bodily transgressions that the makeover must redeem. The shame projected onto the physical body also extends to its habitus. *Queer Eye* attends to the bodies, habits, and domestic spaces of usually young men at moments of professional and romantic uncertainty. Audience responses to this show were striking in that they rarely critiqued the show's disciplining gaze, instead almost always seeing it as necessary and functional. One woman said of the straight men on *Queer Eye*, "You have to laugh because sometimes these guys are just so pathetic. I mean, you know, they're taking a shower in a bathtub with six inches of grunge on the bottom. I mean, you gotta kinda laugh at that." The unusual spectacle of male reform is made possible because the advice comes from men with an expressly queer gaze; coming from women hosts it would be seen as nagging.

Even if audiences generally believed that seeing oneself from the outside could be uncomfortable, many people mentioned that this could be useful in making changes to oneself. Erving Goffman argues that when a person behaves against the expectations of the group, "he may become embarrassed and chagrined; he may become shamefaced."[20] When we lose face we must do "corrective" work in order to reestablish a social equilibrium. Elspeth Probyn sees shame as potentially having a positive social value: through experiencing shame we recalibrate our behaviors to align more fully with social norms.[21] This was an assumption shared by many of the people with whom we talked. When they saw candidates as transgressing socially valued norms of self-presentation and behavior, they thought that exposure and shaming were appropriate methods of promoting positive change.

None of the regular viewers, however, mentioned the relationship between shaming on the shows and the maintenance of narrowly defined gender, race, or class norms. Angela McRobbie argues that the upper-class women hosts in the British version of *What Not to Wear* employ a "post politically-correct" irony to shame working-class makeover candidates and the norms they value.[22] The class differences in US shows work somewhat differently, however, where hosts are usually exemplars of meritocratic success rather than inherited cultural capital, and where candidates are usually lower middle or middle class. With the exception of the more sensational talk shows, US audiences rarely see poor people on television. One interviewee, Cathy, discussed her feelings of embarrassment watching a rare appearance of poor people on *What Not to Wear*:

> In a very recent episode . . . they did the worst-dressed family. And I really think that they went into that thinking, "Oh, we're just going to find some hicks and whatever, tell them that wearing leather chaps to school isn't right," and it would be a big joke or something. And I really think Stacy and Clinton were surprised with how emotional they got, and how real it was, and the family definitely had a lot of—they just were sad, more or less. I hate to say that, but they were. They didn't have very much money, and they weren't dressing [well] because they didn't have any money and they didn't know what to do. It wasn't just, "Let's make fun of these people." It was much more the wife crying, saying how she's so insecure and it's like, "Oh, wow, okay."

Expecting to have a giggle at some "hicks" who were unaware of the norms of appropriate dressing, Cathy seemed caught by her emotional response to this family as "sad." In their study of women viewers of lifestyle shows, Wood and her colleagues discuss the double meaning of the word "sad," meaning both sorrow and a negative judgment of another as "shocking, deplorably bad or incorrigible."[23] As did the women in Wood and her colleagues' study, Cathy used the word "sad" in both senses, identifying and sympathizing with the candidates' struggles while simultaneously judging them for failing to uphold basic standards of self-care and domestic organization: "*I hate to say that*, but they were [sad]."

At the same time as the makeover shows produce shame for particular candidates, they also vicariously shame audience members who see people on the screen with whom they share characteristics. Although explicit references to race were rare in the shows, *What Not to Wear* frequently critiqued women of color for being "too hoochie," and here and in *Starting Over* Black women were shamed for having "attitude." For example, an African American interviewee was embarrassed by the behavior of a Black housemate on *Starting Over*: "The first [housemate], her name was Deborah, and she was just an embarrassment. Yeah, but watching the stuff that she did, and the things she said, I just thought, 'Oh my God, please get her off because people are watching this now and they're going to think that's what all Black women are like.'" This woman described a double burden that afflicts people of color and other marginalized groups: they are already stereotyped in particular ways and, because there are fewer examples of these groups in popular culture, specific individuals tend to stand for the group. Consequently, some audiences were embarrassed on behalf of the candidate, themselves, and the whole group that the candidate is supposed to represent.

I was also curious about whether gay people watching *Queer Eye* would be embarrassed by its campy representations of the five gay hosts. As I mentioned earlier, one young interviewee's family would not let him watch the show because of Carson's "flamboyant" behavior, but none of the people who participated in this study expressed their own shame about *Queer Eye*'s campy gay hosts. One gay male interviewee did mention this as a common criticism of the show, however:

Carson is a little more flamboyant than the rest. I've seen more flamboyant gays than that. But if you're living in Tennessee he's not the kind of guy you see every day. So a lot of gay guys that I know are sort of like, "I'm not gonna watch that show, it's the *Amos 'n' Andy* of gay TV." And my take on that was like, you know, what are you talking about?! We know people like that. What the hell? And Harvey Fierstein says something along the lines that he feels that any coverage is good coverage. As long as we're out there and we're being seen, somebody is being affected by that and somebody who sits down to watch *Queer Eye* or catches it accidentally, who is inclined to dislike us or be opposed to our lifestyle . . . somebody out of thousands is gonna watch it and be like, "Wait, maybe we misjudged."

This interviewee addresses the struggles around *Queer Eye* about how to position the openly gay and sometimes quite outrageous hosts vis-à-vis discussions about stereotyping among gay communities. On one hand, the visibility of people who have been symbolically annihilated is important for social and political progress. On the other, too often these representations are framed by stereotypes that reproduce some of the shaming qualities attributed to the group. Members of the group themselves are positioned within an unequal economy of emotional labor.[24] They must work emotionally to absorb and transform the feelings associated with these representations in order that, they hope, the whole group may be seen in a better light.

More comparison group viewers than regular interviewees were quite critical of these shows' shaming of candidates. Discussing the sample episode of *What Not to Wear*, one man said that he didn't like the hosts' "negative talk and attacking [the candidate] and criticizing her. And making her feel that there was a problem. And like the whole kind of group mentality thing, where they were saying, 'Everybody else thinks this, like your friends think you have a problem, and this is what you should be doing.' Personally, I didn't think the people that were hosting the show looked good either." Another comparison group viewer saw the *What Not to Wear* episode as "sex-phobic, size-phobic; about size and all this. It was pretty problematic, and then it was just annoying, like, people watch that for real?" He continued:

In the beginning of the show they're like, "Look at all the rolls. Looks like she has eight hundred rolls [of fat]." I mean it's one thing to emphasize ways to wear your clothing to make you feel better, or to not look a certain way you wanna look. It's another to have a skinny woman tell you that you look like a grizzly bear might attack you because you have on a puffy coat. That's fucked up. A lot of their comments were just real crazy.

Comparison group viewers were somewhat more likely to dispute the fundamental premise of the shows—that the candidates needed to change—as well as the shaming strategies the hosts and producers employed to convey this need.

For most regular viewers, however, makeover shows afforded important moments of self-reflexivity in the candidates, where the technologies of surveillance prompted the shame necessary for the journey to self-improvement. Few participants discussed the role of shame in reaffirming social hierarchies of gender, race, or sexuality, or mentioned how class shame promotes the kinds of upward social and professional mobility that our current economic times demand. Shame was seen as socially useful by most of our regular viewers; humiliation, however, was seen as exploitative and evoked sympathy in many of the people with whom we talked.

Hell Is Other People

Viewers' endorsements of the functional uses of shame did not prevent them from being highly critical of some of the representational techniques used in the shows. Audiences perceived both shame and humiliation in candidates as a result of them falling short in standards of attractiveness and behavior. They were distinguished, however, according to how useful these representational routines were seen to be. Shame was constructed as a useful lesson in social alignment; humiliation was a gratuitous display of shortcomings for the purposes of entertainment. Shame involved looking at oneself through the eyes of another and seeing one's shortcomings; humiliation was being seen to fail with no hope of reform. Shame was for the benefit of candidates and their loved ones; humiliation served the audience's baser pleasures and the economies of television. There was nothing inherently different about the representational routines audiences discussed as shaming or humiliating; indeed, different interviewees saw the same events as examples of each. Shame and humiliation were distinguished according to whether they were perceived to prompt a socially useful, transformative self-reflexivity.

Although critics of makeover television tend to assume that audiences enjoy the humiliating aspects of these shows and distance themselves from the candidates on-screen, the regular viewers we spoke to expressed a great deal of discomfort about how the producers represented the candidates, were ambivalent about its effects on other viewers, and were often sympathetic to those people they saw as gratuitously humiliated. Many respondents criticized *The Biggest Loser* for its routinized exposure of the contestants' overweight bodies, including making them strip down to weigh in at the end of each episode:

> I always thought it was weird that they put these people on *The Biggest Loser* in what I would consider somewhat skimpy outfits. Like to some degree that I wouldn't even feel comfortable wearing those and I'm a normal-weight person. Like they have the women in these sports bras and little shorts so their stomachs are hanging out, and they have the men take their shirts off to get weighed. And they're just these little flimsy shirts, so why would they make them take off their shirts? I felt like it was a sensationalism aspect to really kind of go, "Look at how fat these people are."

Many people thought that the exposure of the contestants' bodies on *The Biggest Loser* was gratuitous and unnecessary, and therefore expressed sympathy for them. Some also felt that the stunts in *The Biggest Loser* "are kind of degrading":

> One that sticks out is where people had to—this is in the second season—where they had to run up and down these stairs. So, anything to do with running—like if they have to pace or carry something or carry something heavy or have to bring buckets from the water into the bucket and Matt has to hang onto it or something like that, those don't bother me. But it's the big running things they have to do. I think they want to show the world that fat people can't run and they can laugh at them. That's my impression of it. I don't like those ones.

Audiences were particularly concerned when they thought that producers were humiliating candidates in order to meet the economic needs of the television industry. Talking about *What Not to Wear*, Justina discussed how the need to produce "good television" played out in the candidates' personal transformations:

> INTERVIEWER: How does the show convince the people who come on that they need to make a change?
> JUSTINA: How do they? I think they try to point out a videotape of what they've worn in the past in front of their friends or a group, and show that people don't think it's necessarily flattering on them.
> I: And do you think it's an effective way?
> J: I think it makes for good television. I think sometimes it's not always effective because it's kind of bringing the people down. Who would want to see that—themselves on TV in front of their friends, being made fun of? So then it brings you down and then you feel like, "I have to be made over. Obviously, everybody thinks this way about me."

The perception that candidates were represented in an unkind way in order to produce "good television" was fundamental to the idea of humiliation. *Starting Over* was particularly criticized for doing sometimes quite intense psychological work that viewers worried "shouldn't be on TV." Some interviewees were critical of the techniques used by the life coaches to stage dramatic enactments of housemates' psychological problems. They were particularly concerned that some of these "stunts" were psychologically damaging for the housemates who were already vulnerable and effectively trapped in the house. A few interviewees commented on the economics of *Starting Over*, whereby the women submitted to shaming and humiliation to gain access to free therapy. One woman said, "It's something that most people, especially the women there, could never afford—that kind of therapy. And even though there are things that you would have to trade, like your privacy and being vulnerable." As did a few other *Starting Over* respondents, she acknowledges a trade in which the housemates exposed themselves in return for benefits they could not otherwise access.

Only one *Starting Over* interviewee frankly acknowledged the entertainment value produced through manipulative editing on that show. When we asked her whether the editing accurately portrayed the women in the house, this woman said, "I really don't care. I don't really think about it, as long as they just show me the stuff that's going to make me laugh." This woman was a rare exception among our participants; there was very little evidence that participants in this study watched the makeover shows featured here primarily to get pleasure from witnessing the humiliation of others. This is not to say, however, that contempt and schadenfreude are entirely absent from people's enjoyment of makeover shows. There were three conditions in which interviewees mentioned audiences' contempt for people in the shows: other people's unkind attitudes, especially online; their own ambivalent reception of the cosmetic surgery subgenre of makeover shows; and their perceptions of celebrity seeking by makeover candidates.

Many of the *Starting Over* participants we recruited from Starting-OverSupport.com said that they had left the official *Starting Over* message boards because these had become so bitchy about the housemates. One woman worried that she had been influenced by the hostile discussions of the housemates on the boards:

> There's just a lot of meanness in the message boards. And they take every person on that show—I shouldn't say every—but it seems like they take a majority of people on the show, and they just cut to something that— you know like they'll complain about what they wear. And that's why I'm influenced by the message board when you ask me this question because one of the people that they've made a big deal about is Kim or Kimmy, about her ulterior motives. They made a big deal about Alison, after she got cancer that she was there whining and trying to get more money or something. I'm not so sure I would have come to those conclusions if I hadn't read the message boards.

Some *Starting Over* interviewees were especially disappointed with what they saw as negative criticism on the message boards being at odds with the supportive, affirming ethos of the show itself.

Some *Starting Over* viewers we talked to were involved in the Television Without Pity (TWoP) website, which has threads for many current television shows that make funny, acerbic reviews into an art form. These interviewees were more likely to express an ironic distance from the content of the show, but even here they weren't especially cruel about the housemates on the show. Bill described his participation on the *Starting Over* TWoP board:

> I enjoyed being able to snark on the people, the presences on the show. It's that thing of, like, with shows like this, do you call them "characters," the houseguests, the housemates? Like if one was particularly annoying, that would be where I would go to vent, or I would enjoy watching other people vent about the show. The board, when I followed it, had the most hostility for the life coaches, especially Iyanla, and a lot of love for Dr. Stan, with Rhonda being sort of the also-ran, sort of not getting as much heat or as much love. And certain houseguests really did bring out the fire of the board, which was always sort of fun.

Although Bill acknowledges his snarkiness about *Starting Over*, the hosts came in for more express criticism than the housemates. This might suggest that laughing at the housemates, the show's "characters" who had less power in that setting, was less acceptable than lampooning the hosts. Outside of TWoP, however, the audiences we talked to who were quite active in online discussions about *Starting Over* distanced themselves from other people's bitchiness toward the housemates, and even TWoP posters seemed more measured in their discussions of housemates than of the hosts.

The second place where people were somewhat more likely to express contempt or hostility for makeover candidates was regarding cosmetic surgery shows such as *Extreme Makeover* (not the *Home Edition* version that later became popular) and *The Swan*.[25] Even people who told us that they themselves had undergone cosmetic surgery were critical of the shows. Marci, a *Biggest Loser* interviewee, told us:

> I had a mastectomy in '93, and I just last year had my breast reconstructed. And then of course, they have to make the other one match so you get a nice lift and, I'm fifty-two but my breasts are a year old [laughing]. I'm going to be a very popular old lady, I'm so excited. So I really don't have any problem with plastic surgery at all. I'd love to go in next year and have them suck something out of my belly, too, no problem. It's just on some of those shows, I just think—the face thing, I just hate the way the faces come out.

INTERVIEWER: So if they had plastic surgery that made the women's faces
   come out in a way you thought was beautiful, you'd enjoy shows like
   The Swan more?

M: Oh, I didn't say I didn't enjoy it!

I: You're right.

M: I loved it! [laughing]. I just don't like the way they turn out so many
   times; they just look freakish.

Interviewees discussed surgery shows along a number of themes, many
of which were summarized by Seth, the regular *Biggest Loser* viewer
who opened chapter 1. When we asked him what he thought of the surgery shows, he responded:

> This is a hard question to answer because [laughs], conceptually, I don't
> like them. I don't think that it's healthy as a society to put these people
> on display for manufacturing their appearance. I think that's damaging,
> probably to a whole segment of people, whether it be women with low
> self-esteem, or teenage girls, or just people in general, I just think it's a
> bad idea to make that so readily available.

Like many other viewers, Seth expressed concern about the moral value
of putting on display the vulnerabilities of some of the people on the
surgery shows. Seth disliked the way that the surgery show genre "preys
on the low self-esteem of people, people who are ugly, or feel inferior, it
preys on them and gives them a false sense of hope where—to juxtapose
that with *The Biggest Loser*, I know that I have the ability to lose weight
because I see other people doing it on their own merit." As with other
respondents who positively compared the non-surgical shows in this
study with *Extreme Makeover* and *The Swan*, Seth felt it was important
that viewers could act on the instruction in the show and have agency
over their own transformation. Yet at the same time, he admitted that
he had watched a surgery show, albeit ambivalently:

> *The Swan* was just the craziest show I've ever seen in my life, and I was
> glued to the tube. I mean I don't respect it at all. I know a whole segment
> of people that we thought the show on a moral level was just depraved,
> just sick. But we would watch it like it was crack. It's just unbelievable,

the changes that these women went through, and what they did to themselves to do it. And I think a lot of what we watched it for was basically just to judge these people, just to be like, "You're so stupid for doing this! You need mental help; you don't need physical help if you're unhappy with how you look!" It's like watching a car accident, you can't turn away.

Seth's discussion of the surgery shows epitomizes two central modes through which people talked about what they considered the unkind, damaging, or "sick" aspects of the makeover genre: third-person effects and ambivalence. Third-person effects describes the tendency that people assume media will have stronger, usually negative effects on other people, often those they consider to be more vulnerable than they imagine themselves to be.[26] Concern about how *other* people would respond to humiliating representations of makeover candidates came through most strongly in reference to surgery shows. A *What Not to Wear* interviewee said of *Extreme Makeover* and *The Swan*, "I think it's a freak factor. I think that's what it is, and it makes them [other viewers] feel superior. Like, 'See I might have problems in my life, but I'm not so pathetic and ugly that I have to go on a TV show.'"

Most people attributed unkind attitudes about makeover candidates to other people, and were usually extremely reluctant to admit that they may sometimes have found themselves sharing this view. Even though Seth began by worrying about what effect surgery shows will have on other people, especially teenage girls and people with low self-esteem, he concluded by acknowledging his own and others' complicated attraction to *The Swan*. He and his friends talked about this show as "depraved" and "sick," but nevertheless watched with the kind of compulsion associated with "watching a car accident" or being addicted to drugs: "We would watch it like it was crack." Seth was one of the few people who expressed his own overtly judgmental attitudes to the women on surgery shows, whom he saw as stupid and needing mental help, not physical surgeries. Yet even as he did so he reflected on what he considers the moral turpitude of the shows and his own inability to turn away: he was "glued to the tube." Marci and Seth were among the very few respondents who acknowledged any pleasure in watching the surveillance and humiliation of makeover candidates, and even here it is with much ambivalence. Schadenfreude is not a particularly socially acceptable attitude, especially in the context of academic surveys and interviews, a point I will return to later.

The fact that makeover candidates had volunteered to be on the shows helped mitigate some interviewees' discomfort with watching their unkind representations. The presumably "ordinary" people who participate in reality television shows were seen to have traded their right to privacy in return for celebrity, however fleeting. When the interviewer asked a comparison group viewer if he knew anyone who he thought would be a good housemate on *Starting Over*, he said:

> Obviously, a lot of reality show participants have that "I want to confess my problems to the world. I wanna come lay it all out there." Which I'm not sure it's—that's not necessarily healthy, you know? I think it's kind of, on some level, like they want the audience to sympathize with them, but at the same time there's something a little kind of voyeuristic about "We're gonna listen to the phone calls. We're gonna watch the therapy sessions," et cetera, et cetera. But I mean, it's reality TV. I guess that's just how it is.

When these nonactors were seen as seeking celebrity and airing their dirty laundry on-screen, audiences felt less ambivalent about their contempt for them. Bill, for example, considered some *Starting Over* housemates to be on the show for the "right" reasons, whereas others were there for drama or publicity. It was precisely this combination that yielded much of his enjoyment of the show:

> I think that's part of the pleasure of the show, is the train wreck aspect. I think on the one hand, there's the possibility of watching people legitimately change their lives. I think on the other hand, the producers are interested in watching people who are really just a mess. So I think there's about half and half: people whose lives can legitimately change for better, and then other people who just sort of like having a camera and are just willing to put their dirty laundry out.

By hanging one's dirty laundry out, *Starting Over* participants produced the circumstances of their own humiliation.

Some people saved their unabashed ridicule and contempt for those shows that featured D-list celebrities, such as *Celebrity Fit Club*.[27] A

Biggest Loser regular viewer, Marci, commented, "Well it's totally fake, *Celebrity Fit Club* [laughs]. And I watch it because to me it's just hysterical. And I think they edit to their little hearts' content once they decide what somebody's going to be like. And I never want to see Willie Aames's boobs bounce like that again, it was so disgusting." Committed to the value of *The Biggest Loser* and sympathetic about the struggles of the contestants there, Marci nevertheless took a very different view of *Celebrity Fit Club*. This show is remarkably similar in aim to *The Biggest Loser* but features people who have already given up the right to be treated sympathetically because they are already famous (or have been and want to be again).

Interviewees were thus willing to acknowledge contempt for candidates in three circumstances: other people's contempt, especially online; their own judgments of candidates on surgery shows; and their derision of candidates they saw as celebrities or as seeking celebrity. Overall, however, both comparison group and regular viewers expressed a great deal of ambivalence about watching scenes and characterizations that they perceived as humiliating or degrading in the four shows we studied. They were reluctant to admit hostility, contempt, or schadenfreude toward these shows' candidates. This left me wondering whether audiences in general are less hostile than journalists in the popular press assume, or whether this was an artifact of the research process. The lack of expressed cruelty might be attributed to self-selection, where only those viewers who felt positively about the show and wanted to present themselves as a sympathetic person volunteered for the study. However, some data challenge this assumption of sympathetic self-selectivity. First, there was no more evidence in the survey than in the interviews of unkind perspectives, even though the survey respondents were anonymous and may have had less need to appear sympathetic. Second, where people did express contempt for makeover shows, this tended to be directed toward the producers of surgery shows for exploiting candidates who were suffering. Third, if the self-selecting regular viewers were more invested in seeming kind than the comparison group, we might expect to see more expressions of contempt within the comparison group. Mostly, however, the comparison group interviewees were even more sympathetic toward the makeover candidates, worried about their exploitation, and expressed stronger concerns about third-person effects than did the regular viewers. This does not rule out the possibility that survey respondents, regular viewer interviewees, and comparison group interviewees played down a socially unacceptable sensibility such as schadenfreude in describing their perceptions of the shows. But I also wonder whether people might be kinder than journalists assume, or the interviewees assumed of other people, for that matter. Like the negative effects of violent images attributed to other people, humiliating representations on makeover shows dehumanize everyone but the self.

Through the Eyes of the Camera

The audiences in this study were thus highly reflexive about the media contexts in which the shows were produced, and how they used surveillance and shame to meet the industrial and economic demands to produce "good television." They used this media reflexivity to distinguish helpful shaming (done for the benefit of the candidate) from exploitative humiliation (done for the purpose of increasing ratings). But surveillance and shame come to play in self-reflexivity as well. Critics of the governmental aspects of makeover television have argued that the surveillance techniques in makeover shows encourage the audiences' application of these techniques to themselves. Gareth Palmer, for example, argues that makeover shows shift from the surveillance that characterizes reality television in general to *self*-surveillance. He writes, "To be filmed by [hidden] cameras is suddenly to share the look of the other, to objectify yourself from a vantage point in which this look is inscribed within the seemingly 'objective' gaze of the surveillance footage."[28] Palmer describes a shift within the shows from surveillance by hosts and cameras to the candidates of themselves; he also assumes that audiences will adopt this internalized self-surveillance. To what extent did viewers of the four shows we considered here discuss applying the monitoring gaze of the hosts, camera, and imagined audience to see themselves as if through the eyes of another?

Of the four show cohorts, viewers of *What Not to Wear* were the most likely to talk about adopting surveillance techniques from the shows. One regular viewer described employing the perspectives afforded by

What Not to Wear in her own shopping practices as a result of seeing candidates on the show:

> When I go shopping and they have a three-way mirror I usually try to look and see what I look like in that—but as a normal course, I don't normally look at myself from behind. I do more now since I've been watching the show. But a lot of people don't know how they look other than when they look straight ahead at a mirror, and a lot of people don't even own a full-length mirror, so they don't get the whole picture. I mean I see a lot of people out and about and think, "If they knew how they looked from behind, would they really be wearing that?"

This woman applied the rigors of the three-way mirror, one of *What Not to Wear*'s primary techniques to get candidates to look at themselves as if from the outside, not only to herself but to other people she sees in public. (The *What Not to Wear* message boards had a very active thread devoted to fans sharing clothing faux pas they saw in public—another online example of contempt for others.) Another viewer commented about posts on the *What Not to Wear* message boards:

> If you watch the show often enough and you look at it from that [the hosts'] point of view, I do think that you'll find that, at least a lot of people would find, that they are actually taking a second look at themselves. They may not have the guidance that they need within themselves to be able to see what their good points are, that's the only thing. But I know that on the discussion board . . . I've read people who say that, many people who say they have Stacy and Clinton in their heads when they're getting dressed or going shopping or whatever.

This borrowing of the shows' various monitoring techniques was most succinctly articulated by Robert, the "fan–expert" from chapter 3:

> When [the candidates] get away from their friends and family, and they're with complete strangers who really have no vested interest other than the interest of the show, and they're like, "Here, this is what a total stranger looking at you thinks." Because all of a sudden, they're seeing

themselves through the eyes of the camera. You know, that happens to me a couple of times: I'll be walking by a mirror, and it's like, "Oh, wow, am I that heavy?"

Seeing himself as if through the eyes of the camera, the scrutiny of the hosts, and the reflection in the mirror, Robert wondered if he catches himself as he "really" is.

Starting Over interviewees were also likely to describe seeing themselves from the outside in the same terms as the candidates on the show. A woman described watching *Starting Over* as an experience of "recognizing herself":

A lot of times when you're watching it, there are issues—it might just be like a small portion of an issue that one of the houseguests has, that you recognize yourself. And you realize, "Oh! It never really occurred to me that that was a problem." . . . Once you see these women going through it, it's like, "Oh!" It's like a light bulb going off. It's kind of like that cataclysmic event that causes you to make a change in your own life.

Another *Starting Over* interviewee discussed recognizing behaviors in herself through seeing them in the housemates on-screen:

I learned more from [Kelly], watching her in some ways, and caught on because she did. It was kind of like watching myself. When she would get mad, I would go, "Oh my God, that's how I am." Or when Kim would do something, I'd go, "Oh my God, that's how I am." And you know, when you're alone watching this or even if you have other people with you, you're just relating to yourself, you can be honest with yourself. You don't have to admit it to your therapist; you don't have to admit it to your husband or anything else.

Starting Over respondents fairly often reported identifying with housemates' problems and adopting strategies for change they saw on the show. In contrast, however, *Queer Eye* and *Biggest Loser* participants very rarely described applying the shows' representational techniques to themselves, perhaps because these shows were more likely to be seen as entertaining and motivating, respectively.

These interviews thus challenged the idea that helpful shaming in the shows would be adopted by audiences. When audiences mentioned using the shows to see themselves from outside it was very show-specific. The explicit focus in *What Not to Wear* is on techniques of looking (the hidden camera, the 360-degree mirror, the hosts' inspection), making this the show most available for self-scrutiny. Critics' assumption that governmental strategies of surveillance that characterize makeover television cultivate a self-monitoring, self-disciplining orientation may be particular to specific shows. *What Not to Wear* may be the most governmental of the shows we looked at in this research, in the ways argued by Palmer and others, but this model cannot be seen as paradigmatic for the genre.

Although some candidates described adopting the shows' representational techniques, what came through most strongly was many people's horror at the idea of being represented that way. Comparison group viewers were especially critical of these surveillance strategies, distancing themselves from that representational economy. One male interviewee said of the sample episode of *What Not to Wear*:

> I mean, shit, they put them—what woman of size wants to be in a room surrounded 360 degrees by mirrors? Nobody wants to do that. Like, you'd see something, everybody would see something that they never saw before in that room. It's probably gonna be upsetting, you know?

Even regular *What Not to Wear* viewers who were more likely to regard the strategies on that show as promoting a useful self reflexivity were horrified by the idea of seeing themselves on camera or in front of the 360-degree mirror. Many of the survey respondents mentioned that they were tempted to be on the show, but that the mirror and the hidden camera would put them off. One woman wrote, "I am very self-conscious and shy—the two weeks of surveillance freaks me out. I would not like the 'dressing-down' (pun intended) in the 360-degree mirror and I would feel very uncomfortable with such close scrutiny. Also, I do not photograph well and look even worse on video."

In contrast to the contemporary assumption that everyone wants to be a celebrity, many survey participants across all four shows responded that they would not like to be on the show because of anxieties about being exposed and humiliated. Men who responded to the *Queer Eye* survey, for example, frequently said that what didn't appeal to them about being on the show was "being on television," that "they make fun of you," and "having so many cameras recording everything." Only *What Not to Wear* survey respondents said that they would want to be on the show more often than not. Whereas the majority of respondents to the other three surveys did not want to be on the show because of concerns about exposure and humiliation, *What Not to Wear* respondents were more likely to say they didn't want to be on this show because they would have to give up their existing wardrobe or because they didn't like some of the hosts' suggestions of how to dress. This suggests that *What Not to Wear* audiences may be more accepting of its shaming techniques as a useful corrective of their flaws. Collectively, however, these participants' responses counter assumptions about the general population's wanton search for celebrity: more people than not rejected the idea of being on television, precisely because of the exposure this would likely bring.

The two frames through which makeover shows are assumed to have negative social effects—promoting schadenfreude and cultivating obliging self-surveillance—are thus complicated by the data from this audience research project. The people we spoke with articulated complex moral hierarchies of shame and humiliation according to what they thought the candidates deserved and what the motives of the shows' producers were. They were highly reflexive about media conventions that humiliated candidates for the sake of profit. They did not, however, critique the normative elements of shaming that affirm conventional modes of gendered, raced, and classed self-representation. They reserved their contempt for surgery candidates, albeit with ambivalence, and for celebrities, who were assumed to have traded respect for publicity. These complex engagements begin a conversation that the next chapter develops: the role of affect in audiences' identifications with makeover candidates, and how their perceptions of emotion temper viewers' assessments of the realism of the shows.

5

Feeling Real

Empirical Truth and Emotional Authenticity

[When I'm watching *Starting Over*] I'm usually crying or whatever when they're crying. And I think it's wonderful! I think it's
real TV and you don't see that often. There's no real TV in many
places. One of the reasons I really, really like the show, it's because
you can see those real intimate moments and there's so many people that I come in contact with who are just so afraid to be real,
to be heard, to be vulnerable. And so sometimes seeing that is a
breath of fresh air.
—Julie, *Starting Over* viewer

Julie's discussion of her emotional engagement with the housemates on
Starting Over frames the intertwined themes in this chapter. For Julie,
the housemates' expression of emotion, particularly crying, signals the
authenticity of the show, a rare value in most television. This authenticity is underpinned by her sense of the housemates' vulnerability,
where Julie presumes they are showing their real selves to the audience.
And through this perception of the housemates' emotional authenticity, Julie also experiences her own emotional release: "I'm usually crying . . . when they're crying." Julie's appeals to "real TV" and "be[ing]
real" emphasize a taken-for-granted association between emotional
expression and authenticity that underpins the realness of reality TV.
This chapter investigates the conditions in which audiences perceive
the genre of makeover television, its candidates, and their feelings to

be "real." On one hand, audiences were skilled at critiquing the artifices of the reality genre; on the other hand, this media reflexivity paradoxically reinforced their sense of the genre's emotional realism. How do the ways audiences talked about emotional performances on the shows, and their responses to these, help us understand the ambivalent status of "reality" in reality television? Or, what makes reality television real for audiences?

Much has been written about realism in television and film, and especially about the fraught question of the relationship between reality television and the real. Writing just before the 1992 debut of *The Real World*, Bill Nichols reviewed debates about the construction of realism in a variety of forms. He argues that:

> realism builds upon a presentation of things as they appear to the eye and the ear in everyday life. The camera and sound recorder are well suited to such a task since—with proper lighting, distance, angle, lens, and placement—an image (or recorded sound) can be made to appear highly similar to the way in which a typical observer might have noted the same occurrence.[1]

Since both documentary and fictional film use cameras and sound equipment that allow for a high level of verisimilitude between life and recording, both can offer a seductive indexical relationship that presumes that we see and hear events as they actually happened. However, Nichols argues, as have others, that documentary doesn't represent "life" and fictional film "stories," but that both use representational strategies to present different stories about reality: "In fiction, realism serves to make a plausible world seem real; in documentary, realism serves to make an argument about the historical world persuasive. Realism in fiction is a self-effacing style, one that deemphasizes the process of its construction."[2] In contrast, "documentary realism is not only a style but also a professional code, an ethic, and a ritual."[3] In both documentary and fictional films realism is a strategy, albeit differently pursued in each.

In her audience study of factual, reality, and fictional programs, Alice Hall argues that realism is a highly adaptable value that shifts in meaning according to the audiences' expectations of the text and its genre.[4]

She found that audiences could perceive a text to be realistic if it was found plausible (I can imagine the story taking place in the real world); typical (it might happen to me or someone I know); factual (it is faithful to what "really happened"); and had "perceptual persuasiveness" (I can't see how the fictional violence is faked). Hall found that people could perceive texts as realistic even when they were implausible (as in science fiction shows) as long as the story was internally coherent. She also found that audiences discussed texts as realistic when the emotions expressed by the actors were seen as authentic, what Ien Ang calls "emotional realism."[5]

Reality television plays with two kinds of latitude: the flexibility of reality as a code, and the breadth of audiences' willingness to read texts as realistic. Further, the metagenre complicates the distinction between documentary approaches and entertainment genres. It combines both observational, "fly-on-the-wall" types of unobtrusive recording, as well as more participatory and reflexive techniques that emphasize the subjects' awareness that they are participating in a mediated event. As John Corner writes, "Much reality television . . . mix[es] moments of self-conscious and playful artifice with moments of intensive commitment to the truthfulness of their images, the 'reality claims' of which at least equal the much-discussed 'ideology of transparency' of classic observational work."[6] For Corner, the friction between the fantasy of the window on the world and the revelation of the window frame itself opens up the potential of reflexivity in audiences. However, Corner remains doubtful that this new attention to performance "involves a new reflectiveness on the part of program makers" or "a new refusal on the part of audiences to accord reality status to what they see on television."[7]

Drawing from her audience research project, Annette Hill also argues that contradictions within the aesthetics of reality television open the possibility for a consideration of the realism of the metagenre. She suggests that reality television's uneasy location between transparency and artifice demands that viewers reflect on its truth claims: "The intermediate space of [reality television] can be transformative, and at times we will personally connect with something in a program, reflecting on what that person or real event means to us, creating a powerful self-reflexive space."[8] For Hill, reflecting on the realism of reality television is an outcome of the metagenre's precarious position at the interstices of fact and fiction. She

calls her respondents' skepticism about reality television a "chain of distrust" and argues that because of the slippage between information and
entertainment, viewers are more critically engaged with the truth claims
of reality television than those of news programs and documentaries.[9]
Although both Corner and Hill are ambivalent about the virtues of reality
television, its frank acknowledgement of its production processes might
be one of its more progressive aspects, offering audiences space to reflect
on its claims to represent the real world. To what extent did audiences
in this current study perceive the makeover shows as real, and in what
terms did they discuss this realism? How does reality television's position
between fact and fiction challenge the perception of realism among the
people we spoke to here?

Challenging the Real

The audiences in this study manifested a high degree of media reflexivity in their challenges to the realism of reality television. These challenges included elements of the makeovers they saw on-screen, as well
as their knowledge about production and editing processes that went
into the production of "good television"—shows that were visual, entertaining, and profitable for the producers. This involved a number of different critiques, some of which were particular to the individual shows.

Many people in both the regular viewer cohorts and the comparison
group commented that because the shows are edited, "Nothing's really
100 percent reality; this show has a producer," and "You never really
can tell, can you, what you're getting." They saw the producer's hand in
many of the events that played out on-screen, and were well aware of
how scripting, editing, and even genre expectations not only shaped but
also challenged the realism of the makeover shows. Robert, for example, spotted producers' sleights of hand on *What Not to Wear*:

> When it comes to the unreality aspect of the show—and as I told you, I
> am a freelance writer and there's spots where I can tell that [the hosts']
> responses are completely scripted—typically it's when they're coming
> up with these really smart-ass zingers. I mean, yes, some of those are
> real. But particularly when you see them watching the makeover shop-
> ping on the day when they go out shopping alone. . . . If you look, the

way the lines come out, it's definitely scripted. I think what happens is, they sit down, they look at everything, and Stacy and Clinton will make comments—I think the comments Stacy and Clinton originally make as they're watching it are genuine. And then the scriptwriters get it and they tweak it a little bit.

Drawing on his own background as a freelance writer, Robert assessed the extent to which the writers shape the content of the shows:

> In *The Biggest Loser*, I think they have to grab, go for the most dramatic [story]: it is a commercial product. I hope that people watching realize that. Sometimes certain individuals have been portrayed, like sort of vilified, like this is the mean one, this is the nice one. You know it's focusing on certain characteristics of any one individual, so that you'll have the dynamics while they're together, when in fact even the nice one has a bad day. So I'm skeptical, I assume it's done for commercial value, to get the biggest bang for the buck.

Another *Biggest Loser* viewer recognized the entertainment conventions of needing to create a narrative in order to make a commercially successful product. The producers "have to create a story every episode, so they're going to pick and choose toward a storyline." The show involved shaping the story of the candidates losing weight to "have an audience for their marketers. They're trying to make money."

Both regular viewers and comparison group interviewees commented on the sometimes strained visual metaphors that *Starting Over* drew on to visualize the makeover. One of the more critical among our interviewees was Edna, a mixed-race woman with a master's degree who was a regular *Starting Over* viewer. She said:

> I think a lot of what they do with the women is constructed—you can kind of see the core of it being maybe based in some kind of idea of helping. But then they—I mean they had a woman dress up like a baby for a week. I don't think that that's necessarily something that would be that great for change. This would probably make most people very angry. But the help that they provide on the show is certainly crafted with the audience in mind, again with the spectacle.

After watching the sample episode of *Starting Over*, a woman from the comparison group commented:

> The sort of kind of ridiculous symbologies that they employed were pretty intense and I think that was—it may have made it—clearly there was a representative function. They tried to get this across to the viewer: "We want this to be very clear that this is how we're outlining your problem and representing your problem." So things like making that slideshow when Antonia came into the house and things like that. I doubt that a group therapy session would—I mean, it maybe does—but would run in the way that involved PowerPoint.

Starting Over has particular representational challenges because so much of the makeover involves "inner" transformation. One of the few men we talked to who watched *Starting Over*, Bill, wondered, "If somebody's working on hard issues for a while, how can you keep it entertaining?" In contrast, *Biggest Loser* viewers saw the candidates' diminishing bodies as both compelling viewing and evidence of the realness of the show: "I think most of the reality shows are really scripted, and I don't know how they could script this, because how could you be sure they're going to lose weight? I mean they actually lose weight." Yet all the shows use highly visual rituals to represent transformation: the graduation ceremony in *Starting Over*, the moment of reveal in *What Not to Wear* and *Queer Eye*, and the weekly weigh-in in *The Biggest Loser*.

Bill offered the most sophisticated analysis of how *Starting Over*'s production routines linked with existing genres:

> [It] blends the two great things about daytime TV, which is the self-help focus of a talk show with the hyperbolic drama of a soap opera. . . . What's refreshing about soaps is that people get hysterical, and that's sort of fun, it's sort of nice. . . . [On *Starting Over*] it's often like someone's had a horrible fight with another houseguest, and they get all worked up trying to talk to somebody on the phone or one of the other houseguests. And that I find interesting, because it definitely does have that reality show thing of people that get used to having cameras as a part of their world, so if it's not completely manipulated, it's definitely like their guard

is down and something's happening in front of the camera, and there's something thrilling about that.

As I discuss further below, even with the awareness of the genre conventions that *Starting Over* draws on to shape the reality represented on-screen, Bill nevertheless credits some moments as real: "Their guard is down."

Many people we spoke to were highly reflexive about the role of production processes and commercial demands in shaping the realism of these makeover shows. This kind of media reflexivity was facilitated by audiences' social interactions about the shows as well as the aesthetic of reality television that reveals its seams to the audience. As I discuss in chapter 3, audiences collaborated in critiquing the advice and consumer appeals of the shows. Similarly, they discussed with one another the production conventions of the shows:

> You wonder how much of the negative stuff they've edited out about someone who appears to be a fan favorite. And I'm sure the show has their people who monitor the chat rooms and blogs and stuff. And they can kind of see who's a fan favorite, as opposed to someone who is not a fan favorite. And maybe that plays a part in how the show is edited and how the—I can't call them characters—but how some of the contestants' behavior is edited.

This woman was highly reflexive about how certain contestants (or "characters" as she wants to call them) are shaped according to online fans' chats about them, recognizing a circuit of feedback whereby producers attend to online discussions of the shows.

Many respondents mentioned their online interactions as cultivating a more reflexive approach to the shows. This may have been especially true for Bill, who was a regular participant on the website Television Without Pity (TWoP). TWoP pays "recappers" to provide hilariously snarky synopses of episodes, which "often focus on production details such as lighting and editing, thereby helping to direct the attention to the formal aspects of the shows they describe."[10] Andrejevic argues that part of the pleasure of participating in TWoP is in the construction and representation of the self as "savvy," duped neither by the artifices of the production processes nor by the promise that their activities will have any influence on the producers.[11] Yet Andrejevic concludes that savviness does little to protect TWoP participants from the extraction of labor entailed in the work of being watched while watching shows, to paraphrase Dallas Smythe's famous phrase.[12] On the contrary, the pleasures of critique intensified their investment in and loyalty to particular shows.

According to many of our interviewees, much online discussion was devoted to commenting on the production processes of the shows. Yet although Corner, Hill, and others suggest that audiences enjoy their awareness of reality television shows' constructions, this was not always welcomed by the audiences in our study.[13] Roberta observed:

> You'd think they'd do it like *Big Brother* and put cameras all over the [*Starting Over*] house and do away with the people that were wandering around the house. Because once in a while, you'll catch one of them in one of the scenes, or somebody that's in there to clean. Of course it gives the people on the message board a lot to talk about. You'd think they'd just put the cameras all around the house; that's what I would do.

For Roberta, being able to see the processes of the production was distracting from the observational, "fly-on-the-wall" style of reality television that she prefers.

Genre conventions that encourage reflexivity in audiences may not then be entirely welcomed by them, nor are they wholeheartedly embraced by producers. A few *Starting Over* respondents mentioned an example of the limits producers put on a reflexive mode of representation in the shows. A housemate in the second season, Sommer, was forced to leave the show for reasons that were not explained to audiences (the failings of most housemates who do not graduate are usually made all too clear). The gossip on the *Starting Over* message boards was that she was removed because she kept on interacting (or "flirting," as one respondent put it) with the camera crew, making the footage from these scenes unusable. The housemates are also not allowed to talk about the process of filming, or what they think producers are going to do next. It's not that housemates aren't allowed to acknowledge the camera; indeed, they are required to visit the "diary room" regularly, where they share their thoughts and feelings directly with the camera. But the show maintains a division between the "observational footage," shot around the house where the participants act as though the cameras aren't there, and the "reflexive" moments in the diary room.[14] Further, in neither observational nor reflexive moments do the candidates acknowledge the means of recording (i.e., the camera or crew); audiences either see a window on a world unfolding without our involvement, or have a direct audience with the housemates. For all the reality genre's stylistic conceits that it offers a glimpse into television's production processes, Sommer's ejection from the show draws attention to the limits of this. Bill, the TWoP member quoted above, used this event as leverage in a larger reflexive moment concerning the limits of what audiences are allowed to see:

I think the big mystery of Sommer, and what actually happened to cause her to be evicted the first time, like there's an awareness that there's stuff that we don't see. There's times when you see, "Okay she did not have braids when this was happening, so the diary room with her wearing braids, that sort of throws things off." So I think there's an awareness that the editing, the diary room editing in particular, and some of the obvious post-narrations from the life coaches . . . Granted, I have a slightly more sophisticated ear and eye for some of these things than, say, my mom does. But any time I point it out to my mom, who's also started watching Starting Over not long ago, she's always going, "I thought that was sort of weird." So there's an intuitive awareness of the manipulation, without the experience to call out particular proof of it. So, I have no illusions about the editing. I think it's the nature of editing that these kinds of things. Like there's some times when gold is captured, and it's able to be put out there right as it happened. But then there's other times when they have to fit it into the chunks; you sort of know that it's there. I certainly don't think it impedes the realism, it's just part of the product.

Bill discussed being aware that there is "stuff we don't see," made most apparent through the continuity disjunctures between the diary room footage and the events being discussed there. He acknowledges that he might have a "more sophisticated ear and eye" than many viewers (not only is he a TWoP regular, he indicated in the survey that he has a doctorate degree). But even less informed viewers, like his mom, have an "intuitive sense" that the show is edited, sometimes manipulatively—a sense that Bill's discussions with his mom may have developed. But even with this acute perception, Bill nevertheless recalls moments of "gold," spontaneous interactions that don't have to be "fit[ted] into chunks." Even further, his awareness of the editing does not impede what he sees as the realism of the show. So what is the gold? What remains real even for someone as highly reflexive about media production processes as Bill?

Emotional Realism

> So I suppose that's why I like it, because it strikes me that it's actually happening, that it's real. You know it's not one person and then a skinny person coming in at the end. You watch them sweat like crazy; you watch them cry; you watch them laugh; you watch them develop these friendships.
> —Marci, *The Biggest Loser* viewer

> I think [*Starting Over*] showed us what [the housemates'] emotions were. And I thought their emotions were real, I just didn't think they were realistic. You know what I mean by the difference? That it's not realistic to expect that just because two people walk in the door, you're going to be friends—no, that's not the case. You're not going to like everybody and not everybody's going to like you.
> —Amy, *Starting Over* viewer

Many of the viewers we talked to were quite knowledgeable about the production processes of the show and were reflexive about the impact these have on what they saw on-screen. By recognizing elements usually used in fictional shows—scripting, editing for drama, drawing on generic tropes from fictional genres—audiences questioned whether the shows represented events as they really happened. A striking element of the data from the survey and the interviews with regular viewers (and some of the comparison group) was that skepticism about the empirical realities of the shows' production existed alongside—and sometimes reaffirmed—a profound investment in the genre's emotional realism. Marci's and Amy's discussion of the emotional realness in *The Biggest Loser* and *Starting Over* condenses many of the ways in which the audience members we talked to addressed the representation of emotion in the shows: whether housemates expressed their "real" feelings; whether these feelings were based on realistic expectations of human relationships; whether these were transmitted faithfully by the editors; and whether even experts can distinguish "genuine" from fake feelings. Audiences saw emotional realness as central to the authenticity of the shows.

Hill summarizes the criteria for authentic talk in broadcasting. What is perceived by audiences as authentic is speech that "does not sound contrived, simulated or performed," that "seems truly to capture or present the experience of the speaker," and that "seems truly to project the core self of the speaker."[15] This relationship among expression of genuine feeling and the relation to the "true self" comes through in many of the audiences' descriptions of the shows. This woman valued the emotional portrayals on *Starting Over*:

> When they let it out, when they come to the realizations, they're real about it. The women on the show are not acting. I believe they're being their true selves. They forget the cameras are there and they really try. And when they come to the realization of certain things through the process, they're open about it, they cry, they scream, they get mad, they throw fits. They're real people.

Respondents tended to see expressions of emotion, and of crying in particular, as evidence of genuine feeling. This was especially so with the serial shows, in which viewers could see candidates' emotional disclosures over time.

Viewers of the episodic shows also appreciated the emotional authenticity they found there. Another woman enjoyed seeing the heterosexual men's expressions of appreciation on *Queer Eye*:

> At the end of the episode, how they always thank the *Queer Eye* guys for making the effort—they always seem to get really choked up, and that always kills me! Not to mention the fact that you are talking about five gay men on television—the perception of maybe not wanting to be

portrayed as sensitive, or fear of what people might think. It's just nice to see people in a genuine manner. And you can tell when you look at them on TV that they are being genuine. You can just tell by the expressions on their face and the emotion in their face when they're speaking that they're gonna get something out of it.

Crying is assumed to represent an authentic commitment to the makeover process; its absence suggests a cynicism, "just want[ing] to be on TV," as another *Queer Eye* viewer said.

Authentic emotional expression was seen by many as both the necessary condition for and evidence of a successful makeover. Donna said of the candidates on *Queer Eye*:

I think [crying] means that they're getting through to them, that [the candidates are] truly grateful about everything that is being either given to them or done for them or done with them. And they get it. They get that this could alter their lives for the better.

The expression of authentic emotion had a direct link with the transformative powers of the makeover for many respondents. Some saw emotional release as a sign that the makeover had been a deeply affecting process, necessary to achieve anything but the most superficial changes to the outer self. One female regular viewer saw the most successful transformations on *Queer Eye* and *What Not to Wear* as those:

where the cast member has a big emotional realization or change. I think that there are some [episodes] where they go in confident. They're cocky; they're arrogant. Maybe they're really in shape, they're successful in their career; the changes that are brought are just going to make them more so. But for me the ones that have a bigger impact are the ones where they see themselves through new eyes, where they're touched by the transformation, where they can see how their paths have changed because of their experience.

Another linked the expression of feeling in *The Biggest Loser* not only to competitive success but also to the success of two contestants' personal relationship on season 2: "It's funny that the two who were the most emotional people on the show were two of the finalists, and now they're engaged [to be married]." Through the expression of genuine feeling, both the finalists could forge a lasting union.

Conversely, an inability to express feeling was seen as the cause of a range of psychological and physical problems that brought candidates to the makeover shows in the first place. This was most explicit with *The Biggest Loser* viewers (both regular and comparison group), who linked emotional expression and transformation through the concept of "emotional eating." A *Biggest Loser* comparison group interviewee saw crying as a direct cure for what ailed that show's contestants:

> I know when I get personal, I overeat. . . . A lot of people do, like any type of breakup, people go and get some chocolate ice cream. But [the contestants] did good. They didn't eat. They cried, but they didn't eat. And that was a good sign that they're not looking toward food to help them go on.

A regular *Biggest Loser* female viewer echoed this view: "If you're upset you should cry, because if you don't cry you're going to eat because you are stuffing your emotions with it."

The association between emotional expression—especially crying—and health emerged with *Starting Over* respondents as well. A regular viewer talked about initially feeling alienated from *Starting Over* because of all the emotional outpouring there. She went on to explain her alienation as relating not to the hyperbolic emotionalism in the show itself, but as an example of her own struggles to express her feelings:

> The very first day I saw the show, everybody was crying. And I said, "There is no way I am getting myself hooked on a show where everybody cries every day." I mean, I had absolutely no interest in that. And then I tuned in another day, and all of a sudden I saw all the work that was being done. . . . I think you have to somehow tolerate some of the emotionalism. And I'm not berating the women for it. You know that was one of my issues anyway [laughing]: "You don't cry!" I do think so. I told my psychiatrist about it. And I'm seeing him for medical reasons; I mean I've got chronic medical problems. I just think . . . it follows a lot of the stuff he's worked with me on, you know.

In the examples both of *The Biggest Loser* and *Starting Over* is the underlying view that expressing feeling is necessary, and that not to do so creates health problems. Since obesity is increasingly seen as an illness of epidemic proportions, the assumption that it has its root in an inability to express feeling, specifically sadness and loss, suggests that this kind of bottling up is similarly epidemic. This view is reminiscent of the metaphors Susan Sontag wished to dispel surrounding tuberculosis and cancer.[16] She argues that TB was evidence of too much passion that the will had not managed to wrestle into shape, but the appearance of which was proof of sensitivities unsuited to modernity. In contrast, cancer is seen as evidence of suppressed passions that must nevertheless find expression: the body tells the truth when the inner voice isn't permitted to. Sontag writes, "With the modern diseases (once TB, now cancer), the romantic idea that the disease expresses the character is invariably extended to assert that the character causes the disease— because it has not expressed itself."[17] Silencing the true inner self produces physical pathology.

It is striking that even among audiences who were savvy about the production artifices of these shows, many of the people we talked to remained highly invested in their emotional realism. This describes audiences' attribution of emotional authenticity to a television drama (*Dallas*, in Ien Ang's research) that is also seen as highly artificial at the "empirical" level: in terms of setting, apparent wealth, plot, and so on. Based in the Netherlands, Ang's respondents' worlds were far distant from that of the rich, oil-baron, ranching Texas family, yet "many fans do find [*Dallas*] 'realistic.'"[18] Although the series drew on the conventions of "transparent narrativity" of classically realist television (much more so than the more reflexive style of reality television), this was not enough, in Ang's view, to account for her respondents' pleasure in the realism of the text. The fundamental feature of audiences' engagement was not the show's empirical realism—how true it was to the lives of the Dutch audience—but with its emotional realism: "What is recognized as real is not knowledge of the world, but a subjective experience of the world: a 'structure of feeling.'"[19] Through the perception of emotional realism in *Dallas*, women viewers connected with a felt experience of emotional community, not only with the characters in the show but also with other audiences.

However different in time, place, and genre from Ang's *Dallas* study, many of the makeover audiences we talked to similarly based their enjoyment of the shows on their perception of the authenticity of the participants, predicated on their emotional genuineness. As with some *Dallas* characters, makeover show candidates who were perceived to be "'caricatures' or 'improbable' are not esteemed, [whereas] characters who are 'lifelike' or 'psychologically believable' are."[20] In contrast to the *Dallas* study, however, the believability of the makeover candidates in this study hinged on a perception of their ordinariness. A sense of ordinariness was produced in a reciprocal relationship between nonactor status and the perception that a candidate's expression of feeling was authentic. Regular viewers were highly invested in the participants not being actors (at least in the makeover shows they discussed with us). For example, Marci commented:

> On many of them, like on *The Real World*—I watch that with my daughter—and on *The Real World*, I sit there and look at that and go, "Oh my gosh, they're just totally doing it because that's what got them on the show." And that I think is just, "I want to be an actor, so I'm going to go be on *The Real World*." I don't know if the people on *The Biggest Loser*—I mean I really don't think Dr. Jeff went on there to try to be an actor. You don't see him on talk shows; you don't see him on anything. I think he looked at it as a way to lose the weight.

Another *Starting Over* interviewee said, "I think kind of, a little bit, it's real. Meaning that these are everyday women. They look like me. They look like you. They look like not celebrities. These are everyday women, young, old, successful entrepreneurs, corporate, the whole gambit. And I think that it relates—it's gonna relate to somebody." And ordinariness means not being paid: "I think it's great. It's real; it's not like they're being paid to cry on the air and stuff like that."

Respondents distinguished those candidates they considered "real" people, who were nonactors and there for the "right" reasons, from those they thought were only interested in wanting to be on TV, to further an acting career, or to promote their product or business. Of the *Starting Over* housemates, a regular viewer commented:

There have been some women who are on there who are really on there
for the attention, and for the fame and fortune. I don't think that that is
everyone who's been on there. But I do think that there are some women,
that that is definitely the case. And, they just seem to be kind of on, all
the time. Then there are other ones that I think have just reached a point
where they are just unhappy. Everything that they've tried hasn't worked,
and this is like their last-ditch effort, because it's an out of the ordinary
kind of thing to do, to have cameras following you around twenty-four
hours a day.

For Amy, it is precisely the extraordinary circumstances that can be
productive for ordinarily unhappy women.

Mostly, regular viewers remained confident that the expressions of
emotion were produced by nonactors and were therefore authentic. Of
What Not to Wear, Robert said:

I think for the most part what you see expressed there is absolutely real.
There are sometimes when you just, you see them breaking down emotionally. And if you're not paid as an actor, you can't fake that. And so
yeah, I think what you see for the most part is real, although sometimes
it's been tweaked a little too much.

Even when they acknowledged the "tweaking" of production processes,
respondents remained highly invested in the ordinariness of the candidates, where emotional authenticity was predicated on the participants
not being actors. On the one hand, some viewers assumed that the candidates are not actors, and therefore their emotional expressions are
genuine. On the other, the apparent authenticity of candidates' feelings
was taken as proof of their ordinariness: this person could not be an
actor because his or her emotions were so authentic.

Only Seth was somewhat skeptical that one candidate from the first
Biggest Loser season was an actor:

A lot of reality TV, you get skeptical that 50 percent of the cast puts
on their resume bogus jobs, and the reality is they're just struggling
actors from LA trying to get a TV show. So I was curious to see if he
was an actor before the show, versus his new body image gave him the

confidence to do it. I never really got anywhere with that. I wasn't able to figure that out.

Comparison group viewers were more likely to question the supposed ordinariness of the candidates on the shows. When asked whether he knew anyone who would be a good candidate for *Starting Over*, a comparison group interviewee responded, "Sure. In fact, I know some struggling actors that could really use the work." Another commented more extensively on his skepticism prompted by the emotional expression on *The Biggest Loser*:

> DEREK: Like at the end the guy was crying when the guy who voted him
>   out was crying and the other guy—I don't know. He just—the other
>   guy said, don't worry about it, it's nothing, and you had to do it. . . .
>   A few points there, I was thinking: These are all actors. These aren't
>   real, just heavy people. These are all actors and actresses.
> INTERVIEWER: What made you think that they were actors and actresses?
> D: I didn't think just regular people would be like that.
> I: You mean like that emotional?
> D: Yeah. And show their feelings. I don't know. I just see people not like
>   that.

The degree of emotional expressiveness exhibited by both women and men on *The Biggest Loser* seemed so at odds with Derek's experience that it undermined the very premise of the "reality" of most reality television: that the shows cast ordinary people.

Grindstaff discusses how hard talk show producers work to ensure the ordinariness of the guests. Ordinariness here means guests who are "outsider[s] to the production apparatus" and who are thus most likely to produce spontaneous expressions of feeling, the "money shot."[21] Nonactors' lack of television experience makes them harder to work with than celebrities and experts, but at the same time this inexperience is their ticket to media visibility: "Emotional expressiveness—the capacity to convey, on camera, raw, real emotion—is the ordinary guest's greatest form of cultural capital, the element most desired and anticipated, yet, in the final analysis, the one producers perceive to be most beyond their control."[22] This cultural capital is a rare commodity in talk shows, where wary producers must be vigilant about the threat of impostors—not only aspiring actors, but also guests who have been on other shows and thus know the routines of emotional expression, those who lie about or exaggerate their stories in order to get on the shows, and other "talk-show sluts" in the words of one producer.[23] For the regular audiences we talked to, ordinariness was produced within a reinforcing circle of authenticity, where candidates' outsider status in the production process guaranteed that their expressions of feeling were authentic. In turn, perceptions of the authenticity of their feelings affirmed that the candidates can't possibly be actors because they seem so real. But like talk shows, reality television displays a peculiar kind of ordinariness: "The most significant feature that talk shows share with other media . . . is the tendency to deny ordinary people routine access unless they engage in exceptional behavior."[24] In order to seem ordinary, candidates must express highly emotional and authentic-seeming feeling, displays that most people we talked to would not want to do on television (see chapter 4).

This perception of emotional authenticity predicated on ordinariness is what enables, or prompts, identification with characters and provides viewers much of the emotional pleasure of watching the shows. A *Starting Over* viewer said, "There have been some [episodes] where I'm just sitting there bawling—that may be another reason I don't watch it with my husband [laughs]. I don't want to go there." Another *Starting Over* viewer recalled one episode that she found "memorable because that's when Iyanla shared her story about how Alison's life had impacted her. You know, and she shared that, the loss of her [own] daughter to cancer and things like that. I really cried. I cried on that one."

Not only regular viewers but also comparison group viewers mentioned crying at some of the shows (as did our interviewers, for that matter). When the interviewer asked a *Biggest Loser* comparison group interviewee how she felt about the contestants in the sample episode, she said:

MAYA: Good. They gave me a strong, positive attitude. Like I cried.
INTERVIEWER: Yeah? Oh, I didn't know this. What made you? Do you
    remember when?
M: Yeah. I just did.

ɪ: Me too.

ᴍ: So when people cry on TV, tears start.

Some people suggested that emotional identification precipitated necessary change in the audience. This interviewee discussed *Starting Over*
along these lines:

> There are times if you're really getting into the show you can actually
> sit there and cry with them. Depending on what the problem is, there's
> probably been somebody in that house that's in a situation similar to
> yours or you've gone through something similar to that in your life. I
> think it's a learning tool for all women, myself included.

Misha Kavka argues that the sense of intimacy produced by reality television is predicated on what she calls "affective identification": "Affective
identification . . . is not the same as empathy; where empathy involves
sharing in the feeling of the other, affective identification refers to *having* the feeling itself."[25] Many respondents discussed their affective identification with candidates, not only in terms of feeling for the candidate,
but also having the feelings themselves: crying as the candidates cry
on-screen, feeling shame or humiliation on their behalf, experiencing
their struggles and triumphs as their own, and so on. Kavka argues that
audiences identify with candidates not only because of the details of
their lives but also because of their emotional experiences: "We viewers
identify with the affective situation."[26] Similarly, Bill Nichols sees identification as "a form of emotional proof tied to the particulars of situation
and character. . . . Rather than being presented from the exterior only,
identification requires that characters be presented from the interior as
well."[27] Reality television thus does particularly well what documentary
often eschews on the basis of objectivity: it offers access to the inner
experiences of the people represented. The expression of interiority,
exemplified by crying, is not only evidence of the authenticity of the self
but also fundamental to the identification with and imagined intimacy
between the viewers and their on-screen proxies.

Earlier audience research suggests that identification between viewers and candidates might be the norm, despite sometimes very different
class positions and in contrast to the assumption that schadenfreude

epitomizes reality television viewing. Skeggs and Wood found that for all the punitive class representations on *Wife Swap*, both working- and middle-class British women found, or struggled to find, points of identification even with people who were represented very unsympathetically (e.g., as fat, eating too much, racist):

> Some of our working-class women quite forcefully took the high moral ground afforded to them as non-working mothers by privileging care for children. There were also often quite lengthy attempts made by the middle-class women to reach for a point of connection beyond that which might be obvious, in order to care for, and about, television participants.[28]

Similarly, identification with emotionally expressive candidates was the norm among our respondents across varied education levels.

Big Boys Don't Cry

Emotional authenticity also seems to be gendered in a way that was initially surprising to me. Men's expression of emotion, particularly crying, was valued as especially authentic:

> I'm always touched by—for some reason, men crying is certainly more of a tearjerker than a woman; you expect a woman to. And when you see a man that in touch and that willing to let go, I think that there's something moving about that. I think that, again, it's just so intensely personal—weight, yeah it's about what you eat, but there's so much more emotion underneath it. There's abuse, or there's just a hundred things underneath it. So it's not surprising to me that the men cry. I think that it's a burden that they're carrying as much as when a woman is in that situation. And it's just all a release.

One of the most expressive men among our interviewees, Seth, identified with Matt, the eventual winner of *The Biggest Loser* season 2, who had been quite open about his frustrations about his weight gain, alcoholism, and life choices:

I couldn't imagine a better guy to go through that process and to be as real as he was, and I really kind of thought at some point, he's really just going to be an asshole like everyone else, every other alpha male guy that starts to run away with it. And this guy just really wasn't posturing, he wasn't pretending, he wasn't just saying, "I'm doing this because"—he wasn't giving all the right answers, he was really conflicted about it: "I feel like a failure because I was a wrestler, and now look at me. I feel like I can't talk to my old friends because I feel uncomfortable in their presence. And I've had relatives that have died, and to think that they saw me in this condition and have no chance to see me rectify my life." Plus he was also a guy who felt like his life was not going anywhere he wants it to go. And to share that, and know that what he's doing, that he's revealing himself to millions of people, I just thought it was brave and added a dynamic to the show I wasn't expecting. I mean I really did fall in love with the guy—not in a gay way—but it just really was like, "This is a cool guy, like I would like to know a guy like that." And I guess everybody, when they watch a reality show, kind of looks for the person's that them, or who they want to be. . . . You're kind of like, "Man I wish I could just, if I needed to, cry openly in front of someone else about that situation without feeling self-conscious about it."

For Seth, *The Biggest Loser* offered a model for how men might deal with their feelings, even while he acknowledged the difficulties of doing this, including the pressures on men to keep their feelings to themselves and the threat of male affection being perceived as "gay." Participants' valuation of men's expressiveness conforms to a deeply held self-help doctrine that expressing emotion is healthier than bottling it up, and that for both women and men emotions must be worked through and managed. Their engagements suggest some of the ways that makeover candidates' emotional expression, perceived to be genuine, promotes intense identifications and pleasures that extend feminine, middle-class norms of emotional expressivity among their audiences.

For Seth and other regular viewers, men who cried were seen as especially authentic, in part because of the contrast with the stoic images of masculinity usually found on television. A heterosexual male *Queer Eye* viewer said:

I think the unemotional part of being a man is sort of a fallacy in American culture. It's the way you're supposed to be or whatever, but, man,
there aren't many guys who are. When it comes to the show, a lot of guys
get emotional, whether they want to admit it or not. . . . I think it's good.
I think the more we can do that, the better. I'm one that doesn't think
guys should hide their emotions.

Although many people saw crying as evidence of emotional authenticity, men crying was a much more stable sign of this than women crying:
as a female interviewee put it, "You expect a woman to [cry]." Interviewees were more likely to see women's emotional displays as false or
manipulative. A male comparison group interviewee commented about
Starting Over:

I thought it was kind of cheesy, kind of contrived. . . . Like, I don't know,
I thought Kelly's emotional displays seemed really contrived or the
whole, like, being really excited about getting a key, that whole thing, it
felt really like public and performed. And in the whole thing, watching a
lot of these shows, especially ones that are about women in this way, or
women's lives are about people kind of performing emotion or all sharing emotion in this really touchy-feely way—it feels really not real to me.

Another male comparison group viewer also saw a female *What Not to
Wear* candidate's tears as manipulative:

The hosts don't really have a lot of positive things to say, and they really
just threw that woman into the fire, and she started crying and that's
when they started then like, "Ooh, maybe we shouldn't talk about how
big she is." Like you gotta shed a few tears to, like, get them to be nice
and considerate to you. That's crazy.

This was echoed by some of the regular viewers as well. One *Starting
Over* survey respondent said that one thing she didn't like about the
show was that "some of the women are so fake. Too much crying."
Another wrote that she didn't like one *Starting Over* housemate in particular: "Lisa from Florida. So insincere, didn't seem to care. Her tears
were crocodile tears. I did not like her at all." Men's emotionality was

generally framed as being moved (crying) and occasionally being angry or mean. Women, on the other hand, were much more likely to be characterized as catty, bitchy, competitive, whiny, and fake.

The premium put on men's emotional expression helps to make sense of how emotions function in the production of realness in these makeover shows. Rather than seeing men's expressivity simply as a valuable opportunity for identification and modeling for men in the audience, this is also an example of how makeover shows offer male viewers training in the kind of emotional work that women have traditionally done. In contrast to the assumption of emotional expression as a mark of spontaneity, Hochschild argues that we can make sense of expression in terms of "emotional management." This describes how we work on our feelings to either generate or suppress emotion in line with what we consider the expectations of the moment. We can see men's crying as a violation of gendered "feeling rules," in which women are expected to fall apart and men to remain stoic, certainly in front of (millions of) others.[29] The expression and interpretation of feeling "operate within a larger social context in which some expressions are by custom scarce and others abundant. The general 'market' of expression thus influences the value we impute to a particular smile as well as the probability of perceiving it as true or false."[30] The violation of the feeling rule that "big boys don't cry" affirms another fundamental premise of the shows: their emotional authenticity. Men's expressions of feeling aren't more authentic because they are rare, but their rarity imbues a valued impression of authenticity to both the candidate and the show as a whole.

Gender expression here is intertwined with class hierarchies. Laura Grindstaff differentiates two kinds of talk shows: those "largely for, and about, middle-class white women," and which "increasingly legitimate contemporary discourse about the therapeutic benefits of emotional expressiveness"; and those that are more physically confrontational and in which "emotional expressiveness [is] a breach of taken-for-granted norms that transgress acceptable therapeutic limits."[31] Makeover shows draw from similar, class-inflected feeling rules that value expressions of feeling framed within therapeutic discourse and, at the same time, bring male candidates within these feeling rules.

If men crying epitomizes the positive values of authenticity and identification, audiences' discussions of "attitude" serve as an interesting contrast. Respondents frequently said that having the "right attitude" was a precondition for a successful makeover, as though the elements of this were self-evident. When candidates "had attitude" or had a "bad attitude," this included talking back to hosts, rolling their eyes at the advice offered, and storming off. A white *Starting Over* viewer commented:

> It disappoints me that the naughty [housemates] are Black, but I think sometimes when you're talking about attitude I think that's totally true; sometimes a lot of Black women do have naughty attitudes or attitudes that are like, you look at them like they're from outer space. Sometimes I think there are a lot of Black women who get the idea that they need to have everything done for them.

Here "attitude" was associated with two familiar stereotypes of Black women: the person of color as childlike ("naughty"), or as a "welfare queen" (who needs to "have everything done" for her). Similarly, when we asked another white woman whether she thought that people of all races are treated similarly on *What Not to Wear*, she responded, "Yeah, I haven't noticed anybody being treated differently. I have noticed some of the makeovers [candidates] really kind of have bad attitudes, but you know . . . "

The only person to complicate the racialized construction of attitude was Sally, a Black woman who recalled an episode of *What Not to Wear* that presented a Black woman in a warmly funny light:

> I just loved that sense of humor that they showed because so often—I hate to say it—is that [the media] do to Blacks what they did to that one girl, Laura, who was Hispanic. Which is they portray us as angry and upset and bad attitude, and it's like, "No!" [laughing]. So I would say, really I haven't seen that much of a difference as far as Blacks and whites are treated on [*What Not to Wear*]. I would say just because of that one Hispanic girl, I would say that's where they probably need to work on some improvement and get away from stereotypes.

Here Sally saw the representation of women of color on *What Not to Wear* as having a bad attitude as more associated with Latinas than with African Americans, but as a problem of racial stereotyping nonetheless.

"Attitude" thus seems to describe a failure of emotional management, particularly attributed to women of color in this research but also to teenagers, which says a great deal about the assumptions of emotional maturity of nonwhites by whites. White, middle-class norms of emotional management are endorsed by referring to belligerent, complaining, unwilling behavior as "attitude." "Having attitude" is a way of chastising the behaviors of people who have few other means of resisting norms that are not their own.

Producing Feeling

The audiences we talked to were highly invested in the ordinariness of the makeover show candidates and the authenticity of their emotional performances. This was the case even when they were quite skeptical about the conditions under which this emotional realism was produced. As with talk shows, makeover programs capitalize on ordinariness and extraordinary displays of feeling by producing the "money shot," usually through the moment of the reveal.[32] Many of the viewers we talked to were aware of how producers intervened in order to precipitate candidates' emotional expressiveness. They observed how scripting, editing, and even genre expectations not only shaped but also risked challenging the emotional realism of the show. Some viewers criticized the shows for what they saw as formulaic editing that manipulated the emotional ups and downs of the episodes. Cathy, a *What Not to Wear* regular, said:

> I think there is a pattern, and I think they could be more creative with their editing on the pattern, because it's almost like after a while, they've just kind of gone into a pattern, more or less. Like, the start is [candidates] are resistant, and by the middle they're being a little more emotional and softening up, and then by the end they're saying how great Stacy and Clinton are. That's pretty much across the board.

Many people questioned the impact of editing on the representation of emotion in the shows. A male regular viewer questioned whether the heightened emotions were products of casting or of editing in his testy discussion of *The Biggest Loser*:

Sometimes it just seems to me that there are certain people who just constantly cry or people who constantly get angry at random things and then there's a part of me that wonders if this is what they are showing me, you know, the editing, I wonder that, too. So I don't necessarily know if it's a realistic portrayal of who those people are.

Similarly, a woman responded to the question "Do you think that the way emotion is expressed [on *Starting Over*] is realistic?" with the following:

You know, yes and no. Do I think they edit it to get the most from it? Yeah [laughing]. But at the same time, I think any time you are making that change, and because it's such a micro-environment, and so much [is] thrown at you, I think it has to have that—you know, I think you would have just a huge level of emotion, just from being so centered and so isolated, you know. But yeah, I do think that they edit it.

Like other viewers, this woman saw the residential setting as likely to produce strong feelings, but also that the show edits the material "to get the most from it."

Critiques of the formulaic structure bring us to another challenge to the realness of the makeover shows: genre. *Starting Over* regulars in particular complained about how the structure of the episodes leaned toward drama, which many likened to soap opera:

This year, I think what really disappointed me was when they started bringing back the ones that already graduated, because most of us, you know, we hate Alison. And she came back for the second time, and it just seemed ridiculous that she came back because it made you think, "Well, this show's nothing more than a soap opera." And they just started going too dramatic. I mean, if I wanted to watch drama, I could turn a soap opera on.

Some participants were highly critical of *Starting Over*'s producer in part of the second and the third seasons, Millee Taggart-Ratcliffe, who replaced Mary-Ellis Bunim after she died in January 2004:

My major, major problem is with Millee Taggart-Ratcliffe. She comes from a soap opera background, and up until I think it's this season, or even last season, when they brought her on board, the show was definitely reality. With her in there now, I feel that it's more for ratings on her plate. I mean, yes, I know ratings are major to a show, but the way she is having the show edited and everything, she is having it edited for drama rather than real life. . . . You know, they're editing it like we're six-year-olds and we don't get it. Come on, folks; we're adult women. We do get it. We know what's going on. Just let the show play out; let the drama unfold as it will. Don't necessarily edit it to make it more than what it really is.

Some interviewees were critical of the ways that the editors reproduced genre conventions from soap operas; others likened *Starting Over* and other shows to daytime talk shows. A *Starting Over* regular viewer railed against these strategies: "There have been little blurbs here and there that are so *Jerry Springer*, I mean I just want to [say], 'Noooo . . .' Like having John Davidson show up for Cassie. It's like, 'Who can we pull strings to get to show up for the audience to watch?' That sort of thing. You can tell it's a set up, for ratings." Even if they might distance themselves from trashy talk shows, the attribution of soap opera to *Starting Over* would not be unwelcome to the show's producers, who described it as a "reality daytime soap" on the Bunim/Murray website.[33]

Only a few people explicitly appreciated that the editing on *Starting Over* was done for viewers' benefit, such as this woman interviewee:

There's twenty-four hours in a day, and I saw one hour of it. Oh my God, I can't imagine what happens in that place; what they cut out. . . . They can only show you so much, and they have to give you aspects, like they have to keep the drama going so that you're interested and want to keep watching, along with the exercises to make the show valid.

For this regular viewer, the editing for drama and interest is what keeps audiences watching the exercises, which are the raison d'être of the show.

Despite their savviness, many respondents nonetheless remained highly invested in the emotional realism of the shows. Viewers tolerated a dissonant position between an investment in the makeover shows' emotional authenticity and their reflexive understanding of them as objects constructed by media producers in order to appeal to audiences. Further, this reflexive position actually enhanced their investments in the shows' emotional realism. There were surprisingly few instances where viewers assumed that candidates were *less* emotional because they were on television. A *Biggest Loser* comparison group viewer described the sample episode thus: "There were instances where I think there's genuine feeling, but I think there are also instances where they kind of try to over-compose themselves because they're on television." When regular viewers mentioned cases where candidates had been less expressive because of the production context, they usually went on to say that this "front" was impossible to sustain over time and eventually candidates revealed their genuine feelings. Most people who assessed the influence of the production context on the candidates' emotional expressions saw this as precipitating *more* authentic (if more extreme) emotions than candidates would express in their daily lives. One woman favorably compared *The Biggest Loser* with *The Real World*: "It seems more genuine to me. I think when you're going through a process like that, it can be really emotional, and that having to do it on TV, I can't even imagine how emotional that must be." Another *Biggest Loser* interviewee said:

> I think [the emotions are] realistic because of the intensity of their circumstances. . . . They might pick people who are more emotional, or people who express themselves well because obviously they want people who are going to be expressive because otherwise the show might be boring. So partly it's the selection process, but I also think it's the circumstances that bring out emotion—anybody would be emotional in such circumstances when they're making these dramatic changes in their lives and they're in these intense circumstances with competition and exercise and diet [and] getting weighed on national TV on the world's most gigantic scale [laughing].

She here acknowledged that the *Biggest Loser* producers might cast a particularly expressive group of contestants, but nevertheless the processes of the show, including the ritualized weekly weigh-ins, produced heightened emotional expressivity.

Most respondents endorsed the view that the very artificiality of the shows' circumstances encouraged strong expressions of feeling, especially among men not usually allowed to cry in ordinary life, and this was to the benefit of both candidates and audiences. There were, however, a few examples of criticism of the production of strong feeling. One of the most skeptical among the *Staring Over* interviewees, Edna, was concerned about housing six women in a small space with little privacy for long periods:

> I think it's sort of a cult thing almost. I guess it's kind of like summer camp. You're trapped together in this little house, and you're all experiencing the same things, and you're basing this love and affection for each other on these false pretenses that you truly understand each other when actually, no, you've just gone through a very bizarre and emotionally draining experience together, not necessarily something founded on the real things friendship is founded on. It's like they all got trapped in an elevator during a fire and bonded. Once they're let out of the elevator, who knows if they'll ever talk to each other again?

Edna did not see the expression of feeling on *Starting Over* as fake, however, but as a genuine response to highly artificial circumstances manufactured for the sake of the television show and its audience. Among the most relatable housemates for Edna were those who resisted parts of the *Starting Over* process. She recalled one housemate who:

> was pissed at other people when they were insensitive to her situation. She had more natural reactions I guess. . . . There's something authentic about their reaction to other people and the situations, and questioning, too, like, "Why am I doing this?" Like, if someone tried to put me in a little dress, or have me talk with sock puppets, I'd be like, "Are you kidding me? What are you talking about?"

As with other respondents in this study, Edna shared the view that the artifices of production did not undermine her investments in candidates' emotional authenticity, but instead produced a heightened sense of real feeling.

Media Reflexivity and Emotional Realism

Regular viewers didn't watch the shows believing that everything they saw on-screen happened naturally, or was conveyed without a significant amount of mediation by producers. They recognized that editing conventions, generic formulas, the need to produce good television, and the demands for high audience ratings and lucrative corporate sponsorships shaped what they saw on-screen. In her study of the production of *Sorority Life* (a kind of *Real World*, fly-on-the-wall docusoap based on a university Greek house), Laura Grindstaff argues that:

> to speak of reality programming as "re-presenting the real," or *mis*-representing the real, as some scholars and critics are wont to do, is misleading. A reality show like *Sorority Life* does not re-present anything other than the outcome of its own production process, because it does not simply take a pre-existing reality and transform or alter it; rather, the various activities, practices, and technologies of production actively construct *for real* what participants experience. And then, beyond this, there is a second-register packaging of that reality intended for television and internet audiences.[34]

Not only the sorority participants in Grindstaff's study, but also the audiences we talked to in this research recognized the production processes that shape the very rationales of the shows, as well as how the packaging of those processes rework material to produce a very odd kind of "reality."

Yet there are strong elements of these shows that audiences found very real. Accounting for this sense of reality requires moving away from standards of realism in documentary film and factual programming. As Bill Nichols writes, "Subjectivity and identification are far less frequently explored in documentary than fiction. Issues of objectivity, ethics, and ideology have become the hallmark of documentary debate as issues of subjectivity, identification, and gender have of narrative fiction."[35] Because reality television explores identification and subjectivity through a style that draws heavily on documentary aesthetics (if not ethics), this makes it of dubious moral value for critics. Kavka, however, looks to earlier feminist research on debased cultural forms to argue that there are important elements in reality television that communicate women's lived, relational, affective experiences that can't be communicated easily through traditional representational conventions.[36] Reality television blurs the divisions between fact and fiction, the real and the staged, that are used to distinguish (masculine) factual television from (feminine) fictional forms. Commenting on the convention that reality shows reveal their own constructions, she surmises that "viewers find truth not in the transparency or erasure of the media frame, but rather in social or intersubjective truths that arise out of this frame's manipulation."[37] To show the workings of the production process *adds* to the sense of immediacy, of "being there."[38] Even the most highly media-reflexive audience members we spoke to credited the emotional expressions as authentic, immediate, and intimate. Indeed, their ability to see the artificiality of the makeover situations and the manipulations of the editing enhanced their valuation of the emotional authenticity they perceived in the candidates. They could see what was fake; correspondingly, they could attribute realness to the core expressions of the candidates. Their media reflexivity endorsed their ability to gauge the authenticity of the candidates and their feelings. Thus there is less a tension between the intimacy of identification and the distance of reflexivity, as Corner suggests, but rather a way that reflexivity intensifies the emotional intimacy of the viewing experience.[39]

What is real in reality television is that which is perceived as access to the candidates' true inner selves, the evidence of which is their expression of feeling. Media reflexivity becomes folded into a larger reflexive project in which audiences are able to see themselves, including their media environments and their emotional lives, in context. As I discuss in the next chapter, the shows affirm, and many of the viewers we talked to endorse, a grand project of self-reflexivity and expression, in which the true inner self must be expressed in the world. This project is not a governmental regime of adaptation and flexibility, but reworks much older values of Romanticism through the context of contemporary labor, emotional, and mediated economies.

6

Mirror, Mirror

The Reflexive Self

That's why this show is good: it's because it's not a makeover show.
It's not really to make over your clothes because you're just terrible. They're trying to give people tools to move through life better. And that makes it so much better, especially when you have all
this resistance from people. . . . But that's the best part, is to see the
people make the transformation internally, even if they didn't mean
to. They're like, "Gosh, I'm so surprised." And I know that's a little
bit of the producers, leading them to say certain things. But you do
get a sense that they feel different.
—Danica, *What Not to Wear* interviewee

Danica here draws together some of the themes from the preceding
chapters. She disputes that *What Not to Wear* is a makeover show, suggesting a narrow definition of this genre that focuses only on physical transformation. What she enjoys instead about *What Not to Wear*
is its attention to "internal" change, despite the candidates' conscious
intentions. Although she is aware of the producers' interventions in
what happens on-screen, she maintains that such a transformation has
indeed taken place, that candidates "feel different" about themselves.
The preceding chapters considered media and self-reflexivity in audiences' engagements with the shows. In chapter 3, audiences drew on
their knowledge of the production contexts of the shows to appraise
their instruction and consumer appeals, representing themselves as
experts in the process. In chapter 4, respondents constructed moral

hierarchies of representation, parsing out necessary shaming from exploitative humiliation in order to affirm the shows' project: to get the self to see the self as if from outside. In chapter 5, participants used their critiques of the empirical realism of the shows in order to affirm their emotional realism, with the pleasure of identification that came with this. This chapter draws on these themes of reflexivity to consider how the people in this study mobilized the shows as a resource in an extended conversation about what it means to be a self.

As I mentioned in my introductory chapter, I was initially surprised by how prevalent references to interiority, the inner self, and the problem of its manifestation in the social world were in the survey and interview data. Returning to the shows, I found many instances of these types of references too, although there were differences among the four shows in terms of the frequency and types of address of an inner self. Audiences drew on the shows' self-reflexive motifs, narratives, and rituals to cultivate an intimate and intense engagement with the self. Contrary to contemporary scholars of reality television who argue that reality television produces a new mode of rational, self-governing subjectivity, I argue instead that the self-reflexivity encouraged in makeover programming invokes a much older, Romantic model that values interiority, authenticity, and expression. The contemporary self is reflexively produced as a moral and mediated accomplishment, for which makeover shows are one of a number of resources.

So fundamental is the idea of an interior self to a Western, contemporary mode of being that we tend to see it as a natural and historically continuous fact: "We in the West still take it for granted that we can talk about an inmost self and conceive of it as an inner world, a sort of private interior realm where we are most at home and most ourselves. Many still find this concept indispensable, as if we human beings would lose sight of some important part of ourselves without it."[1] Yet this sense of the self as having interiority has developed historically. The Greek injunction to "know thyself" was, in Roy Baumeister's words, "purely functional," concerning how to "appraise one's talents and capacities accurately so as to be able to carry out one's [civic] duties effectively."[2] In the fourth century Augustine conceived the self as an interior space as a solution to a theological problem: how to know God. Augustine imagined the inner self as a space into which one could retreat and look within and up toward the divine. This idea of the self as an interior space expanded in the Romantic era, in response to the rationalities of the Enlightenment and the pressures of the Industrial Revolution.[3] The inner self as an interior space with depth became something that could be explored and expressed. As Charles Taylor writes, "Only with the expressivist idea of articulating our inner nature do we see the grounds for construing this inner domain as having *depth*, that is, a domain which reaches farther than we can ever articulate, which still stretches beyond our furthest point of clear expression."[4] Augustine's invention of interiority would be reworked and increasingly secularized, but nonetheless provided the foundational model for what we now think of as the inner self.

Anthony Giddens has elaborated the modern self as not only in possession of an interior, but also as reflexive toward that interior. He argues that the disruptions of the industrial revolution, the move toward increasing social mobility, and the demise of religion as the dominant narrative to explain the social world destabilized the self in modern times. This process was enhanced in the second half of the twentieth century, as identity movements, reflexive turns in anthropology and other disciplines, post-structuralism, postcolonial thought, and postmodern theory facilitated an increasingly reflexive approach to the self. No longer could people look to grand narratives that presumed a universal self—a loss that can be welcomed, perhaps, because that universal self was implicitly male, white, Western, heterosexual, and rational. Indeed, Giddens, as well as Ulrich Beck and others, argues that the dislodging of this universal self is to be welcomed.[5] As the idea of the self has become increasingly unstable, self-identity "is not something that is just given . . . but something that has to be routinely created and sustained in the reflexive activities of the individual."[6] I draw on Giddens and Beck here not to describe the modern self as fact but as a heuristic to help identify some of the features of self-reflexivity that are manifested in makeover television. Makeover candidates must consider their own interiority, construct themselves as coherent subjects, and narrate integrative stories about themselves. I conclude that makeover shows do not simply offer resolutions to crises of interiority and congruence, but precipitate a crisis of the self that candidates must resolve through appropriate ways of appraising (and shopping for) the self.

Keeping My Door Open inside of Me

Many of the people in this study were highly invested in the idea of the interiority of the self that could be investigated and articulated. One example comes from this *Starting Over* survey respondent, who said that the show reminded her to "keep my door open inside of me [and] know that I am the artist of my life." Another wrote that "there is generally something about each of the housemates that will make you explore within yourself." A *Biggest Loser* participant wanted to nominate her friend for that show because "she is overweight and I think this would give her confidence to deal with issues within." Another surmised, "When you lose weight you gotta change your insides first." A *What Not to Wear* viewer commented that what she liked most about the show was "to see the people make the transformation internally, even if they didn't mean to. They're like, 'Gosh, I'm so surprised.'" Another respondent wrote, "I like that the physical transition tends to affect the person on the inside as well as how they look on the outside. Some of these people don't know how beautiful they are, or how professional they look." *Queer Eye* participants were less forthcoming about the inner self, which may reflect the show's emphasis on male makeovers and the presumption that, with men, "what you see is what you get." With the other shows, the frequency with which participants referred to an inner self as a taken-for-granted reference point suggests that makeover shows give a vocabulary for and orientation toward this inner self.

A frequently repeated character that *Starting Over* audiences invoked to describe the inner self (or part of this inner self, at least) was that of the inner child. Freud's splitting of the inner self into the ego, the id, and the superego precipitated a rapid fragmentation of the self in psychology, psychiatry, and psychotherapy throughout the twentieth century, complicating the Romantic idea of a unified inner self. The identification of multiple inner selves proliferated through the psychological movements of the twentieth century, making possible a whole genre of literature concerned with the inner child's welfare.[7] Because of its indebtedness to popular psychology, it is not surprising that the

Starting Over life coaches and audiences invoked this metaphor. One survey respondent wrote that she particularly remembered a *Starting Over* episode that involved one housemate, Niambi, "beating up the girl inside with the exercise that included the bat and punching bag. I took [that] with me: Beat yourself up once, let it go, forgive yourself, begin to move on." Another took advice from the show "about telling our inner child the positive things we never heard growing up."

In addition to expanding the realm of interiority, the Romantic era also began a process that shifted the truth of a person from how she or he behaved in public to the inner self as the source of authenticity. Most romanticized was the figure of the artist, whose "conduct that violated social expectations . . . was justified by the presence of a unique and private source of meaning."[8] Inner authority was privileged over the authority of others, and the inner self became the real self. In many cases, revealing the authentic inner self is the purpose of the makeover. In *The Biggest Loser*, this real self is a slim self presumed to exist inside the false self of the overweight body. Having not seen him for a number of weeks of weight loss, a contestant's wife tells him, "You are finding yourself again." In the season 2 finale, Matt Hoover, who would go on to win, reflected, "More important than the weight I lost was finding out who I was again, and that I didn't have to settle for the life I was leading" as an overweight, unfit alcoholic. After one *Queer Eye* makeover, the candidate's wife tells him, "Everything is so you. It's like they captured your whole inner self. It's the 'you' you should have been for years and years." The audiences in this study echoed this discourse of inner authenticity. Discussing a *Starting Over* housemate, a survey respondent wrote, "Jill Tracey tells it like it is and wasn't afraid to dig deep to find her authentic self."

The authenticity of the inner self is augmented by the value placed on the inner voice: the source of moral integrity and truth of a person. Taylor notes that for Rousseau, the inner voice was "the voice of nature within": because the inner voice is founded in nature, which is inherently good, "the inner voice of my true sentiments *define* what is good: since the élan of nature in me *is* the good, it is this which has to be consulted to discover it."[9] References to the inner voice as the source of authority, authenticity, and moral value were especially common with *Starting Over* participants. As one *Starting Over* survey writer put it,

"The biggest [lesson] was to slow down and listen to the voice inside you." Another described what she had learned from the show: "Mostly I've remembered to listen to and honor my own inner voice. I've learned to not let fear drive my career goals and education decisions." Here the inner voice is the true expression of the self, doing battle with fears that aren't "real" but rather obstacles to the expression of the self in the world. Sometimes the inner voice is characterized as coming from a physical place, most commonly the "gut": "The most common [thing that I've learned from watching *Starting Over*] would probably be to listen to your gut, realize who the true you is inside and live as that person, and search to find your passion, what gives you energy, drive, and motivation and do everything in your power to live that passion." By asserting the authority of the inner voice or the gut, the women who make up the bulk of these shows' audiences can assert passions and resistances that they might not otherwise. The interior voice of authority can speak up for needs that might run counter to the demands of their intimate others.

References to the inner voice draw on Romantic ideas of the inner self as the source of goodness. Against the corruptions of the outer world, the moral person looks within, to his or her essential inner nature that communicates the true state of being to consciousness. For Rousseau and his successors, a radical inwardness enabled a self-determining freedom, where the inner nature is essentially beneficent. The idea of the "inner voice," however, quickly took many forms: for some, the inner voice was the voice of the natural self unencumbered by social expectation; for others it gave expression to the beauty and goodness of nature; for others it was the expression of a universal sympathy among beings and things. John Gagnon argues that the inner voice became fragmented into a squabbling cacophony during the twentieth century, the product of psychoanalysis and, later, the competing claims within both the 1970s human potential and social equality movements.[10] When audiences refer to the inner voice in makeover television, however, it is assumed to be a coherent and untroubled source of authority.

The audiences we talked to for this study repeated the shows' claims that inside the wayward outer body is an authentic, inner self that needs to be expressed. Self-reflexivity is the means by which this inner self can be explored and understood. However, with the investment in the inner self comes the risk that there is a discrepancy between this inner and outer self, the possibility of deception, and a crisis of coherence. The resolution of this discrepancy is the makeover genre's express project.

Trapped in the Wrong Body, and Other Crises of Congruence

When viewers responded to makeover shows such as *What Not to Wear* with statements like "I love that nearly every makeover results in a person's inner transformation," they articulated a long-standing assumption that there is a correspondence between the inner self and the physical body. There are two main constructions of the relationship between the inner and outer selves, both of which reemerge in makeover shows and how people talk about them. In the first, predating Augustine, the body was in a reciprocal relationship with the soul. According to Foucault, increasing attention to the care of the self in the first centuries of the Christian era arose from the belief that physical ills were manifestations of disturbances of the soul: in turn, treating the body badly resulted in inner disease. Talking about technologies of the self that attended to diet, sleep, and sexual activity, Foucault writes, "The focus of attention in these practices of the self is the point where the ills of the body and those of the soul can communicate with one another and exchange their physical distresses: where the bad habits of the soul can entail physical miseries, while the excesses of the body manifest and maintain the failings of the soul."[11] In another, more expressly spiritual frame, the New Thought movement drew direct parallels between physical and spiritual well-being. In the 1890s, Ursula Gestefeld wrote, "The visible physical body is not the seat of disease but only the plane of its visibility. By the relation of subjective and objective, the objective body is the means by which is made visible what is held in the subjective soul."[12] For Gestefeld and other New Thought advocates, physical problems, including disease, were merely manifestations of an interior, spiritual dis-ease.

This view of the wayward body as evidence of a troubled soul underpins the rationale of *The Biggest Loser*, in which fat represents what Eve Sedgwick calls "an epidemic of the will."[13] One *Biggest Loser* comparison interviewee, for example, said that "for most of the people that get overweight, it ain't medical. . . . It comes from within." Audiences read the crisis of the overweight body in *The Biggest Loser* as proof of laziness and a lack of willpower, themes constantly repeated throughout the series. The opening montage's text asks, "Do you have the willpower?" and each episode tests contestants' wills though the show's competitions of physical endurance and trials of psychological commitment. This emphasis on work was much of what respondents liked about *The Biggest Loser*. One interviewee told us that the successful candidates "have to put forth the effort—the show just gives them the vehicle to do it. But they actually have to do the work." The focus on work and determination was transparent to comparison viewers, too. One male interviewee said the show's producers "attempt to drive home that kind of message to the viewer that if you want to make changes in your life you have to work at it and put your mind to it." Much of this emphasis on will and productivity is gendered. With the cast of *The Biggest Loser* equally split between women and men, masculine values of hard work prevail; trainers emphasize the need for contestants to push beyond their perceived limits, and to "work out like a man," as one trainer tells the all-female team in season 2. By linking working with masculinity and laziness with femininity, *The Biggest Loser* characterizes the epidemic of the will as a feminization of American culture for both women and men.

The perception of the fat body as marking external evidence of inner dysfunction is not new. As early as 1914 a popular magazine declared, "Fat is now regarded as an indiscretion, and almost as a crime."[14] For both women and men through the twentieth century in the United States, the "crime" was to indulge in increasingly available bodily and consumer pleasures, the proper response to which was self-discipline evidenced by weight control. This moral focus on controlling bodily appetites was most pronounced in Christian dieting books. Marie Griffith observes that by the twentieth century, "an increasingly moralistic pursuit of extreme slimness would vie with the focus on health as a supreme religious value, a notion aided by the accelerating belief in spirit-body correspondence that steadily advanced the body as an expressive language revealing the interior soul."[15] Only the slim body was an acceptable vessel for Christ. Makeover shows secularize the relationship between the overweight body and the problem inner self, but remove little of the moral burden that comes with this relationship.

In makeover shows, being overweight is less a punishment from God or an accident of fate than a manifestation of inner conflict that becomes the person's responsibility to resolve. This responsibility for physical problems is not reserved for weight: Susan Sontag recognizes how this assumption has shaped social constructions of tuberculosis, cancer, and AIDS, irrespective of developments in medical understanding that have taken place.[16] But the responsibility for weight has particular personal and social implications; sloth is not only a crisis for the individual, but for the nation as well. As Kathleen LeBesco writes, "To be fat is to fail to do one's duty as a productive worker: 'Already the US economy loses $100 billion from weight-related sickness . . . what chance has America in the long run, if [fat acceptance prevails], that it can ever compete with those wiry Filipinos and Koreans?'"[17] She continues, "More interesting than the *accuracy* of this claim is the intensity with which it signals a failure on the part of the fat body to register as a fully productive body in a capitalist economy."[18] *The Biggest Loser* reproduces anxieties about the US economy posed by global outsourcing of labor in late capitalism by positing the unproductive, fat American body as a problem to be solved. *The Biggest Loser* reworks the moral imperative to be, or look, slim, detaching from an earlier, expressly religious framework and linking with the demands of neoliberalism for empowered, employable, consuming citizens.

If seeing outward problems as a manifestation of inner dysfunction is one way of articulating the relationship between the inner and outer selves, another version is that the body fails to represent adequately the true state of the soul. In some instances, the beautiful inner self is misrepresented by a less attractive appearance. This was most dramatically expressed by the "trapped in the wrong body" trope. Respondents to *The Biggest Loser* survey, in particular, frequently commented that trapped inside the contestants' overweight bodies were their beautiful (i.e., slim) selves dying to get out. One survey writer offered a typical example: "I like it when women who have felt ugly and fat their whole lives discover a brand-new attractive person inside themselves!" This perspective assumes that the makeover candidates have an essentially beautiful inner self that the shows' training can help them discover. This process of discovery can also be adopted by audiences: a survey respondent liked *The Biggest Loser* because "it teaches [that] everyone is a beautiful person, you just have to find that within yourself." In the season 2 finale, the finalist Suzy Preston described herself as always believing she was "a thin girl trapped in an overweight body." (Only days later, on *The Larry King Show*, Suzy reversed this metaphor and worried that she was still a chubby girl trapped in a slim body.) The motif of the trapped self was represented visually in *The Biggest Loser*'s season finale, when all the contestants came back to the show after having spent three months continuing to diet and exercise on their own. As a dramatic example of the before/after reveal, each newly svelte contestant burst through a paper screen on which was printed a larger-than-life image of them- selves as they were when they started the season, tearing through the preexisting wrong body in which they had been trapped.

The idea of being trapped in the wrong body was neither exclusive to *The Biggest Loser* nor reserved for women. A *What Not to Wear* viewer described one candidate on that show as follows: "There was another [candidate] named Ken, who was a biker. And he dressed so tough on the outside, but he was just such a puppy dog on the inside." Here the candidate had to reclaim his sweetness and (feminine) vulnerability to become his "true" self, a puppy dog, rather than a hypermasculine biker. Not all viewers took to heart the trapped-self metaphor, however. One woman wrote that one thing she disliked about *What Not to Wear* was "there are only so many times that I can hear 'Be your inner sexpot' before I must change the channel."

The expression, to be "trapped in the wrong body," is most familiarly used to describe transgender experience, and scholarly work on this from a transgender perspective is helpful to contextualize the experi- ence of having an inner and outer self at odds. Jay Prosser acknowl- edges the strategic deployment of the "trapped in the wrong body" trope in persuading medical experts about the necessity for hormone treatment and surgery. He contends, however, that "transsexuals con- tinue to deploy the image of wrong embodiment [beyond a point when it is medically strategic] because being trapped in the wrong body is simply what transsexuality feels like."[19] He argues that people who choose to fully transition to their new gender are not "dupes of gender," reactionary gender recidivists who want to reify essentialized gender norms, but are resolving what is too frequently experienced as an ago- nizing sense of being alienated. He argues that the physical experience of the body as being at odds with the self is "a psychic projection [that is] nevertheless deeply felt."[20] Prosser's account acknowledges gender as socially constructed but nonetheless viscerally and psychically experienced as real. I am not equating transgender people's experiences with those of people who undergo or watch televised makeovers, but Prosser's analysis is useful in two ways. First is the possibility that the sense of the body comes from the experience of the inner self, rather than seeing that inner self as defined by the body and its legibility. Second, Prosser reminds us that the sense of an inner self at odds with the body is not merely a discursive issue, but demonstrates how discourses of self, identity, and embodiment are deeply and importantly felt. I draw from Prosser an unwillingness to see the inner self as a phantom that has no experiential reality, to argue that even as the sense of the inner self is worked through discourse, it nonetheless has significance and emotional import for our experiences of ourselves as legitimate and legible beings.

The trapped in the wrong body metaphor was one way that the shows and their audiences talked about the relationship between the inner and outer selves; in another version, inside an apparently attractive exterior lurked a disturbed inner self that needs attention. This self is both self-deceiving and deceiving of others. Talking about *What Not to Wear*, one survey respondent asserted, "Appearance can be the first sign of inner demons. And we all have them." Jill, a housemate on season 3 of *Starting Over*, was framed by a survey respondent in these terms: "She was really leading a good life, it appeared on the outside, but on the inside she was a mess." Another *Starting Over* housemate, Jodi, struggled with her feelings of shame about how she had behaved to the other women. Iyanla, one of the life coaches, told Jodi that she is facing her "shadow self," which is "where all the darkness is." An ongoing theme of her time on the show was to "destroy the mask" that kept her from authentic relationships with people—a mask that was both psychological and made literal (and televisual) by a plaster cast of Jodi's own face. The fake self, the mask, must be removed: late in the season Jodi was deemed ready to destroy her mask and, in a characteristic *Starting Over* ritual, she dropped it from a balcony and it shattered on the terrace below. The mask metaphor was adopted by this *Starting Over* viewer, who wrote that as a result of the show she saw the value of "stripping away phony outer appearances to see what really lies within the psyche. I have been forced since watching the show to see who I really am." Here the outer presentation is symptomatic of the inner self insofar as it is inauthentic. Only by expressing the struggles of the inner self can one produce a more authentic self.

In contrast to male candidates, who tend to be represented as pathetic but without guile, women have been traditionally seen as agents of deception, particularly through appearances. Kathy Peiss argues that anxieties about feminine mysteries became entwined with nineteenth-century social mobility: "That a woman with rouge pot and powder box might practice cosmetic sorcery suggests both an ancient fear of female power and a new secular concern: In a rapidly commercializing and fluid social world, any woman with a bewitching face might secure a husband and make her fortune."[21] The gold digger epitomized this strategic deployment of appearances. In contemporary makeover media, women are caught between two competing demands: to learn the codes of upward mobility and to know their place as gendered, raced, classed subjects. The removal of the mask naturalizes this tension, where women candidates must reveal their real inner selves that are, paradoxically, highly normative. The metaphor of the mask, the body as evidence of a diseased soul, and the soul trapped in the wrong body are each reworked in the makeover genre to describe a crisis of authenticity, where the implicitly good, moral, inner self is not adequately expressed. The work of the makeover show is to produce a coherent subject whose inner and outer selves are congruent.

Feeling Beautiful, Inside and Out

Both the shows and the audiences' conversations about them most often assumed that congruence between the inner and outer selves was achieved through internal transformation. A *Biggest Loser* interviewee discussed how contestants' changing image of themselves came second in importance to the internal shifts taking place:

> I think they are doing a lot of internal work, in that they are learning to persevere through this, and become more confident. It's very clear that the trainers do a lot of psychological, emotional work with them along

the way. . . . I think that when they see themselves, finally, it's more like a plus that all their work has been worth it, [but] they start feeling better about themselves first.

The shows, too, emphasized the need for inner change. A contestant from the first season of *The Biggest Loser* returned on season 2 for a pep talk, telling the cast, "You can't physically appreciate yourself if you don't appreciate yourself on the inside." In an episode of *What Not to Wear* the hosts made over Kathryn, a Mormon artist whose modest outfits they considered "frumpy." Afterward, her husband observes, "She is on the outside what she is on the inside now." Similarly, when a housemate is about to graduate from *Starting Over*, the show's style expert gives her a makeover so "the outside reflects all the work she has done on the inside." The priority given to the inner self as driver of positive outer change affirms the Romantic view that the inner self is the source of authenticity.

Participants also, less frequently, discussed change between the inner and outer selves in the reverse direction, where transformations in the outer self precipitated inner changes. After his makeover on *Queer Eye*, the straight guy Philly Rojas thanks the Fab Five for having "touched so many aspects of my life, from the exterior to the interior. I was in a rut, and now I see, I hope I see endless possibilities. I know I can get my life back." This theme was especially prevalent with *What Not to Wear*, which focuses on improving candidates' self-esteem by training them in new consumption practices. One candidate had put on a lot of weight after a bad breakup; as a result of her makeover, she says, "You really change more internally than you know. . . . I feel like a different person—I feel beautiful inside and out." Here the external transformation precipitates a change in this candidate's sense of herself "inside." This emphasis was shared by *What Not to Wear* audiences, too: "I am a believer that changing the outside can effect changes on the inside. Many women feel ugly and lacking in confidence. There's nothing like a new outfit and a great haircut to make you feel wonderful." Some respondents commented that external change can be a behavioral push to make deeper changes on the inside. One interviewee said that on *What Not to Wear*, "what you see is as they get an outer change, that builds them up to their own potential, . . . it begins an inner change.

You know, it's kind of like 'do it, and then you'll feel like doing it.'" Later, the same interviewee commented, "If I can change how I appear, I can change other things about myself." Occasionally candidates contradicted the assumption that the makeover returns them to the real self they were supposed to be. After her makeover, a *What Not to Wear* candidate said, "I know I'm me, but I don't feel exactly the same, because I'm way more glammed up than I was. We'll see after I do this for a week or two whether I feel like me or if I feel like I'm in somebody else's shoes." Even if the shoe fits, some candidates might not necessarily wear it.

Respondents, however, rarely linked their discussions of congruence between the inner and outer selves to having to produce a particular *kind* of outer self that is compatible with the demands of the environment. The makeovers don't simply offer candidates tools to align their inner and outer selves but provide a framework for culturally normative adjustments. In a very rare reference to racially inflected style, an African American *Starting Over* viewer said that she cut her dreadlocks as a result of identifying with a Black housemate, Jill, who had decided to cut her hair: "I've taken those dreads out of my hair, because I always felt like if people didn't want to look at anything else, they could look at my hair. So, now I'm kind of like, I'm revealing my face, who I am." Dreadlocks here represent a false kind of evidence; by choosing a hairstyle associated with an assertion of Afrocentric identity, Black women hide their "real," that is "unraced," self. Not only is there a higher premium on looking attractive and respectable for Black women, but to be authentic means dispensing with a distinctively ethnic style, reflecting what Brenda Weber calls the "ethnic anonymity" of the shows.[22] Makeover shows position the purpose of the transformation as expressing the true, integrated self—a much easier pill to swallow than finding ourselves having normative gender, class, and race standards imposed on us.

Whether changing from the inside out, or the reverse, many people assumed inner/outer congruence has moral value. Some of the people we talked to argued that looking better produces a better person. A *What Not to Wear* interviewee said, "I am sure that some of the makeovers have done psychological good, because my grandmother had an old saying: 'When you look good, you feel good; when you feel good, you do good." The shows also reassured viewers that paying attention to their appearance would not compromise their moral inner self. A survey respondent wrote that *What Not to Wear* "shows me that looking good on the outside does not undermine your being a good person, that you can be tough and good looking, instead of vain." Part of the shows' education is to work against the negative associations of paying attention to appearances and insist instead that "good people" can look good, too.

Starting Over respondents based the moral value of this show on the manifestation of inner authenticity. One woman described watching *Starting Over* to help her "look deep within myself in order to become a better person." Another wrote, "When the women graduate from that show they have truly been helped from the inside out. The change is permanent and everyone that is in their life are better for it." This emphasis on inner change in *Starting Over* was so profound that some respondents resisted including the show in the makeover television genre, despite the fact that "graduating" housemates get a one-day makeover before they leave the house. One survey respondent wrote:

> *Starting Over* is not a makeover show. It really should not be in this category. It is true that they "make over" the graduate before graduation, but that is making the outside match the new inside—and frankly most of us were pretty darn critical about just how talented [style adviser] Andy Paige is on makeovers (not). If they skipped that feature, none of us would have cared. It wasn't about "makeover," it was about inner change.

Inner change has its own moral worth, irrespective of whether the housemates looked different at the end of the show. Yet even this viewer recognizes that the *Starting Over* makeover is supposed to make "the outside match the new inside," acknowledging a relationship between these.

The moral questions that external transformation posed were exemplified by audiences' discussions of makeover shows that involved cosmetic surgery. Surgery was usually seen as completely superficial and thus useless or suspect. A *What Not to Wear* interviewee criticized the candidates on *Extreme Makeover*, saying, "I'm like, 'You're not really working towards it. You should want to look on the inside.' I mean everyone has something they don't like about themselves. But that ends up being something you embrace and ends up being like a characteristic about you." The quirks of one's appearance reveal a uniqueness "on the inside" that people should come to celebrate, not change.

Biggest Loser interviewees offered the strongest version of this argument, one that endorsed this show's emphasis on hard work: "Gastric bypass, or liposuction, I really disagree with those methods because it's a quick fix. It doesn't solve the root problems that are making the person overweight. Because I think overweight is a total mental thing unless you have a diagnosed thyroid problem." Another *Biggest Loser* interviewee criticized *Extreme Makeover* for its radical approach to physical transformation:

> I don't like the idea that people need to have a whole bunch of surgery to feel okay about themselves. . . . *Extreme Makeover* really bothers me because people are having so much work done, and it's like, come on! Do you really need nine surgeries at once and tooth caps and everything else under the sun just to feel good about yourself?

A *Starting Over* survey respondent commented, "I hate [makeover shows] with surgery or where people go through so much because they hate themselves, either physically or mentally. It should be about bringing out the beauty inside." Another *Starting Over* survey respondent extended this suspicion of outer change to those shows that changed contestants' appearance without resorting to surgery, such as *What Not to Wear*. She wrote, "I love *Starting Over*, but I can't stand makeover shows like the plastic surgery shows or the clothing shows. The premise of those shows is that you're not good enough on the outside and you need to be fixed. *Starting Over* is about internal, lifelong change which I value far more."

The Biggest Loser viewers' negative appraisal of superficial change on the surgery shows affirmed that program's project of inner change through work and struggle. Answering our question about whether there were shows that respondents preferred not to watch, one respondent wrote that she avoided *The Swan* and *Extreme Makeover* because "most of the 'fixing' was done externally to them, not like *Biggest Loser* where the contestants have to work to change." *The Biggest Loser* host,

Caroline Rhea, frequently distinguished this show from cosmetic surgery shows like *Extreme Makeover*. In one episode she emphasized that *The Biggest Loser* "is not about surgery or quick-fix gimmicks, it's about losing weight the old-school way, through diet and exercise only." By emphasizing "old-school" ways of losing weight—diet and exercise— the show affirms the dedication, perseverance, commitment, willpower, and other inner qualities the candidate must develop in order to lose weight. Natalie Wilson found that media portrayals of weight loss surgery characterize this as a lazy option by suggesting that "fat people are not supposed to have a cheater's way out, damnit! They should be made to suffer for their self-indulgence, laziness, and constant eating!"[23] *The Biggest Loser* reproduces assumptions that the moral solution to fat should be physical work and willpower, not surgery.

Makeovers purport to address the crisis of congruence between the inner and outer selves. In one version, the outer self manifests inner disease, a lack of will, a failure of self-esteem: only by working with the outer self and its problems can you bring forth the true, beautiful, inner self. In another, the outer self and inner self don't match, candidates are trapped in the wrong body, hide, are misrecognized, or don't know themselves by their appearance. Only by expressing the good, authentic, inner self may the external self be transformed. Paradoxically, in both versions personal transformation requires the affirmation and revelation of a constant, unchanging interiority. As Rachel Dubrofsky writes, scholars "need to expand notions of the therapeutic to include the idea of affirming self-sameness across disparate social spaces and the use of surveillance to verify sameness."[24] Makeover shows affirm this unchanging self while diagnosing a crisis of inner/outer congruence as candidates' chief ailment. The shows then position their projects as uniquely qualified to address this crisis. Orienting this route to the unchanging inner self is self-reflexive narrativization: the journey from incongruence to authenticity is paved with stories about the self.

Compelling Narratives of Misery

The lack of congruence between the inner and outer selves is a crisis that must be accounted for. In a characteristically apposite *New Yorker* cartoon, a therapist says to a client, "Look, making you happy is out of the question, but I can give you a compelling narrative for your misery."[25] A key element of the reflexive self is the ability to narrate the story of the self, fashioning a coherent trajectory from what otherwise seem to be random and often infelicitous events. Taylor describes the role of the novel as offering templates for self-narrativization, as "canonical" frames—particularly religion—became weaker: "Life has to be lived as a story. . . . But now it becomes harder to take over the story ready-made from the canonical models and archetypes. The story has to be drawn from the particular events and circumstances of this life."[26] Giddens has argued that a fundamental feature of self-reflexivity is the production and revision of narratives. These ground identity when the fixed, stable sense of place that is presumed to have existed before modernity no longer holds: "The reflexive project of the self, which consists in the sustaining of coherent, yet continuously revised, biographical narratives, takes place in the context of multiple choice as filtered through abstract systems."[27] As one of these abstract systems, media offer an array of possible narrative components. Because makeover programs are centrally concerned with the problem of the self, they offer an especially rich archive of narratives of crisis and intervention.

The underlying structure of both episodic and serial makeover shows is based on conventional narratives of candidates' failures and the need for transformation. During the twenty-eight-year-old Philly Rojas's makeover on *Queer Eye*, he tells the Fab Five about his decline: he hurt his leg and stopped working out, put on weight, is stuck in a rut in his job, and was dumped by his second wife, Laurie. Kyan summarizes that this story "sounds like it's affected his self-esteem." To help Philly get himself together and get back with his wife, the hosts emphasize a progress trajectory that underpins self-narratives. Thom says that he wants to transform Philly's home to "impress Laurie and show her who you want to be and where you are going." The narrative gathers the experiences of the past, organizes them into a coherent trajectory, and offers a moment to reorient toward a different future. The shows thus work a general life narrative into the episodic or serial narrative, where earlier crisis becomes the ground on which the current televised transformation can take place, setting up a future of "endless possibilities," as Philly hopes at the end of the episode. Jack Bratich observes that a narrative antecedent of makeover shows is the fairy tale, which "was, in essence, about the powers of transformation."[28] Importantly, fairy tales can both be stories of wonder, hope, and possibility and simultaneously cautionary tales designed to "modify conduct" in their listeners.[29] The reveal at the end of each episode is the "happily ever after" trope of the makeover show. Even those that don't end in heterosexual reunion contain the possibility of an entirely changed future in which all manner of options become available—in love, work, family, health, and so on. The price to be paid, however, is the modification of conduct away from childish irresponsibility toward self-reflexive adulthood.

Many of the viewers we talked to adopted these narratives to make sense of their own experiences. A *Biggest Loser* interviewee discussed her ongoing struggles with weight loss through her involvement with the contestants on that show:

> I've been dealing with weight loss, weight issues, my entire life. Three years ago, I had gastric bypass. And I lost weight through that method, but it wasn't until last fall when I realized that I had spent $25,000 on surgery to lose seventy-five pounds. And I realized this surgery only goes so far. I've got to do something else. And that's where Weight Watchers and working out four days a week came into play. But *The Biggest Loser* is an inspiration because you watch people who are as big as yourself lose it.

A *Starting Over* viewer linked her own devastating experience of being told something unbearable to a housemate's similar experience:

> I understood that Kelly had those issues, and it probably came from her childhood and things that were said to her, how they linger with you. Somebody had said to her that she was being sexually [provocative] with her father, and although that wasn't said to me in that way, my father said he wished I had died when I had cancer. And that has always been with me my whole life, that one thing you can't just let go. So I understood when she said that was one statement that kind of changed her whole life; that one changed me.

Although the specifics of these interviewees' stories diverged from those of the candidates, the makeover shows offered flexible enough narratives for interviewees to organize their own experiences.

Even the most compelling narratives of transformation, however, may not offer all respondents the kind of agency and autonomy from the past that advocates of modern self-reflexivity might wish. A *Biggest Loser* viewer told us her story of a long struggle with weight gain and loss:

> When September 11 happened, I was working on the thirteenth floor, and we had twenty-six flights of steps to go down. I thought I was going to die. And that made me rejoin [Weight Watchers] again, and I lost almost one hundred pounds. And I kept it off, I did great. And then little by little, when stress starts coming into my life, I'm eating nonstop again. This is ridiculous! So, even though the stress was there then, I would look at [the *Biggest Loser* candidates] and say, "Wow, look at how great they look!" And then I'd get a bowl of ice cream. I'm like, I don't understand why I would do that.

Although Giddens and others assume that self-narratives are likely to be empowering and freeing, it may be as important that they conform to what Eva Illouz calls a "culture of suffering," where stories of struggle become the primary means to construct a narrative of the self.[30] Based on the paradigmatic figure of Oprah Winfrey, Illouz argues that suffering has become constitutive of modern identity, especially for women.

Stories of suffering are not the domain of women only, however, nor are they articulated only by participants already committed to the self-project of the makeover show. Terrance, a man in the comparison group who had not previously seen *Starting Over*, related to a housemate's financial problems in the episode. He said, "Thank God I'm not who I was. I'm not who I was, but I'm not who I want to be. But I'm moving toward where I want to be. But I mean honestly, I would have been in that same situation [as the housemate] maybe four or five years ago." Terrance's self-appraisal suggests how much makeover show narratives of the self are not unique to the genre but draw from broader cultural impulses to tell these kinds of stories. Further, he gives weight to Illouz's claim that the twentieth century saw "increased emotional androgynization of men and women."[31] The presence of men in the shows and among the audiences, and the willing engagement of men such as Terrance who may not regularly watch the shows, suggests that the makeover genre may be one cultural form that precipitates such emotional androgynization.

The narrative strategies both in the shows and reproduced by the participants in this study suggest how embedded self-reflexivity is in existing media practices, specifically self-help materials, television genres such as soap operas, and social media. Each of these offers frameworks for narrative self-production. In terms of the narrative conventions of self-help media, Toby Miller and Alec McHoul write, "Self-help is somewhere in between psychology and psychoanalysis. Like psychology, it privileges the empirical, experiencing subject, favoring the expression of feelings without mapping them onto the unconscious. But it is equally caught up in narrative form, as per psychoanalysis: self-help, like Freudianism, likes nothing better than a good story."[32] And it is precisely a good story that makeover shows need, especially the serialized ones that require that audiences return week after week.

Sustaining audience interest during and between episodes also requires drawing on the narrative conventions of other television genres, specifically soap operas. Sonia Livingstone describes the melodramatic patterns of disruption, guilt, restitution, and restoration of equilibrium shared by soap operas and makeover shows:

> A cyclic process occurs where a sociostructural phenomenon (typically, rule-breaking) is transformed to an individual phenomenon of agency (for example, guilt and personal responsibility) and then back to a sociostructural one (e.g., rules mended and penance done). . . . Mythic narrative, from which other narrative forms draw some of their conventions, thus explores threats to the status quo, ultimately creating a heightened expectation of the status quo by showing how one overcomes moral or social challenges to the state of equilibrium.[33]

Significantly, in both soap operas and makeover shows these mythic narratives are given their emotional intensity through melodramatic conventions.

Makeover shows borrow narratives of the self from self-help media and soap operas; some regular viewers then reproduced these through other communication technologies. Some interviewees discussed how they used social media as an intensified means of narrativized self-reflexivity. A *Starting Over* viewer talked about regularly updating her MySpace page:

> I was doing quotations every day; I do it every couple days now. [I'm] thinking about posting a biography that I'm writing but I'm not sure. I posted the links to it. I post about my struggles—like I have anger issues and panic attack issues. . . . I get panicky and then I get angry. I write when I have episodes about that.

Another *Starting Over* interviewee discussed blogging as a technique that helped her make sense of her experiences after she lost her job:

> I just never thought I could do this. I never thought I could stay home. I never saw myself as a stay-at-home mom; I always admired and respected women who could do that, but I was never one of them, and now my daughter's grown and gone and I'm staying home with my dog. Just taking care of myself in a whole new way; when I'm tired, I rest; when I'm hungry, I eat; when I have something on my mind, I journal or blog. I'm trying to be—just *be*—and not do as much. So yeah; and I had some issues with compulsive shopping and spending, and thankfully, because I've slowed down and stopped trying to play the game out there, I've been able to resolve all of those issues as well.

Here journaling and blogging, both forms of technologized self-narration, facilitate an inward turn, to stop "play[ing] the game out there" and learn to "just be." Henry Jenkins is optimistic about the possibilities of convergence and interactivity for audience productivity, where new media technologies offer an unprecedented range of venues, texts, and other resources for self-representation.[34] Mark Andrejevic, however, is suspicious of the role of new interactive technologies as a route to "self-expression and self-knowledge."[35] He warns that the idealized view of democratized media, what he calls "participatory interactivity," is too easily co-opted by media companies, which extract more labor from engaged audiences than from apathetic ones.[36]

I don't intend here to undermine these interviewees' uses of narratives to deal with painful experiences. I do, however, want to consider this in terms of Giddens's assumption that narrativization allows seemingly infinite freedom to self-invent from arbitrary life events, where "the line of development of the self is *internally referential.*"[37] Giddens's only criterion is whether it all makes sense in terms of one's internally generated narrative. However, as Ellen Granberg argues from her research on how people who have lost a great deal of weight construct stories about this process, self-narratives must be recognizable and credible. They tend to draw from "a stock of 'canonical' narratives" and must be met with at least some acceptance from others to whom we tell those narratives.[38] As Foucault observes with religious and sexual confession, Rose argues with discursive practices within the psy disciplines, and Prosser discusses with transgender autobiographies, self-narratives are embodied and felt, and at the same time are institutionally convenient.[39] Far from the freedom to self-invent that Giddens proposes, self-narratives are as likely to deliver the narrator into affective and economic systems unconcerned with her own interests, however comforting these narratives might feel at a personal level.

Like the genre of self-help that preceded them, makeover shows use narrativization to reveal to the self that self's authentic nature. But "self-help's confessional technique is not one that entails the disclosure of an essential or pre-existent identity. Rather, self-disclosure actually becomes a constructed and tailored narrativization of the self. In the process of 'discovering who one really is,' the techniques do the work of self-invention."[40] This work of self-invention is firmly placed not only in a larger culture of self-help but also in mediated and commercial contexts where the invention of the self is both socially normative and commercially profitable. Rather than seeing self-narratives as a *product* of interiority, makeover shows instead help to produce the very sense of interiority that sustains these narratives.

Rituals of the Self

Giddens and Beck argue that self-reflexivity offers freedom from the constraints of history and structure.[41] Both the narrative conventions on which makeover shows draw and their highly ritualized elements, however, alert us to how apparently individualized self-reflexivity is situated within shared norms. The endlessly repeated rituals that structure the formula of makeover television suggest that the self-project of the makeover is less one of freedom from tradition than a reintegration into tradition, albeit in newly mediated forms. Ronald Grimes worries that because "ritual" is so hard to define, it is used either too narrowly to describe specifically religious rites, or too broadly to describe any routinized practice: "Defined too narrowly, its relation to ordinary life is obscured. Defined too broadly, its difference from ordinary interaction is occluded."[42] The appropriate reach of rituals in makeover shows can be defined by those practices that tie together routinized practices and mundane habits. These range from our most intimate rituals (what Pierre Bourdieu calls the "habitus")[43] to borrowed practices from other institutions (religious, social, commercial, and mediated). Makeover rituals also reinsert their practitioners into broader systems of meaning, such as those of belief, faith, or ideology. Makeover shows, and people's interactions with them, rely on ritualized behavior that articulates habits, institutions, and beliefs in the production of a reflexive self.

Each of the four shows in this study borrows rituals from existing and recognizable institutions, most obviously the Christian church. Candidates must confess, are tempted, make sacrifices, experience revelation, and are transformed. The ritual process of the makeovers in all four shows follows most of the criteria identified by Carolyn Marvin and David Ingle for national sacrifice: the sacrifice must be willing; the group must agree on the victim; the outcome must be uncertain; the ritual must have a beginning and end; the sacrifice must be valuable; and successful sacrifice brings commemoration rituals.[44] *What Not to Wear* candidates' willingness is tested when they must choose to give up their current wardrobe for a $5,000 shopping spree. Families on this and other shows nominate candidates and endorse their makeover, suggesting group agreement. Part of the televisual excitement for audiences comes from not knowing the outcome; some interviewees discussed their glee when makeovers were unsuccessful (the occasional failure reinforcing the value of the frequent successes). The beginning of the makeover ritual is marked by the initial crisis—the weight to be lost, the impact on one's career—the end by the reveal. The candidates sacrifice their wardrobe, their weight, their privacy, their time, their earning power, but most importantly their old selves; their families sacrifice time with the candidates during the makeover, their own privacy, and their existing relationship with the candidates' old selves. For Marvin and Ingle, the commemoration of the death of the sacrificial victim rep-resents the conclusion of an Old Testament model of sacrifice. Make-over shows, in contrast, borrow from the Christian New Testament, which emphasizes redemption: the candidate's reveal and return to the family marks the resurrection of her self.

Sometimes the religious elements of the makeover are explicit. Tell-ingly, each episode of *Queer Eye* addresses a "mission," a term that described theological dissemination before it did military operations. In one episode, after peeling the candidate's glued-on toupee from his bald head, Richard and the Fab Five set light to it on the grill, calling it a "ritual sacrifice"—to the god of authenticity, presumably. In another example, a *What Not to Wear* interviewee called the realization that comes with the makeover "an epiphany." Whereas Christian rituals are most obviously borrowed by makeover media, rituals associated with other institutions also appear: the school (*Starting Over*'s review board, grades, and graduations); the police (*What Not to Wear*'s ambush and arrest); the courts (hosts as judges and families as jury, epitomized by the W cable network's *Style by Jury*); and Weight Watchers (*The Biggest Loser*'s public weigh-ins). Makeover shows draw on rituals from these institutions to offer recognizable, visual, and adaptable models that make meaningful the processes of transformation.

Makeover shows' reliance on ritual reveals that their project is less one of producing individual uniqueness than collectivity—or, rather, of producing individuality as an ethic central to modern collectivity. Fol-lowing Émile Durkheim's claim that ritual marks off the sacred from the profane for the purposes of social cohesion,[45] David Chaney sum-marizes that "the essence of a ritual . . . is that a collectivity is postu-lated or affirmed which might otherwise only have an ambiguous social existence."[46] The purpose of ritual is to contain—or to appear to con-tain—the uncertain and hostile elements of human sociability in order for groups to work collectively, at least most of the time.[47] Couldry takes a "post-Durkheimian perspective," arguing that media rituals do not produce social cohesion, but rather only the *impression* of cohesion.[48] In doing so, they situate media institutions and technologies as the privileged definer and distributor of rituals of cohesion. In makeover shows we see rituals reproducing collective assumptions about the self, paradoxically through a highly individualized sense of the self. Just as these rituals affirm the assumption that we concur with the socially normative project of impression management, this cohesion is worked through an intensely personal ritual, the self's relationship with the self. The attractions of this intimacy with the self are part of the intense pleasures of the shows among their audiences.

What connects this sense of intense individuality to the makeover shows is the restorative power of confession. Canonical narratives of struggle, relapse, and restoration affirm confession as a fundamental mode of producing a self. As Foucault famously argues in his first volume of *The History of Sexuality*, there is no preexisting self that then expresses itself; the self—its contours and qualities—is produced through the very act of expression. His concept of the "perverse implantation" dispenses with the idea that there is a "real" human sexuality that can be repressed, in favor of a productive model in which the idea of repression is deployed in order to bring sexual pleasures into the realm of institutional surveillance.[49] By making sex the secret that must be rooted out, the Christian church, medicine, and educational authorities justified going in search of it in the intimate practices of the population, implanting specific deviations from the heterosexual, reproductive norm as perversions (masturbation, sodomy, and so on).

Foucault's concept of the perverse implantation provides a compelling frame for makeover television. A lack of congruence between the inner and outer self is a perversion of the self, a problem that must be identified, explained, and fixed through institutional intervention. A few themes from his argument seem especially useful. First, the proliferation of perversions in the late nineteenth century was not evidence of a more lax society, but of intensified techniques of bringing wayward pleasures under stricter supervision. Similarly, late twentieth- and early twenty-first-century perversions of the self—a lack of will, low self-esteem, a resistance to taking responsibility for the self—are not modern inventions, but become problems to be identified and fixed by the psychological, educational, and self-help discourses that underpin makeover television.

Second, Foucault discusses the "incorporation of perversions" in the late nineteenth century to describe a shift of nonnormative sexual pleasures from activities, to bodies, to the truth of the person.[50] Sodomy, for example, was transformed from a practice to the singular activity that defined the homosexual as a person whose sexuality was "written immodestly on his face and body because it was a secret that always gave itself away."[51] The body in need of a makeover wears its dysfunction on its exterior; fat, frumpiness, and sloth all betray the secret of the ill-at-ease inner self. This body can be read diagnostically: anything but a thyroid problem means that overweight is an externalized moral failing.

Third, for Foucault, the perverse implantation justified surveillance, which both shored up institutional power and produced new pleasures, such as the pleasure of watching and being watched and the pleasure of transgression. Thus nonnormative sexualities weren't only contained and punished, they were also produced by the very techniques designed to control them. As I discussed in chapter 4, makeover shows monitor candidates in part to discipline their transgressions, whether these are the midnight snack in *The Biggest Loser* or the rule-bending article of clothing in *What Not to Wear*. Surveillance becomes its own justification: candidates need to be supervised because they cannot be trusted to supervise themselves, and the successful makeover is one where candidates learn to see themselves as if from the outside, through the eyes of the experts. But surveillance also produces its own pleasures. For reality show participants, being watched by others "serves to intensify one's experiences, and thereby to facilitate self-growth and self-knowledge."[52] Sustaining surveillance affirms the authenticity of our self-presentation. The pains of intense scrutiny at the earlier stages of each show are compensated for in the moments of revelation. These include when candidates see the self in the mirror for the first time, experience the thrill of weighing in, reveal themselves to the hosts, and, most dramatically, display the reformed self to friends and family at the moment of the reveal.

Foucault concludes that "the implantation of perversions is an instrument-effect: it is through the isolation, intensification, and consolidation of peripheral sexualities that the relations of power to sex and pleasure branched out and multiplied, measured the body, and penetrated modes of conduct."[53] Likewise, the implantation of the incongruent self is an instrument-effect of the makeover: the makeover produces in its very techniques the crisis it then purports to resolve. Makeover shows do not discover a problem in candidates so much as they identify problems as problems, thereby justifying the hosts' interventions. In this genre, self-reflexivity does not merely root out problems of the self, it produces a self that has the kind of problems that the makeover show can fix. Through the implantation of the inner self and the assumption of a lack of congruence between inner and outer self, the shows produce a reflexive self on which work must be done.

As I looked to media and self-reflexivity as frames to make sense of these audiences' engagements with the four shows, I was struck by how some of the processes used by makeover shows to promote self-reflexivity were also shared by audience research. Open-ended surveys and interviews rely on a similar idea of the self that has an authentic interior, demands narrativization, involves ritualized self-production, and often veers into the confessional mode. As with other kinds of reflexivity, these audiences described themselves in a context (here in a conversation about the shows), they referred to elements in that context that shaped how they talked about the shows (such as dismissive scholarly critiques of reality television), and they used the research context to articulate a sense of themselves as agents (toward the shows, media in general, and the research exchange). The following chapter looks at research reflexivity—the participants' as well as my own—to appraise the values and limits of audience research.

7

Research Reflexivity

Audiences and Investigators in Context

You really shouldn't ask a two-part question. . . . That's not good
research! I used to design research studies. . . . Tsk, tsk.
—*Biggest Loser* survey respondent

You'll notice, you know, if you've studied the show, and maybe you
need to go back and start studying old seasons again, but you'll
notice most of the makeovers fit in a certain age range.
—Robert, *What Not to Wear* interviewee

In the first quotation, a survey respondent chided us about a badly
designed survey question; in the second, an interviewee told us where
to look for good data about the candidates on a show. As I developed
the frame of reflexivity to describe participants' engagements with
the shows, I realized that they were also reflexive about taking part
in a research study. They were aware of dominant and usually negative views of fans of reality television, drawing on their sensitivities
to makeover television's lowbrow status to contextualize their roles in
the research process. They situated themselves as actors in the research
exchange—as storytellers, experts, and petitioners. Some participants
drew on themes from the makeover shows themselves to reflect on
the research; this included both their media reflexivity about how the
shows were put together and the self-reflexivity valued in the shows.

Participants' research reflexivity offers a frame to reconsider contemporary debates about audience research and the role reflexivity might play in these debates. It also forced me to consider my own investments in a reflexive research practice, which I realized is as much common sense, from a Gramscian perspective, as it is an ethical commitment—indeed, ethical commitments are the densest common sense to unpack. This chapter investigates the ways the participants in this study were reflexive about the research process in order to return to larger questions about the contribution reflexivity can make to audience research. If reflexivity is not an attribute inherent to the modern self but an attitude toward and performance of selfhood, audience research reaffirms this attitude and performance in ways that echo the selfhood privileged in makeover shows.

More Storytelling

Although we did not ask survey respondents or interviewees about how they saw the research process and their own role within it, they nevertheless frequently offered their perceptions about this. I was struck that their comments about the research corresponded quite closely with the modes of self-reflexivity they articulated about the makeover shows themselves. They situated themselves in context, were aware of how they appeared from the outside, were able to narrate their experiences self-consciously, presented themselves as authentic, and asserted their expertise. They were interlocutors; rather than offering a window on their inner thoughts, they shaped their perceptions according to what they believed to be the aims of the interview and larger questions about media fandom. Qualitative research methods continue to struggle with how interviewees shape their responses according to what they perceive to be the preferences of the interviewer. Here I am interested in how they explicitly refer to their perceptions of these expectations and the interview exchange itself as a collaborative event.

Many of the people we talked to were aware of the negative view of a lowbrow genre such as makeover shows, as well as its fans. As one interviewee recalled the details of a particularly memorable *What Not to Wear* candidate, she exclaimed, "God, I watch too much of this show!"

Later she asked, rhetorically, "Why do I even know this, please? It's so embarrassing." Seth, a participant whose critical and emotional investments in *The Biggest Loser* have woven through this book, negotiated between these investments and the popular critique of reality television: "That makes me sound so shallow, to feel so empowered by a reality TV show. But it is—it's the fairy-tale ending that I wanted, and yeah, I was like, 'Yeah, great, good for him, he won.'" This comment suggests that Seth was aware of both the risk of seeming superficial through his involvement in a reality program, and of the constructedness of the show's "fairy-tale ending."

Donna, quoted in an earlier chapter saying that her son would call the sky "teal," described her fandom of *Queer Eye*'s hosts: "I went [to the official website] because I wanted to read about everybody and get to know them because they're now my friends. I know, I'm so sad!" Later she exclaimed that she felt like "the biggest geek on the face of the planet" because she was so passionate about the show. But she also referred to herself as "a reality show ho. I like them all. I like to laugh at the misery of others. That's why I like *Survivor*. The dumber they are, the better it is for me." Her embarrassment about being such an ardent fan of the show may be somewhat offset by her distancing herself from many of the "dumb" characters in reality shows.

A *Biggest Loser* interviewee explicitly acknowledged the perception of reality fans as gullible dupes. When asked whether the portrayals of the contestants were honest, Marci said, "Yeah. I almost hesitate to say that because so much of reality shows, everybody just hates them, or they say they hate them and watch them in private. I don't want it to come out as 'Marci says . . . and boy is she an idiot'!" Because participants acknowledged how close their talk about the shows might look to the negative stereotypes of television viewers as zealous addicts, friendless fans, and media dupes, they were able to distance themselves from these stereotypes.

Interviewees sometimes made it clear that they were aware that they were constructing narratives about the shows for a particular audience: a media researcher. One woman struggled to tell what she hoped would be a coherent narrative about what she saw housemates go through as she watched two seasons of *Starting Over*:

That [question is] really tough because I'm trying to figure out what angle to come at it from. I guess the easiest way for me to break it down in my head is the different seasons; I actually started watching it towards the last part of season 2. I was home and stumbled across it and got hooked. And then on another channel they started showing season 1. So it was kinda cool; I was watching Chicago one day and LA the next. And it was a totally different feel.

This interviewee noted that she consciously selected, both "in [her] head" and for the interviewer, one narrative option among many to describe her watching two *Starting Over* seasons. This attention to narrative may have been particularly strong for *Starting Over* participants because of the serialization of personal life stories in that show. When the interviewer clarified to another *Starting Over* interviewee that she could develop her responses to questions as she wished, this interviewee observed, "So, more story-telling." A *What Not to Wear* interviewee noted that we, as researchers, would be working with her interview as data, assembling it to construct a narrative. She offered, "Take all this [interview material] and muddle it all around." As were many people, this participant was aware of the role of television editors who produce a narrative from raw footage; similarly, she alludes to the work of researchers who produce an analysis from raw data.

This interviewee also affirmed within the research exchange the makeover shows' emphasis on personal authenticity and self-expression. She described empathizing with a candidate on *What Not to Wear*, saying, "That's just the way I think I would feel. I'm trying to be as honest as I can be." Some explicitly acknowledged that, like the makeover process, the interview was an opportunity for therapeutic self-reflection and expression. After a particularly revealing interview with a man in the comparison group, the interviewer thanked him for being "so open." He responded, "You're welcome. I mean, you know what? I believe this was good for me." A comparison group viewer complicated this investment in mediated authenticity in both the shows and the research process. When asked whether she thought the makeover candidates presented themselves as they were in their everyday lives, she said, "I don't know. I was actually—I was also thinking about this because I feel like I'm noticing myself talking differently because I know I'm being recorded."

Some participants thus demonstrated that they were aware of the research exchange as a socially situated encounter, framed both by the usually negative discourses about reality television and by their understanding of the processes of the makeover shows themselves. This included not only the production processes—being interviewed by a professional, being recorded—but also the strategies and technologies of self-production typified by makeover television. Participants drew on these motifs to situate themselves in the interview.

Fan Experts and Lay Researchers

Interviewees drew on discourses of expertise within the research process, echoing both the emphasis on experts within the shows and the cultivation of their own expertise through watching them (see chapter 3). One comparison group interviewee discussed his background in advertising sales for a media company, and how this shaped his response to a question about *Starting Over*. Asked whom he thought the target audience was for the show, he said, "You've gotta understand. My thinking is a little skewed because I'm thinking from the inside of the industry. They're geared toward house women, housewives." Bill, discussed in an earlier chapter because of his involvement with the website Television Without Pity, warned us in an e-mail prior to the interview that he was a professor of theater and performance and was not, therefore, an "average" viewer. He noted, however, that he began watching *Starting Over* as a fan, not a scholar, thus reinserting himself into a role shared by most of the other people with whom we talked.

As demonstrated in the quotations that opened the chapter, both interviewees and survey respondents drew on their expertise to critique the research process. Occasionally survey respondents addressed us as faulty researchers: one person wrote, "This is kind of a vague question, guys :)"; another complained, "Oh come on—Transgender is really not that popular that you would include it on a survey!" A *What Not to Wear* viewer, Barclay, teased the interviewer for posing leading questions to her in a way similar to the hosts on makeover shows:

INTERVIEWER : Do you think that is a theme in the show, that there's a
     "real you" in the end, that wasn't showing in the beginning?
BARCLAY: Yes, that's a good way to put it. You've just done the TV thing.
     Now I'll say, "Yes, it seems like . . ."
I: I'll admit it was leading!
B: You can just use my quote.

This exchange suggests that Barclay was well aware of media conventions whereby unequal distributions of power produce the discursive
outcome of the encounter. But with her offer to "use my quote" she
also jokingly situates herself as a celebrity interviewee, straddling the
gap between ordinariness and fame that provides some of the frisson
of the reality metagenre. Participants' interventions such as this in the
research exchange resist the assumption that credentialed interviewers (makeover hosts, journalists, academic researchers) are entitled to
shape what interviewees (ordinary people) will say and to determine
how this will then be used.

     The question of expertise within the interview played out most
strongly with Jackie and Robert, two interviewees I discussed as "fan–
experts" in chapter 3. Jackie positioned herself as a "lay researcher" by
aligning her expertise not only with the show's hosts, but also with the
research team. She signaled what she considered an important moment
in the interview with her description of "quotable quotes":

> So I really wish there had been a show about what it is to be sisters going
> through a path of recovery. How's that for saying that? See, you can quote
> that one. You should see me doing quotable quotes. My book I'm writ-
> ing is about a woman who, after a child is abducted and sexually abused
> and killed, she becomes aware that one of the reasons this is happening
> is that people no longer sit on their porches. They're all watching TV, liv-
> ing very individual lives instead of looking after each other, so why are
> we horrified? [In the story a young neighbor asks,] "Why do you sit out
> here on the porch?" This is my quotable quote: her response is, "Because
> if you take the wisdom off the street, all you have left is stupidity." And
> I thought it really summed up what's happened to our streets. All the
> wise people went off in their merry ways, and we're wondering why the

kids are stupid. You know? My other quotable quote is, "I wonder if you can really hear a mind shatter." And I'll be talking about a woman with mental illness in that chapter. But that will be her thought, sitting on the porch watching this woman disintegrate: "I wonder if she can hear her mind shatter." See, so I'm right in line with [the *Starting Over* hosts,] Iyanla and Rhonda.

Here Jackie flagged what she considered to be quotable in our research: wisdom she gleaned from the show that she had worked into her own fictional narrative. She then associated this expertise with the show's hosts, claiming membership among a group of quotable women. Jackie did not point out the irony that she drew this wisdom from the very technology she blames for social demise.

There was no sense in Jackie's interview of the unequal power relations usually assumed to structure the interview transaction, where the interviewer controls the process even in semi-structured, open-ended protocols. As this interview was winding down, she warned the (female) interviewer to "be real careful as a researcher not to fall into the male trap of trying to be objective." She then proceeded to turn the tables on the interviewer by asking her opinion of the show, at which point the interview shifted from the interviewer's to Jackie's direction. Ellen Seiter argues that audiences hold "lay theories" of media effects that shape their common sense about television and its dangers.[1] Similarly, some participants in my study have lay theories of audience research, asserting their understanding of the research process and their right to take charge of it.

Robert could also be considered both a fan–expert and a lay researcher. Following his suggestion to look at old seasons of *What Not to Wear*, which opened this chapter, he advised the interviewer:

ROBERT: We've had a few of the makeovers [candidates] come onto the boards, quite often. I don't know how often you monitor the boards.
INTERVIEWER: I haven't actually been on the boards.
R: Well, you might want to do that.
I: Yeah, I see I should from talking to people.
R: Yeah, the boards really reflect a lot of what the viewers feel about the show. Now, run the question by me one more time?

Robert also signaled to us that he was aware that academic research is funded, and wondered if this particular project was by the cable channel that distributes the show: "I'm just curious if this [research] is being funded by TLC [The Learning Channel]. I say, I know enough about business and education and the world of academe that I wondered who had put up the money for the grant." As did Jackie, Robert resisted the "obliging interviewee" role to assert his expertise not only about the show but about the research process and funding as well.

The chance to position themselves as both fan–experts and lay researchers was one reason participants may have become involved in the project. The question of motivation became fraught with the participation of some of the women who watched *Starting Over* and saw themselves as petitioners to save the show. After we had completed the survey phase and were recruiting interviewees, rumors spread on the message boards that the show would be canceled at the end of the third season, as indeed it was. A number of the people we talked to mentioned this possibility in relation to our study, hoping that either we worked for NBC or could at least influence the channel to keep *Starting Over* on the air. One woman wondered at the end of her interview whether it would help save the show if the research was sent to NBC. She had also written directly to NBC and some of the advertisers to plead to save the show. The most explicit reference to this came from another woman:

DIONNE: Is this interview going to help get the show back on? [laughing].
INTERVIEWER: Well, that's not its goal. We're not associated with the
    show at all. So it's possible that when we write this up—I mean, the
    professor writes this up—they would read it, but we don't work for
    the show at all. They don't even know we're doing the research at this
    point.
D: Well it would be lovely if—because I'm sure that the women that
    responded to the interview will have positive talk, that it would be
    lovely if this was passed on to those producers or something, because
    we've even got, a lot of us have written letters to channels like Oxygen
    and WE and Lifetime, saying we think that this would be a good
    show for your network.
M: That makes sense.

D: Because to me, really, what better for a channel for women than this show? So a lot of us have taken, e-mailed and written letters to those networks, too.

Even though Dionne makes this most explicit, the research team became concerned that the motivations of many of the *Starting Over* respondents to keep the show on the air emphasized their "positive talk" about the show as therapeutically beneficial. Although all voluntary participation in scholarly research comes with investments, interviewees' particular investments in *Starting Over* staying on the air may have skewed their responses in a positive light, while they played down their concerns or criticisms. My initial response was to worry that these motives invalidated the interview data from this group. I now see them as part of a fundamental shift in understanding the data not as neutral or transparent accounts of participants' media engagements, but as an account of their awareness of being "an audience" in the research context. As I discussed in chapter 1, "audiences" are constructed among institutions, including the networks and the academy: a construction of which participants in this project were at least somewhat aware. Some *Starting Over* interviewees drew on their awareness of the institutional leverage this provides to attempt to intervene in the show's fate.

The survey respondents and interviewees were thus aware and articulate about their role as participants in this research. This reflexivity reproduced both narrative and representational frames within the shows (telling and editing stories, participating in one's own surveillance) as well as modes of self-reflexivity that the shows encourage (authenticity, expressivity, seeing the self in context). Participants were thus reflexive about the research exchange in ways that parallel the makeover shows themselves, and used the shows as a resource to frame their considerations of their interviews. It is tempting to celebrate research reflexivity, which, like media- and self-reflexivity, can look like an ideal mode of subjecthood: "Look! Audiences have agency! They aren't dupes! They are self-aware!" Investing in the agency of our research participants can be reassuring for those of us anxious about reproducing power hierarchies, systems of organizing people, and frames of knowledge that shape the research enterprise. However, some audience research scholars have problematized reflexivity among their participants in ways that allow us to consider reflexivity as a performance of self that the research exchange invites.

Complicating Reflexivity in Audience Research

Participants in this study were aware of lay theories of media effects, especially the nefarious effects of viewing on more vulnerable groups. They situated themselves in relation to their media consumption, and were aware of these lay theories and how these might frame how we, as researchers, saw them, as "audiences." They deflected some of the worst presumptions of these lay theories, on some occasions flipping the script on the interviewer to assert their own expertise not only as audiences (fan–experts) but as lay researchers, too. It is possible to see this research reflexivity as an endorsement of active audience theory, which has been central to debates in audience research for at least three decades.[2] But as Elizabeth Bird cautions, audience research has paid far more attention to "Kathy"—epitomized by a middle-aged appointment viewer and fan of *Dr. Quinn, Medicine Woman* who had an active social life—than to "Kevin"—an obese, pale, apathetic nine-year-old who watched television all day long, apparently indiscriminately. Because "audience research has been successful in telling us a great deal about the Kathys, and really very little about the Kevins, audience research has become a very optimistic tradition."[3] Active audience theory came about to counter the "cultural dope" view of audiences. "Yet many of us are still ambivalent. As scholars we wrestle with debates about whether audiences are really 'active,' and what that activity actually means in cultural and political terms. . . . We wonder if media are benign 'symbolic equipment for living' . . . or insidious tools of economic, cultural, and political oppression. Or both."[4]

Recent audience research studies have become attentive to how audiences consider their own media engagements. Researchers are ambivalent about the virtues of reflexivity, an ambivalence I share, even though my findings diverge somewhat from these existing studies. These scholars have noticed that a distanced, critical view of media reflects a larger framework of beliefs about television being "bad for you," structured through an implicit class hierarchy. I wanted to pursue this perspective to look at whether there were strong class differences among my participants' levels of reflexivity, whether there was a single dimension between reflexive distanciation and immersion, whether reflexivity produces more selective, discriminatory viewing, and whether highly immersed viewers, the Kevins, are also reflexive. I expected to find significant differences in degrees and types of reflexivity depending on structural factors, where class differences would emerge in levels of media reflexivity, and gender factors would be central to self-reflexivity. Based on earlier research, I had a hunch that people with more education would be more reflexive about media production, realism, and economic factors, and that women would be most likely to discuss the shows in self-reflexive ways. My data from viewers of makeover television, however, suggest that the distinction between the well-educated, reflexive Kathys and the less educated, immersed Kevins needs to be reconsidered within a larger critique of audience reflexivity.

Despite earlier audience research that argues for strong class effects, the degree to which people were reflexive about their engagements with makeover shows depended more in this study on the specific show they watched and the degree of social interaction they had with other people about the show. The four shows mobilized divergent types of self-reflexivity among the participants in this study. People were most likely to discuss *What Not to Wear* and *The Biggest Loser* in terms of self-reflexivity as self-surveillance, whereas *Starting Over* interviewees were more likely to use narrativization as a primary self-reflexive strategy. *Queer Eye* interviewees were not especially self- or media-reflexive; participants were more likely to discuss this show in terms of gay representations and entertainment. Types and degrees of reflexivity also had a great deal to do with social interactions about the shows, where those who were active on Internet message boards were especially articulate in their perceptions of the shows' production conditions and generic formulas.

A number of assumptions about reflexivity are worth considering here. The first is that there is a continuum between reflexive distanciation and emotional immanence. Skeggs and her colleagues looked at how class structured women's engagements with lifestyle television in the UK—a category that includes makeover television as well as home makeovers, cooking and gardening shows, relationship shows, and so on.[5] These scholars found that middle-class women were much more likely to distance themselves from lifestyle content, whereas working-class women were more likely to identify with the candidates on-screen. The middle-class women in Skeggs's research reflected on lifestyle shows' manipulative techniques and lowbrow status, and tended to ally themselves with the researchers, who they assumed shared this view. Working-class women, in contrast, seemed less comfortable with the research process, tended to identify with the women in the shows, and placed themselves in the action by imagining how they would feel or respond, which Skeggs and her colleagues call an "immanent" relation to the text.[6]

I found, however, that many of the regular viewers we talked to took both a distanced and an immanent perspective on the same texts, demonstrating that these approaches are not mutually exclusive. Among people already invested in the makeover shows, immanence–distanciation was not a single continuum determined by gender and class but a range that describes positions held simultaneously by the same person: for example, someone who was emotionally invested in a candidate and saw herself in a similar position, while also critiquing the artifice of the show. Indeed, as I argued in chapter 5, respondents often had quite biting critiques of the empirical realism of the shows (a distanced perspective), which paradoxically endorsed their faith in the emotional realism of the programs (an immanent identification). This affirms Ien Ang's analysis of viewers' engagements with *Dallas*, where their critiques of empirical realism did nothing to disrupt their strong affirmations of the show's emotional realism.[7] In my study, differences among regular viewers according to both immanent and distanced dimensions were less related to their class position or gender, and more to the shows they watched and how much social interaction they had about the shows. In contrast, some comparison group interviewees were more likely to take a distanced, reflexive view that rejected the premises of the show in a wholly oppositional way.[8] Others expressed surprise at how much they had enjoyed the show, even saying they would start watching it as a result of participating in the study!

Implicit in the value ascribed to distanciation and reflexivity among both audiences and scholars is that this promotes more selective viewing and protects audiences from television's most damaging effects. Stewart Hoover, Lynn Schofield Clark, and Diane Alters, however, found discrepancies between how people described the media and its effects, and their actual viewing habits: "What parents *said* to us about the media did not always match up with what they said they *did*."[9] Rather than seeing this simply as a research artifact, a presentation of self as a lay expert of media for the interviewer's benefit, these are instances of how people can hold contradictory views of what they think about and feel in relation to media. Accordingly, there is no clear evidence to suggest that media-reflexive viewers in my study were less immersed in the makeover shows they watched. Like other interviewees, Donna, quoted above, took a distanced view of the "dumb" people on shows like *Survivor*, while she also cruised the *Queer Eye* message boards in search of information about the show's hosts, an activity she considered "sad."

Almost all the interviewees in the regular cohort considered themselves fans of the show, suggesting a commitment to the texts, even when they were also highly critical of some of the representational strategies of and advice offered in the shows. For example, Seth described being a fan of *The Biggest Loser*:

Well, for me it just means that it's something that fills my rotation of TV shows I watch. There's a lot of crap on TV, to be honest, and it's comforting to enjoy a show thoroughly, to the point that you look forward to when it comes back on, and watching it when it's on. I'm older now. I used to be very in tune with watching eight hours of television a day, but now my time is limited. I only have a two- or three-hour window to dedicate to TV per day. And in that, I want to see things that I enjoy to watch. And so there isn't a whole lot. So when that show comes out that I like, yeah, I'm happy that the show's on, and I would say I'm a fan for that reason, then. It gives me everything I want to get from it. I enjoy it thoroughly.

Seth had become quite selective in his viewing habits, a practice that endorsed the value of the shows he continued to watch. Yet he was also aware of his complex and contradictory relations with the representational techniques in *The Biggest Loser*, particularly the double standard in his perceptions of overweight women (see chapter 1).

Reflexive distance does not protect viewers from immersive relations with the text. The paradoxical relationship between critique and investment is especially clear in Mark Andrejevic's work on participants in the Television Without Pity website, discussed in earlier chapters. Here posters produce witty critiques of the shows, including programs they consider to be really bad television. Andrejevic observes, however, that these critiques don't distance their authors from engaging with the texts; indeed, the activity of posting regularly and reading others' posts keeps participants even more closely bound to the text. The media industries care little whether viewers engage ironically or immanently, as long as their activities register as ratings.

Conversely, fandom does not preclude distanced critiques of the texts or self-awareness about viewers' contradictory investments. Although these viewers aren't necessarily "heavy viewers" of television in general (indeed, Seth's comment suggests he is quite selective), these findings complement Hoover and his colleagues' conclusions in their audience research.[10] They assumed heavy viewers (the Kevins) would have the least distance on their media engagements. However "even these families, seemingly highly suffused within the discourses of the media (absorbed, even), can express a nuanced, complex, reflexive positionality vis-à-vis media."[11] As with Hoover's research, the most invested viewers in my study were still reflexive about the texts and their engagements.

A further divergence from existing audience research in my study concerned the influence of structural position—especially gender, race, and education levels—on participants' investments in the shows. The cultural turn to reception studies set in motion by Hall's classic encoding/decoding model situated class as central to understanding media production and reception.[12] This emphasis has been nuanced in subsequent work that also considers gender and, occasionally, race as significant prisms through which to interpret how audiences make texts meaningful. In contrast, I found among the regular viewers in this study fewer differences across gender, education, and race than these earlier studies suggested. Because the regular viewer cohorts were self-selected, they were not representative of the population, or even of actual audiences of these shows: they were more likely to be white, better-educated women than the likely audience or actual population (see appendix II). As a result, the views of this group dominated both the survey and interview data. However, even considering this, I found very few differences among regular viewers irrespective of education, race, or gender. Whereas earlier research found that women higher on the socioeconomic scale were more likely to take a distanced critique from shows, regular viewers across all education levels in my study were active critics of the shows.[13] A woman with a high school diploma said of *The Biggest Loser*, "I think it's edited like every other reality show. Look, I'm sure they take some things out of context, like they chop stuff up, and what they're saying when they talk to the camera privately, but generally it's pretty good, although, like with all those shows, there's too many commercials." A man with some college education but no degree discussed three of the shows and how they edit what viewers get to see:

> On *Queer Eye* and *What Not to Wear* and the weight loss one [*The Biggest Loser*], the editing, because they're not going to show the people freaking out and screaming at the host or whatever you want to call them, they're not going to show that because they want the viewers to think, "Oh, okay, everything is cool; everything is going well." But that's editing, that's the whole thing.

Interviewees across all education groups were reflexive about the production conditions and commercial pressures of the shows.

Women and men were very similar in the ways they mobilized the shows for self-reflexive purposes, drawing on the texts' valuation of interiority, narrative, and expression. This claim is a little more tentative than the first because of the low numbers of male interviewees and the high proportion of gay men among these. For example, one gay man with some college education but no degree discussed the role of *Queer Eye*'s hosts in working with straight men's inner sense of self:

> Yeah, it's just based on the thing that people who take pride in their appearance do tend to feel better. I mean you don't feel like you look particularly good so you don't feel particularly good about yourself, so you don't put any effort into your appearance and it feeds on itself. So I mean it's sort of an effort to break out of that cycle, which I mean I think there was a surprising and almost embarrassing amount of truth that you really do—or most people tend to feel good about themselves if they've invested effort in their appearance.

This quotation complements material from highly invested male viewers such as Seth and Robert, for whom watching makeover shows was an opportunity to consider both the text and their own selves reflexively.

In terms of race, it was striking that no heterosexual men of color volunteered to take part in the interview phase of the study as part of the regular group, although we did have better representation in the comparison group. This suggests that volunteering for an interview about makeover television was not something that heterosexual Black and Latino men had the access, time, or inclination to do. However, among the women and gay men in the regular cohorts I found few differences across racial groups in levels of either media- or self-reflexivity. Danica, an African American woman with a bachelor's degree, watched both *Starting Over* and *What Not to Wear*. She said of the latter show, "That's the best part, is to see the people make the transformation internally, even if they didn't mean to. They're like, 'Gosh, I'm so surprised.' And I know that's a little bit of the producers, leading them to say certain things. But you do get a sense that they feel different." Similarly, Bill, one of the highly reflexive expert viewers discussed earlier, identified himself as mixed race and gay. As with other viewers, Danica and Bill readily invested in the authenticity of the internal transformation even as they were reflexive about the producers' role in shaping how this plays out on-screen.

Among the regular viewer cohorts, I saw very little evidence of structural differences in terms of how reflexive people were about themselves and their viewing practices. It would not have been possible for me to determine a participant's gender, class, or race from their responses alone. In contrast, I found more differences between participants across education levels and gender in the comparison group, in a way similar to that described by Skeggs and her colleagues, although these differences were less marked than in their research. The comparison group interviews were not already invested in the makeover shows in the study (as almost all our regular viewers were), most of them were recruited through a temp agency, and all were paid. The comparison group as a whole made fewer observations about production context, probably because these necessitate some familiarity with the show over time, and there were fewer examples of self-reflexivity in this group overall. Within the comparison group cohort, interviewees with fewer years of education tended to describe the contents of the show with less critical comment than those with more education. There were still moments of media reflexivity among people with less education in this group, however. For example, a white man with a high school education commented on the editing of *What Not to Wear*, saying, "It did look like they made you see what they wanted you to see." Comparison group interviewees with more education tended to be franker and more critical. A white man with a bachelor's degree commented on the editing on *Starting Over*, saying, "I mean it's TV. It's trying to manipulate you. John Forrest said, 'When faced with telling the truth or telling the legend, always tell the legend.' Well, the same goes for reality TV." This comment might be more literary than the first, but I would not claim that it is more reflexive. The middle class–distanced versus working class–immanent associations that Skeggs and her colleagues found in their studies may be somewhat stronger among the comparison group, but not overwhelmingly so.

I was surprised to find few differences among gender, race, or education groups within the show cohorts of regular viewers. Skeggs and her colleagues' research is perhaps the best point of comparison because their study of audiences of lifestyle television in Britain is most similar to mine of makeover show audiences in the United States.[14] Some of the difference in findings can be attributed to our different methods. Skeggs organized relatively homogeneous focus groups of women who shared racial, ethnic, and class positions. This homogeneity in a focus group situation might produce stronger class and race effects than in one-to-one interviews, a problem that the authors acknowledge: "The focus group method *creates* types of class discourse which must be examined before one can interpret the data."[15] We did individual interviews with people we recruited through websites, where people of different backgrounds may be more likely to interact with one another and share values across traditional gender and class lines. Skeggs and her colleagues also talked about a wider range of programs under the "lifestyle" umbrella, whereas we talked to participants usually about a single show. Whereas their research may have emphasized strong group effects, mine might overemphasize individual engagements, stronger effects of particular texts, and the influence of online social interactions among people from different backgrounds. Further, many of the people in this study came from more educated and affluent backgrounds (in part because of the online recruitment method), which means that this group's views are overrepresented in the sample. If educated and afflu-ent people are more likely to be highly reflexive, their dominance in the regular viewer cohort may simply have overwhelmed less reflexive views by less educated viewers, although I have been attentive to this bias among the data. The somewhat wider ranges of reflexivity among the comparison group can be accounted for by their unfamiliarity with the makeover show they watched with us, their lower levels of social interaction about the show, and their more representative gender, race, and education levels than the self-selecting group of regular viewers.

These factors go some way toward explaining the different outcomes of this study from earlier ones, which found stronger class and gender effects. I began to wonder, however, if something else was going on: whether the volunteers in this study shared the value of reflexivity as a performance of selfhood across gender, education, and race groups. This would suggest that reflexivity is less a property of structural posi-tion than something that media texts encourage, both in their struc-tural features (showing the seams of a show's production) and in their privileging reflexivity as a moral and pleasurable orientation to the self. Participants then drew on this privileged mode to present a particular version of a reflexive self in the interview context.

Producing Reflexivity

These discussions of reflexivity, distanciation, and immanence raise thorny questions about the best approaches to studying audiences and what to make of the data these approaches generate. Pertti Alasuutari describes three overlapping phases of reception studies.[16] The first was strongly influenced by Stuart Hall's encoding/decoding model and tended to focus on the interpretations of specific texts by structurally situated groups.[17] The second phase involved a shift from class to gender as a primary frame of analysis, and from particular texts to "the role of the media in everyday life, not the impact (or meaning) of everyday life on the reception of a programme."[18] In the third phase of reception studies, scholars considered media texts as a meaningful place to make sense of the importance of particular genres in the cultures in which they circulated.[19] This approach neither focuses on single texts (the first phase), nor abandons texts entirely in an ethnographic turn toward everyday practices (the second phase), but considers texts and their reception within a broader set of cultural questions. These questions include how audiences consider the activity of reading or viewing, how researchers construct the very idea of "the audience," and how popular media, scholars, and audiences themselves discuss media involvement. This third phase denatures the interview interaction as offering a transparent view into participants' experiences, and instead considers this from a discourse-analytic perspective:

> What is going on in the interview text and in the interaction situation? How do the participants (the interviewer and the interviewee) co-construct and negotiate their roles, definitions of the situation, or different objects of talk? What frames, discourses or "interpretive repertoires" . . . are invoked, and what functions do they serve?[20]

This approach fundamentally disrupts "decoding" as a process that happens between a text and its reader and instead treats interviews as "discourses on the media and everyday life" and, I would add, as discourses about the self in relation to media and everyday life.[21]

As this study progressed, I realized that had I entered it from the perspective of Alasuutari's first phase of reception studies, with a somewhat simplistic approach to interviewing about specific texts. My increasing investment in reflexivity demanded a radical shift to the third approach. As reflexivity became the central rubric with which to understand how audiences situate themselves in relation to the makeover shows, to their own selves, and to the research exchange, it prompted my own reflexive investigation of the process of doing audience research. In contrast to Giddens, who argues that reflexivity is inherent to modern identity, Skeggs and her colleagues, Seiter, and others contend that reflexivity is a performance of a class-based cultural competence.[22] Seiter, for example, argues that a "studied, conspicuous distance from television is a mark of distinction": exercising tight controls over children's viewing habits was evidence of good, middle-class parenting.[23] Skeggs's group situates this performance of selfhood within the research moment itself. They write, "In our research, the groups of women recruited from different classed and raced backgrounds deploy their available cultural resources to produce 'performances' of class, *made* rather than found, in each particular type of research event."[24] For these researchers, middle-class women were more likely to perform a distanced, reflexive perspective in the research situation than were working-class women. I agree that reflexivity is a demonstration of cultural competence, but data from my study suggest that it is not a competence specific to a particular class, gender, or racial group. High levels of reflexivity among regular viewers of all backgrounds suggest a democratization of cultural capital associated with a distanced approach to media consumption.

All research methods that require informed consent involve the problem of self-selection: When people agree to participate, why do they do so? And how does this willingness, this investment, shape the outcome of research? Despite our efforts to recruit a more representative subsample from the survey respondents, these interview cohorts remained predominantly white, fairly well-educated women. This is probably because this demographic group is more likely to have both access to the Internet and the leisure (or independence during the workday) to participate in a study. The group of regular viewers may probably be more reflexive than the general population because it skewed toward demographics for whom reflexivity is already valued. But they were also more likely to be reflexive because the regular viewers were self-selecting; those who volunteered were already invested in reflexive self-performances. This group wanted to talk about the shows, what these meant to them, and how they contextualized them in their own lives. They were aligned with the overarching project of the four makeover shows that encourages, allows, or demands self-reflexivity. The shows' reflexive project flattened the impact of demographic differences among the regular viewers because the research process offered the chance to assert the value of self-reflexivity and the expertise of media reflexivity. Audiences employ reflexivity beyond its traditional gender and class locations so that it becomes a common currency for navigating the mediated world.

The interviewing process affirms this performance of the reflexive self. Interviewing remains epistemologically fraught for audience researchers: we can't quite live with it, but can't live without it either.

The fantasy that research participants have direct access to their motives and meanings and can reproduce these faithfully for a researcher has been fully critiqued. This is particularly so with audience research where interviewees shape their descriptions of their media engagements in part according to what they believe are the interviewers' values. There have been some creative approaches to studying audiences and their identifications with media that aim to circumvent the problems of self-reporting. Seiter recommends supplementing interviews with participant observations of people watching and talking about media, as well as diaries and informal conversations.[25] Elizabeth Bird asked groups to create scripts for a television show that featured at least one woman and one Native American, to see how stereotyping played out in character formation.[26] Helen Wood recorded women's speech and actions while watching television shows to gauge the relationships between their interactions with the texts and how they discussed the texts later.[27] Even with these various attempts to offer alternatives to interviewing, it remains true that ethnographic approaches continue to use interviewing as central or complementary to other methods of audience research. As Martyn Hammersley and Paul Atkinson argue, interviews cannot offer "pure" data about a phenomenon, but they aren't *only* about a social relationship (the research exchange) either: they are situated between these, where understanding the phenomenon and the relationship must be complementary.[28]

Alasuutari's third phase of audience research is situated in this productive intersection between people's sense of their media engagements and the recognition of the interview as a social interaction. In chapter 6 I drew on Foucault's discussion of confession to argue that makeover shows' narratives produce the very crisis of self-reflexivity they purport to solve.[29] Similarly, the interview exchange is not only constrained by discourse—discourses about shame about media consumption, for example—but is productive, an opportunity to perform a particular kind of reflexive self. Audience research reproduces similar demands for introspection and narrativization as the makeover shows I study. Both makeover shows and audience research require that participants produce a reflexive self, someone who can see the self as if from outside, who can tell stories about the self, and who values authentic self-expression. Both offer people across genders and educational backgrounds the possibility of performing a reflexive self, which comes with certain pleasures and privileges. Skeggs writes that self-reflexivity is part of "emotional capital" that has traditionally been cultivated by (upper) middle-class people; lifestyle television encourages social mobility through a particularly reflexive self-performance.[30] Self-reflexivity suggests leisure, reflexivity about media suggests literacy, and both are historically the product of privilege and a performance of status. Makeover shows democratize reflexivity by situating it in the ordinary; audience research privileges ordinary people's reflexivity by bringing it into the realm of the academy. Reflexivity isn't part of modern identity because it's inherent to the modern condition, but because it's pleasurable, valued, and grants status.

Audience research neither demonstrates that audiences are free from textual influences through their reflexive practices, nor offers the opportunity for participants to free themselves from such influences by reflecting on their experiences. Instead, like makeover shows, audience research invests in an economy of knowledge that produces reflexivity for institutionally useful ends, even if these may be ends that we scholars prefer. Recognition of the shared investments of makeover television and audience research, however, should not paralyze scholars interested in making better sense of the sense people make of media. Rather than looking from the outside in, at how media promote productive, expressive, and reflexive performances of selfhood, we can consider how *both* makeover shows and the research interaction encourage reflexivity and expressivity that are part of a larger cultural impulse toward these modes of selfhood. The concluding chapter considers the uses and limits of reflexivity as it is currently worked through both makeover shows and audience research, and the ways both reaffirm a rather old-fashioned idea of the Romantic self within a contemporary, mediated context.

8

Once More with Feeling

Reconsidering Reflexivity

This book began with cautionary tales: makeover shows invoke people's worst impulses toward laughing and pointing at others' misfortunes, produce obedient consumers, and turn people into self-governing, rational automatons. It narrates a story that focuses on some of the people who watch makeover television, and on their reflexive engagements with the programs, the research process, and their selves. This trajectory allows a reconsideration of the makeover genre in light of its reflexive opportunities, and a revisiting of audience research from the perspective of reflexive self-production. But both the contradictions inherent in makeover shows and the challenges of audience research demand that we look back to reflexivity and its limits. I conclude that classic understandings of reflexivity require a disarticulation from institutional contexts, on the one hand, and feelings, on the other. I argue instead that we must rethink reflexivity productively to describe the relationship between these institutional contexts and our participants' expressed sensibilities that cannot be encompassed by those contexts.

The Reflexive Opportunities of Makeover Television

In chapter 2 I offered an analysis of makeover television as a women's genre, and critiqued some of the most normative elements of the texts: implicitly white, professional, responsible, discreetly sexy models of acceptable citizenship abound. Yet looking at the texts in isolation cannot account for how audiences engage with them. The people we talked to for this research described their interactions with the makeover shows not as obligingly rational and self-monitoring citizens, as some critics presume, nor as willing students learning useful skills from the texts, as the British model of public service broadcasting might suggest. Their primary mode of engagement was reflexive: they considered and critiqued the instruction and consumer advice, assessed the representations of the shows' candidates, appraised the empirical and emotional realism in the shows, and so on. In the process, the people we talked to assembled a reflexive self for the purposes of the research exchange as well. This self was knowledgeable about media institutions' demands for audiences and profits, and was aware of editing conventions and other sleights of hand that shaped what they saw. This media reflexivity became part of the reflexive self who is as aware of her social and mediated contexts as she is invested in an authentic, expressive inner self.

The degree to which the regular viewers were reflexive about their engagements with makeover shows depended to some extent on the specific shows they watched and their social interactions with other people about the shows. The four shows mobilized somewhat different levels and types of self-reflexivity among the participants in this study. Regular viewers were most likely to discuss *What Not to Wear* and *The Biggest Loser* in terms of self-surveillance, for example. The emphasis in these shows on scrutiny and surveillance was adopted by some interviewees as a technique they applied to themselves. *Starting Over* interviewees were more likely to construct life narratives that echoed the stories of the housemates profiled on this show. *Queer Eye* interviewees were not especially self- or media-reflexive, which surprised me because it is most like *What Not to Wear* in its style and techniques. Perhaps the emphasis on men's transformations made this show less successful in engaging the kind of self-scrutiny and stories that characterize feminine approaches to the self.

As do other genres of reality television, these makeover shows offered audiences moments of transparency in their production processes. Corner and Hill claim that reality television is situated between different documentary aesthetic modes, on the one hand, and between factual and fictional genres, on the other.[1] This "between" status, they each argue, prompts audiences to consider reality shows' truth claims. Audiences' discussions of the makeover programs suggest that they do indeed engage reflexively with these texts as constructed phenomena, although not necessarily because of the generic frictions identified by Corner and Hill. Many people were well aware of casting, editing, and commercial contexts that shaped how the shows represented the makeovers. They did not, however, question whether the shows were credible according to their position on the cusp of education and entertainment, or between representational genres. Respondents instead discussed sharing with other people their observations about the artifices of the shows, and were also consumers of other media that offer behind-the-scenes glimpses of the production process. Some of the people we talked to used this knowledge and social interaction to present themselves as fan–experts. They described absorbing their expertise into their professional lives and positioning themselves as authorities about the shows in their social and online interactions. Media reflexivity thus seems to be less a product of the shows' revealing (some of) the conditions of their production, and more to do with viewers' social interactions and intertextual knowledge about media routines.

Audiences also used the shows' themes to describe an intimate relation with their selves. Regular viewers made reflexive statements about how the shows encouraged them to see themselves through the mediated frame of the candidates' experiences. This process was enhanced because viewers saw the candidates as real people with whom they often strongly identified. The use of nonactors, the transmission of experience through new media technologies, and the genre's claims to authenticity maximized this process whereby viewers put themselves in the candidates' shoes. Audiences represented themselves as having agency, making choices, appraising their situations, and being able to consider themselves the subjects of their own self-care. They constructed narratives about their life situations, drawing from themes in the makeover shows to deal with their changing circumstances.

Reflexivity thus helps make sense of makeover television as a resource for contemporary discourses about selfhood. Rather than seeing these texts as simply instructional or strictly governmental, the data here suggest that audiences use the shows to mobilize reflexive considerations about media in the context of their lives. But the relationship between media and self-reflexivity is complex. The people we talked to were often quite sophisticated in their awareness of the constructions of the genre. Rather than producing skepticism about the shows and their project in general, however, audiences drew on this media reflexivity to reaffirm a solid sense of self. This self was reflexively produced by drawing on themes within the shows, including an insistence on congruence between one's inner self and outward appearance, the need for emotional expression, a reaffirmation of personal authenticity, and so on. Audiences drew on their shrewdness about what was obviously constructed to reaffirm what they felt to be real: the candidates' authentic selves, evidenced by their emotional expression. Far from challenging audiences' investments in these fundamental appeals to selfhood in the text, media reflexivity bolstered them.

Reflexivity and Audience Research

This study also positions reflexivity as a useful frame to reconsider the challenges of doing audience research. The people we talked to sometimes reflected on the research interaction, commenting on the process of telling stories, framing responses, and interacting with interviewers. They also drew parallels between the processes of audience research, especially interviewing, and those of makeover television. They noted that interviewers in both settings shape the interaction, and researchers and television editors construct narratives from raw data, for example. Andrejevic found in his study of the Television Without Pity website that posters enjoyed and felt empowered by commenting on the shows they critiqued in that forum.[2] They felt that they were part of a feedback loop to the producers, even as they also represented themselves as savvy about the limits of this feedback. The participants in my study intimated that they also wanted to participate in the processes of representation. Some people thought we were market researchers and others thought we worked for the media companies (despite our assurances otherwise), imagining that their input might have a direct effect on the shows. Part of the pleasure of participating in this research was that it offered a chance for the performance of reflexivity, where both media- and self-reflexivity were valuable attributes enhanced by participation in academic research.

Earlier audience researchers, including Ellen Seiter and Skeggs, Thumim, and Wood, have problematized reflexivity and distanciation from texts in the research exchange.[3] Rather than valorizing reflexivity as a natural attitude, they describe it as a performance of cultural capital demanded by the expectations of audience research. Both makeover shows and the research exchange provide opportunities for the performance of a reflexive self, and reward such a performance with goods and status, respectively. Further, the research exchange endorses very similar kinds of reflexive self-production to those the makeover shows encourage. Like makeover candidates, the exemplary audience research subject must be able to consider herself in context; see herself and her media engagements as if through the eyes of another (here the researcher); look within to appraise her investments and motivations; and express herself as authentically as possible.

At first glance, it would be tempting to see these parallels between makeover shows and audience research as paralyzing. If participants simply reproduce norms of self-presentation from the shows in media research, how can we get at the "real" effects of the shows on the people who watch them? Instead, these parallels prompt me to return to some of the ongoing disputes in media reception studies. Debates continue concerning what we mean by "the audience" and how we are to understand the kinds of data yielded by this audience.[4] Scholars have critiqued the concept of "the audience" in audience research as an object that is produced rather than found—and produced as much by media scholars as by market researchers, ratings experts, and media executives. At its worst, this institutional production of the audience has been seen as doing epistemic violence to an otherwise loose collection of people. I have hedged this somewhat in this book by referring not to the *audience* but to specific *audiences*, groups of people who were temporarily assembled because of their voluntary participation in this research. Further, the participants in this study were not necessarily victims of being positioned as "the audience" either by the research process or by media companies. Sometimes they resented being considered a particular kind of audience or market, as in the case of product placement. At other times, however, they seemed to welcome their status as audiences, representing themselves to us as fan–experts. They were also aware of the influence audiences and markets could wield in institutional decision making, as when they petitioned us to keep *Starting Over* on the air, and talked about buying products advertised as a means to demonstrate their support for the show. They were not simply positioned as audiences by the shows or the research process, but were reflexive about the ways that media industries and we as researchers positioned them as audiences, markets, and so on.

As Ien Ang has argued, the more sophisticated audience research techniques become, the more difficult it is to tell what "the audience" actually does with media.[5] This becomes increasingly challenging in a multi-platform media environment, where people consume branded media content across a range of technologies. The features of reflexivity that have underpinned this project, however, allow us to consider how people engage with media without reifying them as "the audience." As Alasuutari argues, audience research cannot simply take a text and ask how audiences decode it, but must understand the way people talk about their media consumption within the context of the research exchange itself.[6] When people talked to us about makeover shows, they were reflexive about how these shows are devalued by both scholarly and popular critics, and shaped their talk as a result, sometimes explicitly. Seeing audiences as reflexive about the research context helps audience scholars dispense with the fantasy that we can gain a transparent understanding of what audiences do with texts, since what they do with texts always occurs in a social context, research or otherwise.

This brings me to another debate in audience studies: the extent to which meanings are determined within the text versus the ways that "active audiences" shape what they take from the texts (see, for example, the debates between John Fiske and David Morley).[7] Elizabeth Bird summarizes a moderate position in this debate, arguing that audiences actively consume some texts over others, and take from particular texts meanings and pleasures not necessarily intended by their producers. However, she also recognizes that the range of media available is limited by economic and increasingly global institutional demands: "Viewers 'choose' [shows], but often it is a Hobson's choice."[8] In my study of people who watch makeover shows, reflexivity was not so much determined but mobilized by the text—when, for example, the shows revealed some of their production processes. Audiences took up and reworked the reflexive demands of the text and drew on intertextual and relational knowledge to critique the texts themselves. As I discuss throughout the chapters, however, there were limits on how reflexive the people we talked to were about the structural conditions of the media they watched and the consumer culture they bought into: they could critique the *parole*, the particular iterations of a makeover, but less easily the *langue*, the underlying structure that gives the genre its rationale.[9] Reflexivity was neither determined by the texts nor produced independently by the people who watched them; rather, reflexivity articulated their awareness of the texts' constructedness with their mobilization of them in the production of a reflexive self.

If audiences are primarily reflexive, audience researchers can be less concerned about inflicting audience status on a motley group of viewers, or about an inability to access an unadulterated understanding of media. Nor should we continue to invest in a continuum between textual determination and active audiences, when these data suggest that both structure and play contribute to people's reflexive orientations to texts, institutions, and their own selves. Having considered makeover television and audience research in light of reflexivity, contemporary understandings of reflexivity must also be rethought in light of audiences' complex engagements with the texts.

Feeling Free

Scholars and practitioners from varied fields of activity have asserted that reflexivity is a desirable orientation. To review my summary from chapter 1, reflexivity describes the ability to see a phenomenon— the self, social structures, a text, or a method—in context, and to be able to consider the influences of this context on the phenomenon. It requires attention to processes, because phenomena and their contexts are always in flux. Advocates of reflexivity across a range of scholarly and creative fields tend to see it as freeing, allowing a distance from the contexts that frame the phenomena: tradition, systems of knowledge, modes of representation, and, I would argue, institutions.[10]

The chapters that make up this book challenge this assumption about the freedoms of reflexivity, however. The audiences here critiqued and contextualized makeover shows' instruction and shopping advice, but not the cultures of expertise and consumption that underpin them. They criticized the representational routines in the shows, but did so to reinvest in what they perceived as necessary shaming of wayward candidates. They recognized the ways that the shows' realism was manipulated, but used this recognition to reinvest in the candidates' emotional authenticity. Audiences' reflexive narratives were not only self-referential, as Giddens presumes, but reproduced canonical narratives that are framed by traditional institutions, including the psy disciplines and Christian rituals. They commented on the similarities between media production and academic research, but nevertheless endorsed the research process through their performance as articulate, self-aware interviewees. Across these different modes, reflexivity did not free these audience members and research subjects from the media, consumer, and educational institutions that produce both the makeover shows and the academic enterprise. Instead, reflexivity can be seen as shoring up an authentic sense of self within the contexts of these institutions.

Far from being freeing, we can see these reflexive activities as requiring certain kinds of labor that are not compensated in traditional ways. As I mentioned earlier, audience activity can be increasingly seen as a form of "immaterial labor."[11] This describes work performed for non-remunerative ends, including pleasure, knowledge, and reputation. Profits are generated from this kind of labor, but do not reward the person performing it. In this research, participants could be seen as working in a number of ways. Many were recruited from websites that included message boards, blogs, and other forms of self-production that require expertise and time. Some people described using their social networks to promote the shows, their advice, and the products represented there. And the research process itself required immaterial labor, where survey respondents and the cohorts of regular viewers participated for free when they shared their perceptions with us. (Only the comparison group interviewees were paid for their time.) This is not to argue that these participants did not benefit from their activities as audiences and research subjects, but that media and educational institutions (and the people who work in them, including me) were more likely to gain material profit from their activities than were the participants.

A particular kind of immaterial labor that both the shows and the research process encourage is what has been called "emotional labor." Conventionally associated with women, Hochschild describes how emotional labor helps to generate capital through a range of often middle-class professions, including social work, health care, and human resource management: "Conventionalized feeling may come to assume the properties of a commodity. When deep gestures of exchange enter the market sector and are bought and sold as an aspect of labor power, feelings are commodified."[12] Emotional labor can be mediated, too. By endorsing the kinds of emotional labor women, especially, perform daily, makeover shows generate profits neither for the (largely female) audience, nor for the (usually female) candidates, but for media production companies and the advertisers that sponsor them. As Wood, Skeggs, and Thumim argue, "'Reality' television, by sensationalizing women's domestic labor and emotional management of relationships, displays the new ways in which capital extends into the 'private,' in which governance and capital become intricately intwined."[13] According to the respondents in my study, "good" candidates are those who manage their feelings according to the expectations of the production context: by showing willingness and application, by being moved beyond the emotional limits that constrain their authentic self-transformation.

Audiences' self-reflexivity in response to the makeover shows suggests that emotional labor is among the more pleasurable aspects of the texts. The shows affirm that through emotional labor women audiences, in particular, can put themselves first, take themselves as their own love object. Radway found that readers gained great solace from romance novels' narratives of being taken care of by a nurturing man, and that the act of "romance reading buys time and privacy for women even as it addresses the corollary consequence of their situation, the physical exhaustion and emotional depletion brought about by the fact that no one within the patriarchal family is charged with *their* care."[14] Makeover shows do not offer advice only for working on the self, but also for caring for the self, even as they remind audiences about the limits of their resources for self-care. Whereas Radway's romance readers could enter a fantasy life in which their emotional and physical well-being became someone else's first priority, makeover shows legitimate women making themselves their first priority, and offer practical advice about how to attain this. As more and more women live alone and as many women have service-related jobs in addition to whatever caretaking they are expected to do at home, the shows' permission to be self-nurturing is among their pleasures.

Responses to the shows by both the women and men who participated in this study suggest that emotional labor has been increasingly democratized beyond traditionally middle-class women's genres. Makeover shows endorse and extend white, respectable, female norms of emotional management, in part through validating men's expressions of being moved: it was men's emotional labor on-screen—their crying, in particular—that was most valued as authentic by many of the people with whom we talked. This can be understood as part of a larger process that Eva Illouz describes as the "emotional androgynization" of work and home life throughout the twentieth century.[15] As feminine values of emotional responsiveness became increasingly important in the workplace, for example in management techniques, the domestic sphere became more rational and systematized. Men were expected to become more emotionally competent, while "feminism called on women to become autonomous, self-reliant, and conscious of their rights inside the private sphere."[16] Illouz's characterization of emotional androgyny points to the mixed blessing of the gendered management of feeling in makeover shows: Viewers welcomed a feminization of men's emotional expression that reflected more realistically an emotional openness that they experienced, or wished for, in their relationships with men in their lives. At the same time, however, men's emotional expressiveness legitimizes an extension of the economies of emotional labor into intimate life, in which now everyone, not just women, must work with feeling.

Reflexivity, then, cannot be considered simply freeing—from history, tradition, or institutions. Instead, we can see the workings of reflexivity in makeovers as rerouting audiences back into the ideologies and

institutions from which they are promised critical distance. Nikolas Rose contradicts the view that through the techniques of the psy
disciplines subjects can free themselves: "Through self-reformation,
therapy, techniques of body alteration, and the calculated reshaping of
speech and emotion, we adjust ourselves by means of the techniques
propounded by experts of the soul. . . . The irony is that we believe . . .
that we are, freely, choosing our freedom."[17] Similarly, makeover shows
affirm that self-transformation promises freedom, but their techniques
of the self join other neoliberal strategies in proffering only limited
spheres of choice and individualism.

Reflexivity: Institutions and Feeling

Rather than freeing audiences from institutional constraints, then,
makeover shows' reflexive frameworks encourage audiences to reinvest in institutions—here consumer, therapeutic, media, and educational institutions. It is tempting to see this as more evidence of
a top-down model of media effects, where textual determinations
dupe audiences who only *think* they have agency in relation to texts
and institutions. One outcome of this would be to believe that "true"
reflexivity is only a hopeless fantasy and that, instead, we are all inevitably constructed through the narrowest of institutional discourses—
a crude form of Foucauldianism. An alternative would be to imagine that there is a "real" sphere of pure reflexivity elsewhere, probably
outside the corrupted domains of commercial media. Bertolt Brecht's
"epic theater," for example, radically refused audiences the pleasures
of being seduced by the semblance of realism or being able to identify with the characters.[18] Instead, it demanded that they reflexively
consider the processes of representation itself. For Brecht, realism did
not mean offering a transparent window on the world but cultivating
a social attitude that considers the relationship between the world and
its representations.

This radical reflexivity, however, depends on a ruthless excision of
sentiment and a corresponding distrust of melodrama. Brecht believed
that emotional identification and expression worked against social
change; instead of satisfying audiences' sentimental impulses, the role
of the theater should be to make clear to audiences the real, exploitative

workings of the social world. "True" reflexivity requires a break from tradition, history, and institutions that can be accomplished only by a disavowal of sentimental attachments. I am, however, suspicious of this move. It represents a long history of disdain for women's media and for female audiences' passions and pleasures, replacing these instead with a masculinist detachment from texts and communities. As Dana Polan notes, rigorous aesthetic reflexivity risks an elitist disdain for the popular, reproducing the very highbrow/lowbrow distinctions that political reflexivity was intended to criticize.[19] His word of caution alerts us to a more general suspicion in theories of reflexivity about the role of feeling, sentiment, and tragic structures of feeling.

The place of melodrama in women's cultures is an ongoing problem for feminist scholars who both resist contempt for women's genres and female audiences and distrust the ideological work that women's genres often perform. Lauren Berlant, for example, argues that melodramas offer glimpses of possibility, even as these are worked through ambivalence, disappointment, and complaint. Her view is that melodrama signals women audiences' needs for connection and reciprocity, even though these needs are thwarted by the text. The compromise represented by melodrama "performs a fear of throwing the whole norm of femininity and heterosexual romance into a crisis; sometimes the fear is of something more abstract, of entering the abyss of not knowing what another kind of life could be."[20] For Berlant, melodrama and other women's genres repeat and rework existing social conditions, offering the promise of change even as the routes toward such change are channeled back into the text and the institutions it endorses. ·

Berlant, Ien Ang, Misha Kavka, and Janice Radway, among others, maintain that there is something important and politically potent in women's genres.[21] Radway argues, for example, that readers' interpretations of romance novels did not suggest contentment with the status quo. Instead, romances offer a vision that:

> reforms those very conditions characterizing the real world that leave so many women and, most probably, the reader herself, longing for affective care, ongoing tenderness, and a strong sense of self-worth. This interpretation of the romance's meaning suggests, then, that the women who seek out ideal novels in order to construct such a vision again and

again are reading not out of contentment but out of dissatisfaction, long-ing, and protest.[22]

We can see the reflexivity that makeover shows facilitate as allow-ing for complaint, bringing candidates and audiences to the edge of the abyss of wondering what another life could look like, but routing these possibilities back through the institutions of mediated consumer culture that prompt dissatisfaction in the first place. Even within this, the shows nevertheless acknowledge longing for a different existence, a utopia of self-ease, love, and fulfillment that is present in the ways audiences talk about the shows. This longing in makeover shows reflects other tradi-tionally female genres. Richard Dyer writes that musicals express five utopian impulses: energy, abundance, intensity, transparency (sincerity and authenticity), and community.[23] As with makeover television, these impulses address their respective deficiencies—exhaustion, scarcity, dreariness, manipulation, and social fragmentation—but, he cautions, make "no mention of class, race, or patriarchy."[24] Dyer's summary offers an apposite commentary on makeover television and its promises:

> With the exception perhaps of community . . . , the ideals of entertain-ment imply wants that capitalism itself promises to meet. Thus abun-dance becomes consumerism, energy and intensity personal freedom and individualism, and transparency freedom of speech. . . . The catego-ries of the [utopian] sensibility point to gaps or inadequacies in capi-talism, but only to those gaps or inadequacies that capitalism proposed itself to deal with.[25]

I argue, however, that the contradictions in audiences' reflexive engagements with makeover shows in the current study suggest that capitalism and the genres that affirm it can never fully contain these desires for a different outcome, for a glimpse of utopia in everyday life. Although makeover shows' melodramatic conventions require emotional labor from their candidates and audiences, these candi-dates' and audiences' experiences are not entirely put to work for the shows and their advertisers. Even the most tragic structures of feeling in melodrama are pleasurable for audiences because of the possibility of another outcome. As Ang writes of soap operas, "Problems are only regarded as problems if there is a prospect of their solution, if, in other words, there is hope for better times."[26] However fanciful the possibility for better times might be in makeover narratives, the people we spoke to nevertheless talked about these possibilities—inspiration, motivation, creativity—in ways that were fundamental to their enjoyment of the genre.

How the participants in this study discussed their engagements with the shows contradicts, first, an interpretation of Foucault that sees every human impulse as contained within the institutions and accounted for by discourse. Their commitments also suggest that a view of reflexivity based on a radical refusal of sentiment risks disavowing important elements of human experience that enliven the texts. To do so reaffirms a view of reflexivity that relies on a disparagement of women's genres, of the importance of intimacy and feeling, and of the possibility of a different life. This project has demonstrated that reflexivity is fundamental to understanding how audiences engage with media and the research process, as well as how they use the shows to produce a self with depth, authenticity, and voice. But as I hope to have shown, reflexivity does not free the self from institutions but can as easily deliver this self back into these same institutions. The danger of reflexive fantasies is that reflexivity fully illuminates the landscape: by being reflexive we will, finally, be able to see what keeps us from full autonomy. But this model of reflexivity is itself based on a particular view of the ideal self as detached, rational, omniscient, and implicitly masculine. The messiness of feeling, the pull of melodrama, alerts us to the gendered dimensions of this fantasy; it requires a condemnation of what are usually considered the feminine attributes of texts and fandom—feeling, identification, suffering, pleasure, immersion. There is no necessary relationship between pleasure and politics, as Ang and Radway argue, but to see feeling as necessarily defeating is its own, troubling political project.[27]

The conventional view of reflexivity imagines a space outside context, text, and ideology. It requires that subjects be individuals unconstrained by family, history, or tradition. Rather than seeing reflexivity as a perspective that affords separation from institutions and illuminates sentimental attachment, however, I have come to see it as a working compromise between institutions and attachments. Reflexivity does not take us beyond institutions, power, and knowledge systems, nor is it hopelessly corrupted by longings for utopia—rather, it holds these institutions and feelings in tension. Audiences engage with media institutions (as audiences, markets, consumers, critics), with educational institutions (as research subjects and fan–experts), and with institutions of the self (drawing on familiar rituals from religion, law, education, the psy disciplines, and so on). Reflexivity does not free us from these institutions but articulates them with those human qualities that cannot be reduced to them. These qualities include optimism, love, generosity, responsiveness, insight, humor, irony, connectedness, longing, playfulness, and empathy. They also include depression, hopelessness, resentment, apathy, melancholy, nostalgia, and inertia.[28] Our discussions with audiences were animated by these sensibilities. The possibility of transformation (and its antithesis, stasis) that makeovers hold for audiences cannot be reduced to a grinding functionalism—either at the level of the individual, as the uses and gratifications perspective can do, or at the level of the state, as in some applications of Foucault's governmentality thesis. In this project, as in all audience research studies, there will be significance in the text that escapes both our participants' and our own abilities to address. Similarly, in all audience research there will be significance in the data that exceeds analysis. These loose threads are to be welcomed. They imbue the data with a sense of plenitude that cannot be entirely routed through more shoes, better therapy, another self-help book, or even a performance of savvy audience activity for a researcher. Reflexivity does not describe a place beyond institutional power or feeling but the mediation between power and a longing for possibility. Neither institutions nor possibilities are reducible to the other in the production of the reflexive self.

Plus ça change

What might be the possibilities of new forms of address to the self within the contemporary demands of our media institutions? This book addresses a specific moment in a trajectory of makeover television in which shows come and go, and the genre adapts to new themes, formats, and production opportunities. *The Biggest Loser* and *What Not to Wear* continue their respective appeals, which have changed little since we collected the audience data presented here. *Queer Eye* and *Starting Over* have both been canceled. More recent makeover programs have reproduced some of the themes of self-production represented by the four shows studied here, including two US shows that represent divergent ends of a spectrum in the cultivation of Romantic ideas of the self.

One end of this spectrum is represented by *Bridalplasty*, broadcast in 2010 on the US cable channel E!, which specializes in entertainment television. *Bridalplasty* exemplifies a recent emphasis on makeovers in preparation for marriage. It joins *Shedding for the Wedding*, *Say Yes to the Dress*, and other shows that make explicit the happy-ever-after romance narratives that underpin the makeover genre. Insisting that wedding perfection requires not only expert planning but also physical reconstruction, *Bridalplasty* portrayed twelve women competing with one another to win the cosmetic surgery of their choice each week—breast enlargements, nose jobs, teeth veneers, and so on. The losers were voted off and told by the host, "Your wedding may go ahead, but it won't be perfect." Strikingly, this show made little attempt to invoke the authentic inner self that audiences in this study so valued. Like some of the other surgery makeover shows that audiences discussed for this project, *Bridalplasty* could be considered resolutely superficial—there was no attempt to insist that the contestants' inner selves must be more appropriately presented to the world.

Watching *Bridalplasty* challenged my emphasis on audiences' sympathetic identifications with candidates on the shows. I have argued throughout this book that the perception that audiences are contemptuous of makeover candidates in general is not borne out by the data here, except perhaps in surgery shows. Although this series aired long after we had collected data for this project, my own enjoyment of *Bridalplasty* affirmed the participants' comments about watching shows like *The Swan*: from the first episode I was hooked. I didn't like what my enjoyment of this show suggested about me, especially as a feminist scholar committed to alliances with other women. The contestants were awful in obvious, over-the-top ways: their concerns superficial, their relationships with their fiancés cringe-inducing, their interactions manipulative and cruel. Despite all my commitments to a generous view of the audience, I found myself situated as Seth and other participants had described: between hilarity and shame.

Bridalplasty represents a more extreme version of the surgery shows discussed by people in this study, insofar as it is unconcerned about the interior self and makes explicit the earlier shows' implicit trajectory toward heterosexual union. In contrast, *How to Look Good Naked* is a newer articulation of the more benign elements of the shows considered here. This show originated in the UK in 2006 and was subsequently adapted for the United States on the Lifetime channel. The US version is hosted by Carson Kressley of *Queer Eye* fame, proving that the gentle, firm hand of the tasteful gay man can reform not only wayward heterosexual men but also sad women with body dysmorphia. Kressley emphasizes that the makeover necessary here is not physical but rather one of "perception reinvention."[29] Even though this show rejects many of the explicit themes of the programs we looked at in this study, it is perhaps most insistent on the need to see the self through the eyes of the other—the host, friends, strangers, and video technology. And for all its apparent kindness, *How to Look Good Naked* still emphasizes that there is work to be done: less on external appearances than on the internal perception of the self. Self-esteem, as Barbara Cruikshank has argued, is neither a natural disposition nor a privilege, but rather a contemporary obligation.[30] An even more pernicious version of this insistence on feeling good about oneself was promoted on a 2008 UK show called *Britain's Missing Top Model.* Here eight women with different disabilities competed to appear on the cover of a top fashion magazine. It was painful enough to watch the contestants with disfigurements undermine the deaf women who, because they were not visibly disabled, did not suffer the same kinds of discrimination. Worse still was hearing the shows' judges criticize the losing candidate each week for not having high self-esteem, and thus not being a good ambassador for people with disabilities.

The contrast between these shows affirms my findings in this study: the makeover shows that seem most benign (and are valued as such by audiences) endorse the reflexive self who can see the self through the eyes of another, whose beautiful inner self must be expressed, and who is emotionally open. Shows like *Bridalplasty* that make no attempt to produce this reflexive self are hard to watch sympathetically. However gentle *How to Look Good Naked* may seem, both these shows continue to insist that the self is a project that takes endless work, and that transformation is not a luxury but a requirement. Whether insisting that surgery is necessary to begin a happy marriage or that resolute self-confidence must be cultivated even in the face of blunt discrimination, makeover demand insist that there is always more work to do. In the words of one woman in her early forties who participated in a pilot focus group interview at the beginning of this study:

> What about the concept of the reality show where it was like I'm done kicking my own fucking ass? We kick ourselves down for the way we look, for the way we dress, for the way we think, for the way we are, and suppose you just went, "Okay, I'm done kicking my own ass. I am what I am."

For all their minor distinctions, these newer shows continue the tradition of makeover media and the genre's valuation of Romantic ideas about the self. Given how long this version of the self has held sway, it was unlikely that we would see radical shifts since the data for this project were collected. We will, however, begin to see changes in how these ideas of the self become reworked and recirculated as media technologies and genres evolve. Whatever their newer iterations, texts that focus on the cultivation and articulation of the self are likely to invoke the kinds of reflexivity discussed here. This reflexivity represents audiences' efforts to align their feelings, their longings for possibility and plenitude, with their experiences of institutional constraint. It also legitimizes the expression of these feelings within the conditions institutions impose. With all the contingencies and compromises this entails, the reflexive self makes utopian aspirations workable.

Protocols

RECRUITMENT

Requests for participation were posted on show-specific and generic reality television message boards and blogs, with the moderators' agreement. These posts linked to a simple webpage that directed respondents to one of four surveys on SurveyMonkey.com: one each for *The Biggest Loser, Queer Eye for the Straight Guy, Starting Over,* and *What Not to Wear.* Below is a reproduction of that recruitment text for the surveys.

Makeover Shows: Are They Trash Television or Inspiring Entertainment?

Love them or hate them, we are looking to hear everyone's view of makeover shows. A team of researchers at the University of Pennsylvania is studying what audiences think about some of the most popular television makeover shows. If you have watched any episodes of *The Biggest Loser, Queer Eye for the Straight Guy, Starting Over,* or *What Not to Wear* and would like to share your opinion—good or bad!—with us, we'd like to hear your thoughts. This survey takes about twenty minutes to complete. All responses are confidential and you can receive a copy of the final report if you want one.

To choose a show you'd like to talk about, please click on the link below:

1. *Biggest Loser*
2. *Queer Eye for the Straight Guy*
3. *Starting Over*
4. *What Not to Wear*

Thank you for participating in our survey. If you have any questions, please e-mail Katherine Sender at [project e-mail address].

THE SURVEYS

There were four surveys from which respondents could choose one. These surveys were tailored from a generic version (reproduced below) that was adapted to the specifics of each show (for example, whether the show was serial or episodic, what the specific terms of the makeover were, how many candidates and hosts there were as well as their gender, race, and expertise, and so on). Closed-ended questions were followed by the options for answers; questions with no options were open-ended and respondents typed their response in a box provided. There were no word limits on open-ended answers.

Questions about the Show

1. About how often do you watch the show during the season?
   Every week
   2–3 times a month
   Less than 2–3 times a month
   Once a month or less
2. Have you watched episodes from earlier seasons of the show?
   Yes
   No
   I can't remember
3. How much do you like or dislike the show?
   I like it very much
   I somewhat like it
   There are some things I like and other things I don't like
   I somewhat dislike it
   I dislike it very much
4. What do you like about the show?
5. What don't you like about the show?
6. Would you like to be a candidate on the show?
   Yes, definitely
   Yes, in some ways
   No
   I don't know
7. What appeals to you about being on the show?
8. Are there things that don't appeal to you about being on the show?
9. Is there anyone you know who you think would be a good candidate for the show?
   Yes, definitely
   Yes, in some ways
   No
   I don't know
10. What is your relationship to this person (are they your sister, wife, friend, coworker, etc.)?
11. What would make this person a good candidate for the show?
12. Is there anything that would make you uncomfortable about someone you know being on the show?
13. How do you feel in general about the contestants on the show?
14. Do you have any favorite contestants on the show? Who are they and what do you like about them?
15. Do you have any least favorite contestants on the show? Who are they and what don't you like about them?
16. Do identify with anyone on the show (contestants or hosts)?
    Yes, definitely
    Yes, in some ways
    No
    I don't know
17. Whom do you identify with and in what ways?

18. Have you ever picked up tips or advice from watching the show?
   Yes, a lot of things
   Yes, a few things
   No
   I don't know
19. What tips or advice have you picked up?
20. Have you ever passed on tips or advice you learned from the show to someone else?
   Yes, a lot of things
   Yes, a few things
   No
   I don't know
21. What tips or advice have you passed on, and to whom?
22. Does watching the show make you want to change anything about yourself? Whether "yes" or "no," please explain.
23. Television executives think about audiences in terms of gender, race, age, income, sexuality, and other characteristics. Thinking about these kinds of characteristics, who do you imagine watches the show?

General Makeover Show Questions

1. We're interested in other personal makeover shows you watch (shows like *Queer Eye*, *Extreme Makeover*, *What Not to Wear*, but not home makeover shows like *Trading Spaces* or *Extreme Makeover: Home Edition*). Aside from this show, have you watched any other makeover shows?
   Yes
   No
   I don't know
2. What other makeover shows have you watched?
3. Are there makeover shows you enjoy more than others? What do you enjoy about them?
4. Are there any types of makeover shows you prefer not to watch? If there are things you dislike about them, please tell us what these things are.
5. Is there anything else you'd like to tell us about watching makeover television or this show in particular?

A Few Questions about You

We'd like to know a bit more about who you are. Please complete the questions below—all answers are confidential.

1. What is your gender?
   Female
   Male
   Female-to-male transgender

Male-to-female transgender
Other
Prefer not to say

2. Are you Spanish/Hispanic or Latino?
    Yes
    No
    Prefer not to say

3. What is your race?
    White
    Black
    Asian
    Other or mixed race
    Prefer not to say

4. How would you describe your sexual identity?
    Bisexual
    Gay or lesbian
    Heterosexual
    Queer
    Other
    Prefer not to say

5. Which age category are you in?
    19 and under
    20–29
    30–39
    40–49
    50–59
    60–69
    70 and over
    Prefer not to say

6. How would you describe your relationship status?
    I am single and not currently dating
    I am dating, but not committed to one person
    I have a boyfriend/girlfriend/partner, and we are not living together
    I am married, part of a civil union, or living with my partner
    Prefer not to say

7. As of right now, what is the highest degree or level of education that you have completed?
    Less than high school
    Some high school, no diploma
    Graduated from high school—diploma or equivalent (GED)
    Some college, no degree
    Associate degree (e.g., AA, AS)
    Bachelor's degree
    Master's degree
    Professional degree (e.g., MD, DDS, LLB, JD)
    Doctorate degree
    Prefer not to say

8. What is your occupation?

9. Where did you find out about this survey? (e.g., if it was a website, which one?).

10. Have you taken any of the other makeover show surveys listed on the front page of our website?

11. Would you be willing to do a follow-up interview?

12. Would you like to see a copy of the final report? (All emails will be kept confidential.)

Thank you very much for participating in this survey—your responses will be very helpful for this study.

If you have concerns about this study or the survey, please contact Katherine Sender [contact information] or [contact information for the University's Office of Regulatory Affairs].

THE INTERVIEW PROTOCOL: REGULAR VIEWERS

The conversation opened with an introduction about the purpose of the interview and assurance about the confidentiality of the interviewee's responses.

Viewing Habits

1. Do you make a point of watching each new episode of the show? Do you tend to tape it, record it on a DVR, or watch it live?

2. When you watch this show, is it usually the only thing you are doing? If you do other things, what are these?

3. Do you watch with other people? If so, who? Do you chat as you're watching it? If so, what kinds of things do you talk about?

4. Have you ever been to the show's official website, or other sites about the show? What kinds of things have you done there?

5. Do you remember any products, services, or stores that have been featured on the show? Why do you think you remember those specific things? Have you ever bought anything because it's been on the show?

6. Have you ever bought a book, DVD, or other product that's associated with the show's name or hosts?

Responses to the Show

1. Throughout the makeover, what kinds of changes did you see the participants/contestants go through?

2. Do external changes the candidates go through say anything about how a person has changed in other ways?

3. How does the show convince participants that they need to change things about themselves? Does this approach seem effective?

4. Do these kinds of changes seem achievable by people in their everyday lives? What, if anything, makes the environment special?

5. Are some makeovers on the show more or less successful? What distinguishes them?

6. Do you think people who participate on the show think their lives will change? In what ways? Do you think this is a realistic expectation?

7. Has the way any participant expressed their feelings surprised you?

8. How do you feel about the way people (candidates/contestants/housemates) express their emotions as the show progresses? (e.g., in terms of their emotional displays).

9. Do you think that the people on the show (candidates/contestants) presented themselves as they are in their everyday lives? Can you think of a time that seemed especially real/not real?

10. Do you think the editing lets viewers see the candidates/contestants as they really were? Can you give me some examples?

11. Were the representations of the makeover candidate/contestant sympathetic/kind? Can you think of examples of anyone who has been portrayed in a more or less sympathetic light? Has there ever been a time when you felt badly for someone?

12. You mentioned in the survey that you identified with _____. What about that person in particular did you identify with?

13. Through watching the show, have you changed anything about your life? What, and with what effects?

14. [A gender-related question depending on the show's format and the gender of candidates.] Do you think that it is as important for men to look good as for women?

15. Do you think people of all races are treated similarly on the show? Can you remember a discussion of race or ethnicity on the show? What happened?

16. Do you consider yourself a fan of the show? What does being a fan mean to you?

Comparisons with Other Makeover Shows

1. Have you watched other personal makeover shows? In what ways are these shows like or not like this one?

2. You mentioned you watch other makeover shows like _____. Can you tell us more about your favorite and least favorite makeover shows, and what you like or don't like about them?

3. Have you watched *Extreme Makeover* or *The Swan*? How do you feel about makeover shows that use cosmetic surgery to attain results? What do you like/not like about watching these shows?

4. How would you feel about someone you know going on a cosmetic surgery–based makeover show?

5. Are there situations in which cosmetic surgery is more acceptable than others?

6. What do you think people get from watching cosmetic surgery makeover shows?

Thank you very much for answering all these questions for me. If you want to add anything or ask anything, you have my e-mail so please send me a message.

THE INTERVIEW PROTOCOL: COMPARISON GROUP

Comparison group interviewees were recruited through a temp agency and local print advertising. Each interviewee watched one episode of one of the four shows that they were not already familiar with and then answered the following questions. They also completed a face sheet in which they indicated their gender, age, education level, and other demographic factors, as with the other participants. Comparison group interviewees were paid $20.

Responses to the Show

1. How much did you like or dislike this episode of the show? What did you like about the episode? What did you dislike about the episode?
2. What is the makeover supposed to do?
3. How did you see the makeover candidate change over the course of the episode?
4. Do you think people who participate on the show think their lives will change? In what ways? Do you think this is a realistic expectation?
5. Do these kinds of changes seem achievable by people in their everyday lives? What makes the environment special?
6. What strategies did the show use to convince participants that they need to change things about themselves? Does this approach seem effective?
7. Would you like to be a participant on the show? What appeals/does not appeal to you about being on the show?
8. Is there anyone you know who you think would be a good candidate for the show? What is your relationship to this person (are they your sister, friend, co-worker, etc.)? What would make this person a good candidate for the show?
9. Is there anything that would make you uncomfortable about someone you know being on the show?
10. How did you feel about the people you saw on this episode?
11. How do you feel about the way the candidates expressed their emotions as the show progressed? (e.g., in terms of their emotional displays).
12. Do you think the candidates on the show presented themselves as they are in their everyday lives? Can you think of a time that seemed especially real/not real?
13. Do you think the editing lets viewers see the candidates as they really were? Can you think of any examples?
14. Were the representations of the makeover candidate sympathetic/kind?
15. Did you identify with or relate to anyone on the episode? If so, with whom, and in what ways?
16. [A question relating to the gender distribution on the show in question.] Do you think that it is as important for men to look good as for women?
17. [A question relating to the race of the candidate(s) on the show.] Can you remember a discussion of race or ethnicity on the show? What happened?
18. Did you see anything on this show that might be useful to you in your everyday life? What?
19. Did you see anything on this show that you could see yourself passing on to anyone else? What, and to whom?
20. Do you think this show could inspire you to change anything about yourself?
21. Did you notice any products, services, or stores that were featured on the show?
22. Television executives think about audiences in terms of gender, race, age, income, sexuality, and other characteristics. Thinking about these kinds of characteristics, who do you imagine watches the show?

23. What do you think fans get out of watching the show regularly?

Comparisons with Other Makeover Shows

1. We're interested in other personal makeover shows you watch (not home makeover shows like *Trading Spaces* or *Extreme Makeover: Home Edition*). Have you watched any other makeover shows?
2. Are there makeover shows you enjoy more than others? What do you enjoy about them?
3. Are there any types of makeover shows you prefer not to watch? If there are things you dislike about them, please tell us what these things are.
4. Have you watched *Extreme Makeover* or *The Swan*?
5. How do you feel about makeover shows that use cosmetic surgery to attain results? What do you like/not like about watching these shows?
6. How would you feel about someone you know going on a cosmetic surgery–based makeover show?
7. Are there situations in which cosmetic surgery is more acceptable than others?
8. What do you think people get from watching this type of show?
9. Is there anything else you'd like to tell us about watching makeover television or this show in particular?

The interviewer then thanked the interviewee and concluded the interview.

Demographic Data

SURVEY RESPONDENTS

Totals of survey respondents by show

Biggest Loser	464
Queer Eye	230
Starting Over	544
What Not to Wear	623
Total:	1,861

Survey respondents (percentages) compared with US demographic data

Gender

	Biggest Loser	Queer Eye	Starting Over	What Not to Wear	U.S. Census 2006
Female	85	75	95	91	51
Male	15	25	5	9	49

Census data retrieved October 28, 2008, from http://factfinder.census.gov/.

Latino

	Biggest Loser	Queer Eye	Starting Over	What Not to Wear	U.S. Census 2000
Yes	2.8	2.2	3.7	3.5	12.5
No	97.2	97.8	96.3	96.5	87.5

Census data retrieved October 28, 2008, from http://www.census.gov/.

Race

	Biggest Loser	Queer Eye	Starting Over	What Not to Wear	U.S. Census 2000
Asian	1.8	1.8	0.0	1.6	3.6
Black	6.2	5.3	7.5	4.7	12.3
White	89.1	88.6	87.1	89.4	75.1
Other or mixed race	2.8	4.4	5.3	4.3	8.9

Census data retrieved October 28, 2008, from http://www.census.gov/.

Education

	Biggest Loser	Queer Eye	Starting Over	What Not to Wear	U.S. Census 2007
Less than high school diploma	1.3	1.7	1.9	1.3	15.2
Graduated from high school with diploma or equivalent	6.1	4.4	11.1	4.5	31.5
Some college, no degree	22.6	22.2	30.8	19.4	19.1
Associate's degree	7.4	7.9	9.2	8.2	8.1
Bachelor's degree	38.3	38.9	27.3	38.5	17.5
Master's degree	13.6	17	14.8	19.7	6.2
Professional degree	5.9	3.5	3.3	5.1	1.4
Doctorate degree	0.9	3.1	0.6	1.8	1.1
Prefer not to say	1.3	1.3	1.1	1.4	

Census data retrieved October 27, 2008, from http://www.census.gov/.

Age

	Biggest Loser	Queer Eye	Starting Over	What Not to Wear	U.S. Census 2006
18-19	2.8	3.5	1.7	3.7	n/a
20-29	25.6	22.9	15.8	33.9	13.8
30-39	43.7	29.1	34.2	34.2	13.6
40-49	19.4	28.2	27.8	18.8	15.2
50-59	6.7	15.4	15.6	7.9	12.8
60-69	0.8	0.9	3.9	0.8	8.0
70 and over	0.5	0.0	0.4	0.2	9.0

Census data retrieved October 28, 2008, from http://www.factfinder.census.gov/.

Sexual identification

	Biggest Loser	Queer Eye	Starting Over	What Not to Wear
Bisexual	2.8	5.3	2.9	2.9
Gay or lesbian	5.5	21.1	3.9	5.5
Heterosexual	89.0	71.5	89.9	89.9
Queer	0.2	1.3	0.0	0.3
Prefer not to say	1.9	0.4	2.8	1.1

Relationship status

	Biggest Loser	Queer Eye	Starting Over	What Not to Wear
Single and not currently dating	27.8	35.0	28.3	29.1
Dating but not committed to one partner	4.4	4.0	3.1	5.8
Has a boyfriend/ girlfriend and not living together	9.9	5.8	6.8	9.5
Married, in a civil union, or living with a partner	57.9	55.3	61.6	55.5

INTERVIEWEES

Regular viewers: Totals of interviewees by show

Biggest Loser	24
Queer Eye	22
Starting Over	37
What Not to Wear	22
Multiple shows	5
Total:	110

Comparison viewers

Five interviewees for each show, twenty in total, comparison group interviewee data in parentheses.

Gender

	Biggest Loser	Queer Eye	Starting Over	What Not to Wear	Multiple shows
Female	20 (3)	11 (1)	36 (1)	19 (1)	5
Male	4 (2)	11 (3)	1 (3)	3 (4)	0
Transgender: female to male	0	(1)	0	0	0
Transgender: male to female	0	0	(1)	0	0

Latino

	Biggest Loser	Queer Eye	Starting Over	What Not to Wear	Multiple shows
Yes	0	2	2	2 (1)	0
No	15 (5)	20 (5)	35 (5)	20 (4)	5
Prefer not to say/ missing	9	0	0	0	0

Race

	Biggest Loser	Queer Eye	Starting Over	What Not to Wear	Multiple shows
Asian	0	0	0	0	0
Black	2 (2)	I (3)	5 (I)	5 (2)	0
White	20 (3)	I9 (2)	28 (4)	I6 (2)	5
Other or mixed race	I	2	4	I (I)	0
Prefer not to say/ missing	I	0	0	0	0

Education

	Biggest Loser	Queer Eye	Starting Over	What Not to Wear	Multiple shows
Some high school, no diploma	0 (2)	0	0	0	0
Graduated from high school with diploma or equivalent	I	I	3	I (I)	0
Some college, no degree	6 (I)	7 (3)	I4	2 (I)	I
Associate's degree	I	0	6	0 (I)	0
Bachelor's degree	9 (2)	8 (I)	6 (4)	I0 (2)	3
Master's degree	4	3	5 (I)	5	I
Professional degree	I	2	2	3	0
Doctorate degree	0	I	I	0	0
Prefer not to say/ missing	2	0 (I)	0	I	0

Age

	Biggest Loser	Queer Eye	Starting Over	What Not to Wear	Multiple shows
19 and under	0	0 (1)	1	0	0
20-29	6 (2)	5 (2)	1 (4)	5 (4)	1
30-39	10 (2)	5 (1)	7	7 (1)	3
40-49	4	9	18 (1)	6	1
50-59	3	3	6	3	0
60-69	0 (1)	0	4	1	0
Prefer not to say/ missing	1	0 (1)	0	0	0

Sexual identification

	Biggest Loser	Queer Eye	Starting Over	What Not to Wear	Multiple shows
Bisexual	0 (1)	0	2 (1)	0 (1)	1
Gay or lesbian	0 (2)	6	2	2	0
Heterosexual	24 (2)	13 (4)	32 (2)	20 (4)	4
Queer	0	1	0 (2)	0	0
Prefer not to say/ missing	0	2 (1)	1	0	0

Relationship status

	Biggest Loser	Queer Eye	Starting Over	What Not to Wear	Multiple shows
Single and currently not dating	7 (1)	7	10 (1)	9(2)	1
Dating but not committed to one partner	1 (1)	2 (1)	1 (1)	2 (2)	0
Has a boyfriend/ girlfriend and not living together	1	1 (2)	3 (2)	0 (1)	0
Married, in a civil union, or living with a partner	14 (3)	12 (1)	23 (1)	11	4
Prefer not to say/ missing	1	0 (1)	0	0	0

NOTES

NOTES TO CHAPTER 1

1. All interviewee names are pseudonyms.
2. Ang, *Watching Dallas*.
3. Biressi and Nunn, *Reality TV*, 4.
4. Ibid.; Giddens, *Modernity and Self-Identity*; Rose, "Governing 'Advanced' Liberal Democracies."
5. Weber, *Makeover TV*.
6. See, for example, ibid.; Andrejevic, *Reality TV*; Palmer, *Exposing Lifestyle Television*; Biressi and Nunn, *Reality TV*.
7. Hill, *Reality TV*; Hill, *Restyling Factual TV*; Skeggs, Thumim, and Wood, "Oh Goodness, I *Am* Watching Reality TV"; Skeggs and Wood, "Labour of Transformation and Circuits of Value 'around' Reality Television"; Wood and Skeggs, "Spectacular Morality."
8. NBC's prime time competitive weight loss series *The Biggest Loser* debuted in October 2004. The show recruits fourteen contestants, seven women and seven men, from among thousands of applicants. Contestants work to lose a lot of weight at the Southern California "ranch" where they live, eat, and work out for three months, before returning home to complete the process. Starting weights range from two hundred to more than four hundred pounds, and over the course of the show candidates have lost more than one hundred pounds. The first season debuted in fall 2004 with almost ten million viewers, and drew sixteen million to the season 2 finale. It has since been franchised to more than twenty countries.

   Queer Eye for the Straight Guy aired on Bravo from 2003 to 2007, with considerable press attention and ratings success, attracting 1.64 million viewers for the first episode—Bravo's largest audience ever. It makes over usually heterosexual men including their wardrobe, grooming, cooking skills, home environment, and taste. The 2006 season dropped "For the Straight Guy" and worked with a broader constituency of gay men, women, heterosexual couples, and a female-to-male transgendered person. *Queer Eye* won an Emmy in 2004.

   Starting Over was a three-season series developed by Bunim/Murray Productions, producers of MTV's *Real World* and *Road Rules*. Debuting in September 2003 as part of NBC's daytime schedule, the show brought the producers' experience with residential, interpersonal reality series together with discourses of self-help associated with talk shows such as *The Oprah Winfrey Show*. Initially based in Chicago and moving to Los Angeles for the second and third seasons, *Starting Over* brought six women into a house to work with life coaches and a psychotherapist. As each woman was deemed ready to "start over" in the outside world, she underwent a one-day appearance makeover and graduated from the house, to be replaced by another woman in crisis. The first season of *Starting Over* drew 1.4 million viewers daily, half of them in the very desirable demographic of women aged eighteen to forty-nine years, and the show won a Daytime Emmy in 2005.

The American version of *What Not to Wear* debuted on The Learning Channel (TLC) in January 2003. It was based on the BBC show of the same name. The show takes a different candidate per episode, secretly films her (occasionally him), makes her take a hard look at her clothes and body on camera and in the notoriously unkind 360-degree mirror, teaches her new dressing rules, sends her out to shop, and then appraises the results before sending her to a reveal to friends and family. By the fall of 2003, the American version garnered 2.3 million viewers.

9. Grindstaff, "Just Be Yourself, Only More So."
10. Heller, *Great American Makeover.*
11. Sender, "Queens for a Day."
12. Sender, *Business, Not Politics.*
13. Ouellette, "Take Responsibility for Yourself'; Ouellette and Hay, *Better Living through Reality TV.* See also Raphael, "Political-Economic Origins of Reali-TV"; Madger, "Television 2.0"; Sennett, *The Culture of the New Capitalism.*
14. Foucault, "Governmentality"; Rose, *Governing the Soul.*
15. Miller, *Well-Tempered Self.*
16. Ouellette and Hay, *Better Living through Reality TV,* 6.
17. Weber, *Makeover TV,* 257.
18. Redden, "Economy and Reflexivity in Makeover Television," 490.
19. See, for example, Radway, *Reading the Romance*; Press, *Women Watching Television*; Ang, *Watching Dallas.*
20. See, for example, Ang, *Watching Dallas*; Bird, *Audience in Everyday Life*; Hall, "Encoding/Decoding"; Livingstone, *Making Sense of Television*; Morley, *Nationwide Audience*; Press, *Women Watching Television*; Radway, *Reading the Romance.*
21. Ang, *Desperately Seeking the Audience*; Bird, *Audience in Everyday Life*; Skeggs, Thumim, and Wood, "Oh Goodness, I *Am* Watching Reality TV."
22. For reality television generally, see Hill, *Reality TV*; Hill, *Restyling Factual TV.* For lifestyle television, see Skeggs, Thumim, and Wood, "Oh Goodness, I *Am* Watching Reality TV"; Skeggs and Wood, "Labour of Transformation and Circuits of Value 'around' Reality Television"; Wood and Skeggs, "Spectacular Morality."
23. Alasuutari, "Introduction: Three Phases of Reception Studies."
24. Taylor, *Sources of the Self.*
25. Cary, *Augustine's Invention of the Inner Self.*
26. Taylor, *Sources of the Self,* 390.
27. Foucault, *History of Sexuality, Volume 1.*
28. Rose, *Governing the Soul,* viii.
29. Ibid., 222.
30. Ibid., 218.
31. Taylor, *Sources of the Self,* 287.
32. Turner, *Ordinary People and the Media,* 3.
33. Giddens, *Modernity and Self-Identity,* 3.
34. Ibid., 78.
35. Dubrofsky, "Therapeutics of the Self," 266.
36. Beck, Giddens, and Lash, "Replies and Critiques," 174.
37. Skeggs, "Moral Economy of Person Production," 633. See, for example, Rieff, *The Triumph of the Therapeutic*; Lears, *No Place of Grace.*

38. Skeggs, "Moral Economy of Person Production," 627.
39. Hill, *Reality TV*; Corner, "Performing the Real."
40. See, for example, Van Maanen, *Tales of the Field*; and Hammersley and Atkinson, *Ethnography* for an overview.
41. Bourdieu and Wacquant, *Towards a Reflexive Sociology*, 36, 214.
42. Ibid., 40.
43. Ibid.
44. Ibid., 215.
45. Gramsci, *Prison Notebooks*.
46. Adkins, "Reflexivity," 22.
47. Radway, *Reading the Romance*; Berlant, "Cruel Optimism."
48. Berlant, *Female Complaint*, x.
49. Skeggs, Thumim, and Wood, "Oh Goodness, I *Am* Watching Reality TV," 6.
50. Weber, *Makeover TV*, 5.
51. Ang, *Watching Dallas*.

NOTES TO CHAPTER 2
1. Sender, "Queens for a Day."
2. Beauvoir, *Second Sex*.
3. Bourdieu, *Distinction*.
4. See, for example, McRobbie, "Notes on *W* l *at Not to Wear* and Post-feminist Symbolic Violence"; Weber, *Makeover TV*.
5. Berlant, *Female Complaint*.
6. Ibid., x.
7. Ibid., 5.
8. Ibid.
9. Heller, *Great American Makeover*.
10. Woodstock, "Cure without Communication," 155.
11. Gurley Brown, *Having It All*; Norwood, *Women Who Love Too Much*.
12. Marketdata Enterprises, "Self-Improvement Market Shifts to Digital, Audio, and Online," press release, November 23, 2010, retrieved March 2, 2011, from http://www.marketdataenterprises.com/.
13. Wood, Skeggs, and Thumim, "It's Just Sad," 137.
14. Livingstone, *Making Sense of Television*, 53.
15. White, *Tele-advising*, 16.
16. Grindstaff, *Money Shot*.
17. Ibid., 19.
18. Gamson, *Freaks Talk Back*.
19. Peiss, *Hope in a Jar*, 144.
20. Moseley, "Makeover Takeover on British Television," 301.
21. See, for example, Weber, *Makeover TV*, 25.
22. Hochschild, *Commercialization of Intimate Life*.
23. White, *Tele-advising*, 55.
24. McRobbie, "Notes on *What Not to Wear* and Post-feminist Symbolic Violence"; Palmer, "The New You."
25. Skeggs, "Moral Economy of Person Production," 627.
26. Bourdieu, *Distinction*.

27. DeBeaumont, "Occupational Differences in the Wage Penalty for Obese Women."
28. Sender and Sullivan, "Epidemics of Will, Failures of Self-Esteem."
29. McRobbie, "Notes on *What Not to Wear* and Post-feminist Symbolic Violence," 106.
30. Ibid., 106.
31. Palmer, "The New You," 189.
32. Schwartz and Brownell, "Obesity and Body Image"; Davis et al., "Racial and Socioeconomic Differences in the Weight-Loss Experiences of Obese Women."
33. Weber, *Makeover TV*, 5.
34. Kelly and London, *Dress Your Best*.
35. Roberts, "Fashion Police," 229.
36. McRobbie, "Notes on *What Not to Wear* and Post-feminist Symbolic Violence," 107.
37. Breazeale, "In Spite of Women."
38. Allen et al., *Queer Eye for the Straight Guy*; Douglas, *Beautified*; Allen, *Food You Want to Eat*.
39. Learmonth, "NBC Feasts on 'Loser' Tie-ins."
40. See, for example, Britten, *Fearless Living*; Vanzant, *One Day My Soul Just Opened Up*.
41. See, for example, Peiss's discussion in *Hope in a Jar* of suspicion about women's use of makeup in the early twentieth century.
42. Cassidy, "Cinderella Makeover," 135.
43. Ibid., 136.
44. Berlant, *Female Complaint*, viii.
45. Kavka, *Reality Television, Affect, and Intimacy*, xi.
46. Bordo, *Male Body*.
47. Illouz, *Cold Intimacies*, 5.
48. Illouz, *Oprah Winfrey and the Glamour of Misery*, 136; Hochschild, *Commercialization of Intimate life*.
49. Berlant, *Female Complaint*, 170.
50. Grindstaff, *Money Shot*.
51. Andrejevic, "Real-izing Exploitation."
52. Ibid., 24.

NOTES TO CHAPTER 3

1. See Hill, *Reality TV* for a discussion of the impact of public service broadcasting on British reality shows and their reception.
2. Ibid., 93–94.
3. Ouellette, "Take Responsibility for Yourself"; Ouellette and Hay, *Better Living through Reality TV*.
4. See Weber, *Makeover TV*; Miller, *Well-Tempered Self*, xiv.
5. This and other *Starting Over* comments should be regarded in light of the suspected cancellation of the series as we were conducting interviews. Some respondents seemed to think we were doing market research for the production company, or had some power to influence the company to revive the series. As a result, the data are likely to be skewed in a positive direction, with negative criticism being reserved in favor of giving the best impression of the show. Given the value placed on education, especially educational television (as Hill discusses in relation to the "idea of learning" in *Reality TV*), *Starting Over*'s educational value might be more emphasized here than had we conducted interviews

while the series was ongoing. I discuss the methodological implications of this in chapter 7.

6. Ouellette, "Take Responsibility for Yourself," 232.

7. See, for example, Britten, *Fearless Living*; Vanzant, *One Day My Soul Just Opened Up*.

8. Hill, *Reality TV*, 85–86.

9. Sender, "Queens for a Day."

10. Hoover, Clark, and Alters, *Media, Home, and Family*, 45.

11. Sedgwick, *Epistemology of the Closet*.

12. Hills, *Fan Cultures*, 16–17.

13. Thornton, *Club Cultures*.

14. Grindstaff, *Money Shot*, 19.

15. Sender, *Business, Not Politics*.

16. Barthes, *Elements of Semiology*.

17. Schudson, *Advertising, the Uneasy Persuasion*.

NOTES TO CHAPTER 4

1. Rodman, "Bring on the 'Losers.'"

2. Turner, *Ordinary People and the Media*, 37.

3. Weber, *Makeover TV*, 89.

4. Mulvey, "Visual Pleasure and Narrative Cinema."

5. Gerbner and Gross, "Living with Television."

6. Andrejevic, *Reality TV.*

7. Wood and Skeggs, "Spectacular Morality," 180.

8. Kaufman, *Psychology of Shame*, 17.

9. Ahmed, *Cultural Politics of Emotion*, 106.

10. Sedgwick and Frank, "Shame in the Cybernetic Fold."

11. Walter Benjamin quoted in Probyn, *Blush*, 41.

12. Snorton, "Trapped in the [Epistemological] Closet."

13. Felski, "Nothing to Declare."

14. Halberstam, "Shame and White Gay Masculinity," 226.

15. John Portman quoted in Watts, "Queen for a Day," 147.

16. Sedgwick, "Shame, Theatricality, and Queer Performativity," 37.

17. Ouellette and Murray, "Introduction," 9.

18. Hall, "Viewers' Perceptions of Reality Programs," 204.

19. Wood, Skeggs, and Thumim, "It's Just Sad."

20. Goffman, *Presentation of Self in Everyday Life*, 8.

21. Probyn, *Blush*.

22. McRobbie, "Notes on *What Not to Wear* and Post-feminist Symbolic Violence," 100.

23. Wood, Skeggs, and Thumim, "It's Just Sad," 144.

24. Hochschild, *Commercialization of Intimate Life*.

25. Cosmetic surgery shows were not included among the four shows we focused on for this study because there were no new episodes of these shows airing during our data collection phase. However, we were interested to talk to people about their perceptions of this subgenre of makeover television, especially in comparison to the non-surgery shows included here.

26. Paul, Salwen, and Dupagne, "Third-Person Effect."

27. *Celebrity Fit Club*, a competitive weight loss show that featured celebrity has-beens, aired in the United States on VH1 from 2005 to 2010.

28. Palmer, "The New You," 183.

NOTES TO CHAPTER 5

1. Nichols, *Representing Reality*, 165–66.

2. Ibid., 165.

3. Ibid., 167.

4. Hall, "Reading Realism."

5. Ang, *Watching Dallas*.

6. Corner, "Performing the Real," 62.

7. Ibid.

8. Hill, *Restyling Factual TV*, 110.

9. Ibid., 140.

10. Andrejevic, "Watching Television Without Pity," 26.

11. Ibid., 38.

12. Smythe, "Communications."

13. Corner, "Performing the Real"; Hill, *Reality TV*; Hill, *Restyling Factual TV*.

14. See Cardo, "Voting Is Easy, Just Press the Red Button" for a discussion of the diary room in *Big Brother* as a special place where contestants reveal their "true" feelings and political strategies directly to audiences.

15. Martin Montgomery quoted in Hill, *Reality TV*, 75.

16. Sontag, *Illness as Metaphor*.

17. Ibid., 47.

18. Ang, *Watching Dallas*, 36.

19. Ibid., 45, alluding to the work of Raymond Williams.

20. Ibid., 33.

21. Grindstaff, *Money Shot*, 71, 19.

22. Ibid., 72.

23. Ibid., 97.

24. Ibid., 252.

25. Kavka, "Changing Properties," 42.

26. Ibid., 27.

27. Nichols, *Representing Reality*, 156.

28. Skeggs and Wood, "Labour of Transformation and Circuits of Value 'around' Reality Television," 568.

29. Hochschild, *Commercialization of Intimate Life*, 82.

30. Ibid., 83.

31. Grindstaff, *Money Shot*, 27.

32. Ibid.

33. Bunim/Murray Productions, retrieved March 18, 2009, from http://www.bunim-murray.com/.

34. Grindstaff, "Just Be Yourself, Only More So," 49.

35. Nichols, *Representing Reality*, 156.

36. Kavka, *Reality Television, Affect, and Intimacy*.

37. Ibid., 5.

38. Ibid., 22.

39. Corner, "Performing the Real."

NOTES TO CHAPTER 6

1. Cary, *Augustine's Invention of the Inner Self*, 9.
2. Baumeister, "How the Self Became a Problem," 165.
3. Ibid.
4. Taylor, *Sources of the Self*, 389.
5. Beck, Giddens, and Lash, *Reflexive Modernization*.
6. Giddens, *Modernity and Self-Identity*, 52.
7. Berne, *Games People Play*; Bradshaw, *Homecoming*.
8. Gagnon, "The Self, Its Voices, and Their Discord," 224.
9. Taylor, *Sources of the Self*, 362.
10. Gagnon, "The Self, Its Voices, and Their Discord."
11. Foucault, *History of Sexuality, Volume 3*, 56.
12. Ursula Gestefeld quoted in Griffith, *Born Again Bodies*, 84.
13. Sedgwick, *Tendencies*, 130; Sender and Sullivan, "Epidemics of Will."
14. Quoted in Stearns, *Fat History*, 22.
15. Griffith, *Born Again Bodies*, 47.
16. Sontag, *Illness as Metaphor*.
17. The *American Spectator* quoted in LeBesco, *Revolting Bodies?*, 55.
18. Ibid., 55.
19. Prosser, *Second Skins*, 69.
20. Ibid., 79.
21. Peiss, *Hope in a Jar*, 26.
22. On race and attractiveness, see ibid.; on ethnic anonymity, see Weber, *Makeover TV*, 5.
23. Wilson, "Vilifying Former Fatties," 253.
24. Dubrofsky, "Therapeutics of the Self," 278.
25. *New Yorker*, December 10, 2007, 92.
26. Taylor, *Sources of the Self*, 288–89.
27. Giddens, *Modernity and Self-Identity*, 5.
28. Bratich, "Programming Reality," 17.
29. Ibid., 18.
30. Illouz, *Oprah Winfrey and the Glamour of Misery*, 111.
31. Illouz, *Cold Intimacies*, 37.
32. Miller and McHoul, "Helping the Self," 148.
33. Livingstone, *Making Sense of Television*, 76.
34. Jenkins, *Convergence Culture*.
35. Andrejevic, *Reality TV*, 97.
36. Ibid., 2.
37. Giddens, *Modernity and Self-Identity*, 80.
38. Granberg, "Is That All There Is?," 112.
39. Foucault, *History of Sexuality, Volume 1*; Rose, *Governing the Soul*; Prosser, *Second Skins*.
40. Rimke, "Governing Citizens through Self-Help Literature," 70.
41. Giddens, *Modernity and Self-Identity*; Beck, Giddens, and Lash, *Reflexive Modernization*.
42. Grimes, "Ritual and the Media," 228.
43. Bourdieu, *Distinction*.
44. Marvin and Ingle, *Blood Sacrifice and the Nation*.

45. Durkheim, *Elementary Forms of Religious Life.*

46. David Chaney quoted in Couldry, *Media Rituals,* 57.

47. Marvin and Ingle, *Blood Sacrifice and the Nation.*

48. Couldry, *Media Rituals,* 7.

49. Foucault, *History of Sexuality, Volume 1,* 36.

50. Ibid., 42.

51. Ibid., 43.

52. Andrejevic, *Reality TV,* 145.

53. Foucault, *History of Sexuality, Volume 1,* 48.

NOTES TO CHAPTER 7

1. Seiter, *Television and New Media Audiences,* 59.

2. For an overview, see Bird, *Audience in Everyday Life.*

3. Ibid., 165.

4. Kenneth Burke quoted in ibid., 167.

5. Skeggs and Wood, "Labour of Transformation and Circuits of Value 'around' Reality Television"; Skeggs, Thumim, and Wood, "Oh Goodness, I *Am* Watching Reality TV"; Wood and Skeggs, "Spectacular Morality."

6. Skeggs, Thumim, and Wood, "Oh Goodness, I *Am* Watching Reality TV," 15.

7. Ang, *Watching Dallas.*

8. Hall, "Encoding/Decoding."

9. Hoover, Clark, and Alters, *Media, Home, and Family,* 75.

10. Ibid.

11. Ibid., 148.

12. Hall, "Encoding/Decoding." See also Morley, *Nationwide Audience.*

13. Press, *Women Watching Television*; Seiter, *Television and New Media Audiences*; Skeggs, Thumim, and Wood, "Oh Goodness, I *Am* Watching Reality TV."

14. Skeggs, Thumim, and Wood, "Oh Goodness, I *Am* Watching Reality TV"; Skeggs and Wood, "Labour of Transformation and Circuits of Value 'around' Reality Television"; Wood and Skeggs, "Spectacular Morality."

15. Skeggs, Thumim, and Wood, "Oh Goodness, I *Am* Watching Reality TV," 18.

16. Alasuutari, "Introduction: Three Phases of Reception Studies."

17. Hall, "Encoding/Decoding." This phase is exemplified, for example, in Morley, *Nationwide Audience.*

18. Alasuutari, "Introduction: Three Phases of Reception Studies," 5. For an example of this approach, see Gray, *Video Playtime.*

19. For example, romance novels (Radway, *Reading the Romance*) and soap operas (Ang, *Watching Dallas*).

20. Alasuutari, "Introduction: Three Phases of Reception Studies," 15.

21. Ibid.

22. Giddens, *Modernity and Self-Identity.*

23. Seiter, *Television and New Media Audiences,* 132.

24. Skeggs, Thumim, and Wood, "Oh Goodness, I *Am* Watching Reality TV," 7.

25. Seiter, *Television and New Media Audiences.*

26. Bird, *Audience in Everyday Life.*

27. Wood, *Talking with Television.*

28. Hammersley and Atkinson, *Ethnography.*

29. Foucault, *History of Sexuality, Volume 1*.
30. Skeggs, "Moral Economy of Person Production," 636.

NOTES TO CHAPTER 8

1. Corner, "Performing the Real"; Hill, *Reality TV*; Hill, *Restyling Factual TV*.
2. Andrejevic, "Watching Television Without Pity."
3. Seiter, *Television and New Media Audiences*; Skeggs, Thumim, and Wood, "Oh Goodness, I *Am* Watching Reality TV."
4. See Bird, *Audience in Everyday Life* for an overview.
5. Ang, *Desperately Seeking the Audience*.
6. Alasuutari, "Introduction: Three Phases of Reception Studies."
7. Fiske, "Critical Responses"; Morley, "Active Audience Theory."
8. Bird, *Audience in Everyday Life*, 172.
9. Barthes, *Elements of Semiology*.
10. Beck, Giddens, and Lash, *Reflexive Modernization*; Bourdieu and Wacquant, *Towards a Reflexive Sociology*; Nichols, *Introduction to Documentary*.
11. Lazzarato, "Immaterial Labour."
12. Hochschild, *Commercialization of Intimate Life*, 102
13. Wood, Skeggs, and Thumim, "It's Just Sad," 136.
14. Radway, *Reading the Romance*, 12.
15. Illouz, *Cold Intimacies*.
16. Ibid., 37.
17. Rose, *Governing the Soul*, 11.
18. Willett, *Brecht on Theatre*.
19. Polan, "Brecht and the Politics of Self-Reflexive Cinema."
20. Berlant, *Female Complaint*, 19.
21. Ang, *Watching Dallas*; Kavka, *Reality Television*; Radway, *Reading the Romance*.
22. Radway, *Reading the Romance*, 215.
23. Dyer, "Entertainment and Utopia," 4–5.
24. Ibid., 7.
25. Ibid., 8.
26. Ang, *Watching Dallas*, 46.
27. Ibid.; Radway, *Reading the Romance*.
28. Cvetkovich, *Archive of Feelings*; Love, *Feeling Backward*.
29. "How to Look Good Naked," retrieved June 5, 2011, from http://www.mylifetime.com/.
30. Cruikshank, "Revolutions Within."

Adkins, Lisa. "Reflexivity: Freedom or Habit of Gender?" *Theory, Culture, and Society* 20, no. 6 (2003): 21–42.

Ahmed, Sara. *The Cultural Politics of Emotion*. Edinburgh: Edinburgh University Press, 2004.

Alasuutari, Pertti. "Introduction: Three Phases of Reception Studies." In *Rethinking the Media Audience*, edited by Pertti Alasuutari, 1–21. London: Sage, 1999.

Allen, Ted. *The Food You Want to Eat: 100 Smart, Simple Recipes*. New York: Clarkson Potter, 2005.

Allen, Ted, Kyan Douglas, Thom Filicia, Carson Kressley, and Jai Rodriguez. *Queer Eye for the Straight Guy: The Fab 5's Guide to Looking Better, Cooking Better, Dressing Better, Behaving Better, and Living Better*. New York: Clarkson Potter, 2004.

Andrejevic, Mark. "Real-izing Exploitation." In *The Politics of Reality Television: Global Perspectives*, edited by Marwan Kraidy and Katherine Sender, 18–30. New York: Routledge, 2011.

——. *Reality TV: The Work of Being Watched*. New York: Rowman and Littlefield, 2004.

——. "Watching Television Without Pity: The Productivity of Online Fans." *Television and New Media* 9, no. 1 (2008): 24–46.

Ang, Ien. *Desperately Seeking the Audience*. New York: Routledge, 1991.

——. *Watching Dallas: Soap Opera and the Melodramatic Imagination*. Translated by Della Couling. New York: Methuen, 1985.

Barthes, Roland. *Elements of Semiology*. Translated by Annette Lavers and Colin Smith. London: Cape, 1967.

Baumeister, Roy F. "How the Self Became a Problem: A Psychological Review of Historical Research." *Journal of Personality and Social Psychology* 52, no. 1 (1987): 163–76.

Beauvoir, Simone de. *The Second Sex*. Translated by Margaret Crosland. New York: Knopf, 1993.

Beck, Ulrich, Anthony Giddens, and Scott Lash, eds. *Reflexive Modernization: Politics, Tradition, and Aesthetics in the Modern Social Order*. Cambridge, MA: Polity Press, 1994.

——. "Replies and Critiques." In *Reflexive Modernization: Politics, Tradition, and Aesthetics in the Modern Social Order*, edited by Ulrich Beck, Anthony Giddens, and Scott Lash, 174–215. Cambridge, MA: Polity Press, 1994.

Berlant, Lauren. "Cruel Optimism." *Differences* 17, no. 3 (2006): 20–36.

——. *The Female Complaint: The Unfinished Business of Sentimentality in American Culture*. Durham: Duke University Press, 2008.

Berne, Eric. *Games People Play: The Psychology of Human Relationships*. New York: Grove Press, 1964.

Bird, S. Elizabeth. *The Audience in Everyday Life: Living in a Media World*. New York: Routledge, 2003.

Biressi, Anita, and Heather Nunn. *Reality TV: Realism and Revelation*. London: Wallflower
Press, 2005.

Bordo, Susan. *The Male Body: A New Look at Men in Public and in Private*. New York: Far-
rar, Strauss and Giroux, 1999.

Bourdieu, Pierre. *Distinction: A Social Critique of the Judgement of Taste*. Translated by
Richard Nice. Cambridge: Harvard University Press, 1984.

Bourdieu, Pierre, and Loïc J. D. Wacquant. *Towards a Reflexive Sociology*. Chicago: University of Chicago Press, 1992.

Bradshaw, John. *Homecoming: Reclaiming and Championing Your Inner Child*. New York:
Bantam, 1990.

Bratich, Jack Z. "Programming Reality: Control Societies, New Subjects, and the Powers of
Transformation." In *Makeover Television: Realities Remodelled*, edited by Dana Heller,
6–22. New York: I. B. Tauris, 2007.

Breazeale, Kenon. "In Spite of Women: *Esquire* Magazine and the Construction of the Male
Consumer." *Signs* 20, no. 1 (1994): 1–22.

Britten, Rhonda. *Fearless Living: Live without Excuses and Love without Regret*. New York:
Perigee, 2002.

Cardo, Valentina. "'Voting Is Easy, Just Press the Red Button': Communicating Politics in the
Age of *Big Brother*." In *Political Communication in Postmodern Democracy: Challenging
the Primacy of Politics*, edited by Kees Brants and Katrin Voltmer, 231–47. New York:
Palgrave, 2011.

Cary, Phillip. *Augustine's Invention of the Inner Self: The Legacy of a Christian Platonist*.
Oxford: Oxford University Press, 2000.

Cassidy, Marsha F. "The Cinderella Makeover: *Glamour Girl*, Television Misery Shows, and
1950s Femininity." In *The Great American Makeover: Television, History, Nation*, edited
by Dana Heller, 125–40. New York: Palgrave, 2006.

Corner, John. "Performing the Real: Documentary Diversions." In *Reality TV: Remaking
Television Culture*, edited by Susan Murray and Laurie Ouellette, 44–64. New York: New
York University Press, 2009.

Couldry, Nick. *Media Rituals: A Critical Approach*. New York: Routledge, 2003.

Cruikshank, Barbara. "Revolutions Within: Self-Government and Self-Esteem." In *Foucault
and Political Reason: Liberalism, Neo-liberalism, and Rationalities of Government*, edited
by Andrew Barry, Thomas Osborne, and Nikolas Rose, 231–51. Chicago: University of
Chicago Press, 1996.

Cvetkovich, Ann. *An Archive of Feelings: Trauma, Sexuality, and Lesbian Public Cultures*.
Durham: Duke University Press, 2003.

Davis, Esa M., Jeanne M. Clark, Joseph A. Carrese, Tiffany L. Gary, and Lisa A. Cooper.
"Racial and Socioeconomic Differences in the Weight-Loss Experiences of Obese
Women." *American Journal of Public Health* 95, no. 9 (2005): 1539–43.

DeBeaumont, Ronald. "Occupational Differences in the Wage Penalty for Obese Women."
Journal of Socioeconomics 38 (2009): 344–49.

Douglas, Kyan. *Beautified: Secrets for Women to Look Great and Feel Fabulous*. New York:
Clarkson Potter, 2004.

Dubrofsky, Rachel E. "Therapeutics of the Self: Surveillance in the Service of the Therapeutic." *Television and New Media* 4, no. 4 (2007): 263–84.

Durkheim, Émile. *The Elementary Forms of Religious Life.* Translated by Carol Cosman. New York: Oxford University Press, 2001 [1912].

Dyer, Richard. "Entertainment and Utopia." *Movie* 24 (1977): 2–13.

Felski, Rita. "Nothing to Declare: Identity, Shame, and the Lower Middle Class." In *Doing Time: Feminist Theory and Postmodern Culture,* edited by Rita Felski, 33–54. New York: New York University Press, 2000.

Fiske, John. "Critical Responses: Meaningful Moments." *Critical Studies in Mass Communication* 5, no. 3 (1988): 246–51.

Foucault, Michel. "Governmentality." In *The Foucault Effect: Studies in Governmentality,* edited by Graham Burchell, Colin Gordon, and Peter Miller, 87–104. Chicago: University of Chicago Press, 1991.

———. *The History of Sexuality, Volume 1: An Introduction.* Translated by Robert Hurley. New York: Penguin, 1978.

———. *The History of Sexuality, Volume 3: The Care of the Self.* Translated by Robert Hurley. New York: Vintage, 1986.

Gagnon, John H. "The Self, Its Voices, and Their Discord." In *Investigating Subjectivity,* edited by Carolyn Ellis and Michael Flaherty, 221–43. Newbury Park, CA: Sage, 1992.

Gamson, Joshua. *Freaks Talk Back: Tabloid Talk Shows and Sexual Nonconformity.* Chicago: University of Chicago Press, 1998.

Gerbner, George, and Larry Gross. "Living with Television: The Violence Profile." *Journal of Communication* 26, no. 2 (1976): 172–99.

Giddens, Anthony. *Modernity and Self-Identity: Self and Society in the Late Modern Age.* Stanford: Stanford University Press, 1991.

Goffman, Erving. *The Presentation of Self in Everyday Life.* New York: Doubleday, 1959.

Gramsci, Antonio. *Prison Notebooks.* Translated by Joseph A. Buttigleg. New York: Columbia University Press, 1992.

Granberg, Ellen. "Is That All There Is? Possible Selves, Self-Change, and Weight Loss." *Social Psychology Quarterly* 69, no. 2 (2006): 109–26.

Gray, Ann. *Video Playtime: The Gendering of a Leisure Technology.* London: Routledge, 1992.

Griffith, R. Marie. *Born Again Bodies: Flesh and Spirit in American Christianity.* Berkeley: University of California Press, 2004.

Grimes, Ronald L. "Ritual and the Media." In *Practicing Religion in the Age of Media: Explorations in Media, Religion, and Culture,* edited by Stewart M. Hoover and Lynn S. Clark, 219–34. New York: Columbia University Press, 2002.

Grindstaff, Laura. "Just Be Yourself, Only More So: Ordinary Celebrity in the Era of Self-Service Television." In *Real Worlds: The Global Politics of Reality TV,* edited by Marwan Kraidy and Katherine Sender, 44–58. New York: Routledge, 2011.

———. *Money Shot: Trash, Class, and the Making of TV Talk Shows.* Chicago: University of Chicago Press, 2002.

Gurley Brown, Helen. *Having It All.* New York: Simon and Schuster, 1982.

Halberstam, Judith. "Shame and White Gay Masculinity." *Social Text* 23, nos. 3–4 (2005): 219–33.

Hall, Alice. "Reading Realism: Audiences' Perceptions of the Realism of Media Texts." *Journal of Communication* 53, no. 4 (2003): 624–41.

———. "Viewers' Perceptions of Reality Programs." *Communication Quarterly* 54, no. 2 (2006): 191–211.

Hall, Stuart. "Encoding/Decoding." In *Culture, Media, Language: Working Papers in Cultural Studies*, edited by Stuart Hall, Dorothy Hobson, Andrew Lowe, and Paul Willis, 128–38. London: Hutchinson, 1980.

Hammersley, Martyn, and Paul Atkinson. *Ethnography: Principles in Practice*. 3rd ed. New York: Routledge, 2007.

Heller, Dana, ed. *The Great American Makeover: Television, History, Nation*. New York: Palgrave Macmillan, 2006.

Hill, Annette. *Reality TV: Audiences and Popular Factual Television*. New York: Routledge, 2005.

———. *Restyling Factual TV: Audiences and News, Documentary, and Reality Genres*. London: Routledge, 2007.

Hills, Matt. *Fan Cultures*. New York: Routledge, 2002.

Hochschild, Arlie Russell. *The Commercialization of Intimate Life: Notes from Home and Work*. Berkeley: University of California Press, 2003.

Hoover, Stewart M., Lynn Schofield Clark, and Diane F. Alters. *Media, Home, and Family*. New York: Routledge, 2004.

Illouz, Eva. *Cold Intimacies: The Making of Emotional Capitalism*. Malden, MA: Polity, 2007.

———. *Oprah Winfrey and the Glamour of Misery: An Essay on Popular Culture*. New York: Columbia University Press, 2003.

Jenkins, Henry. *Convergence Culture: Where Old and New Media Collide*. New York: New York University Press, 2006.

Kaufman, Gershen. *The Psychology of Shame: Theory and Treatment of Shame-Based Syndromes*. New York: Springer, 1989.

Kavka, Misha. "Changing Properties: The Makeover Show Crosses the Atlantic." In *The Great American Makeover: Television, History, Nation*, edited by Dana Heller, 211–30. New York: Palgrave, 2006.

———. *Reality Television, Affect, and Intimacy: Reality Matters*. New York: Palgrave Macmillan, 2008.

Kelly, Clinton, and Stacey London. *Dress Your Best: The Complete Guide to Finding the Style That's Right for Your Body*. New York: Three Rivers Press, 2005.

Lazzarato, Maurizio. "Immaterial Labour." In *Radical Thought in Italy: A Potential Politics*, edited by Michael Hardt and Paolo Virno, 133–50. Minneapolis: University of Minnesota Press, 1996.

Learmonth, Michael. "NBC Feasts on 'Loser' Tie-ins." *Variety*, December 5, 2005.

Lears, Jackson. *No Place of Grace: Antimodernism and the Transformation of American Culture, 1990–1920*. New York: Pantheon, 1981.

LeBesco, Kathleen. *Revolting Bodies? The Struggle to Redefine Fat Identity*. Amherst, MA: University of Massachusetts Press, 2004.

Livingstone, Sonia. *Making Sense of Television: The Psychology of Audience Interpretation*. 2nd ed. New York: Routledge, 1998.

Love, Heather. *Feeling Backward: Loss and the Politics of Queer History*. Cambridge: Harvard University Press, 2007.

Madger, Ted. "Television 2.0: The Business of American Television in Transition." In *Reality TV: Remaking Television Culture*, edited by Susan Murray and Laurie Ouellette, 141–64. New York: New York University Press, 2009.

Marvin, Carolyn, and David Ingle. *Blood Sacrifice and the Nation: Totem Rituals and the American Flag*. Cambridge: Cambridge University Press, 1999.

McRobbie, Angela. "Notes on *What Not to Wear* and Post-feminist Symbolic Violence." In *Feminism after Bourdieu*, edited by Lisa Adkins and Beverley Skeggs, 99–109. Malden, MA: Blackwell, 2004.

Miller, Toby. *The Well-Tempered Self: Citizenship, Culture, and the Postmodern Subject*. Baltimore: Johns Hopkins University Press, 1993.

Miller, Toby, and Alec McHoul. "Helping the Self." *Social Text* 57, no. 4 (1998): 127–55.

Morley, David. "Active Audience Theory: Pendulums and Pitfalls." *Journal of Communication* 43, no. 4 (1993): 13–19.

———. *The Nationwide Audience*. London: British Film Institute, 1980.

Moseley, Rachel. "Makeover Takeover on British Television." *Screen* 41, no. 3 (2000): 299–314.

Mulvey, Laura. "Visual Pleasure and Narrative Cinema." *Screen* 16, no. 3 (1975): 6–18.

Murray, Susan, and Laurie Ouellette, eds. *Reality TV: Remaking Television Culture*. 2nd ed. New York: New York University Press, 2009.

Nichols, Bill. *Introduction to Documentary*. Bloomington: Indiana University Press, 2001.

———. *Representing Reality: Issues and Concepts in Documentary*. Bloomington: Indiana University Press, 1991.

Norwood, Robin. *Women Who Love Too Much: When You Keep Hoping and Wishing He'll Change*. New York: Pocket, 1985.

Ouellette, Laurie. "'Take Responsibility for Yourself': *Judge Judy* and the Neoliberal Citizen." In *Reality TV: Remaking Television Culture*, edited by Susan Murray and Laurie Ouellette, 231–50. New York: New York University Press, 2004.

Ouellette, Laurie, and James Hay. *Better Living through Reality TV: Television and Postwelfare Citizenship*. Malden, MA: Blackwell, 2008.

Ouellette, Laurie, and Susan Murray. "Introduction." In *Reality TV: Remaking Television Culture*, edited by Susan Murray and Laurie Ouellette, 1–22. New York: New York University Press, 2009.

Palmer, Gareth. *Exposing Lifestyle Television: The Big Reveal*. Aldershot, UK: Ashgate, 2008.

———. "'The New You': Class and Transformation in Lifestyle Television." In *Understanding Reality Television*, edited by Su Holmes and Deborah Jermyn, 173–90. New York: Routledge, 2004.

Paul, Bryant, Michael B. Salwen, and Michael Dupagne. "The Third-Person Effect: A Meta-analysis of the Perceptual Hypothesis." *Mass Communication and Society* 3, no. 1 (2000): 57–85.

Peiss, Kathy. *Hope in a Jar: The Making of America's Beauty Culture*. New York: Metropolitan/Henry Holt, 1998.

Polan, Dana. "Brecht and the Politics of Self-Reflexive Cinema." *Jump Cut* 1 (1974). Retrieved June 30, 2011, from http://www.ejumpcut.org/.

Press, Andrea. *Women Watching Television*. Philadelphia: University of Pennsylvania Press, 1991.

Probyn, Elspeth. *Blush: Faces of Shame*. Minneapolis: University of Minnesota Press, 2005.

Prosser, Jay. *Second Skins: The Body Narratives of Transsexuality*. New York: Columbia University Press, 1998.

Radway, Janice. *Reading the Romance: Women, Patriarchy, and Popular Literature*. Chapel Hill: University of North Carolina Press, 1984.

Raphael, Chad. "The Political Economic Origins of Reali-TV." In *Reality TV: Remaking Television Culture*, edited by Laurie Ouellette and Susan Murray, 123–40. New York: New York University Press, 2009.

Redden, Guy. "Economy and Reflexivity in Makeover Television." *Continuum* 22, no. 4 (2008): 485–94.

Rieff, Philip. *The Triumph of the Therapeutic: Uses of Faith after Freud.* New York: Harper and Row, 1966.

Rimke, Heidi Marie. "Governing Citizens through Self-Help Literature." *Cultural Studies* 14, no. 1 (2000): 61–78.

Roberts, Martin. "The Fashion Police: Governing the Self in 'What Not to Wear.'" In *Interrogating Postfeminism: Gender and the Politics of Popular Culture*, edited by Yvonne Tasker and Diane Negra, 227–48. Durham: Duke University Press, 2007.

Rodman, Sarah. "Bring on the 'Losers': New Reality Show Likes 'em Pathetic." *Boston Herald*, October 15, 2004.

Rose, Nikolas. "Governing 'Advanced' Liberal Democracies." In *Foucault and Political Reason: Liberalism, Neo-liberalism, and Rationalities of Government*, edited by Andrew Barry, Thomas Osborne, and Nikolas Rose, 37–64. Chicago: University of Chicago Press, 1996.

———. *Governing the Soul: The Shaping of the Private Self.* 2nd ed. New York: Routledge, 1999.

Schudson, Michael. *Advertising, the Uneasy Persuasion: Its Dubious Impact on American Society.* New York: Basic, 1984.

Schwartz, Marlene B., and Kelly D. Brownell. "Obesity and Body Image." *Body Image* 1, no. 1 (2004): 43–56.

Sedgwick, Eve Kosofsky. *Epistemology of the Closet.* Berkeley: University of California Press, 1990.

———. "Shame, Theatricality, and Queer Performativity: Henry James's 'The Art of the Novel.'" In *Touching Feeling: Affect, Pedagogy, Performativity*, edited by Eve Kosofsky Sedgwick, 35–66. Durham: Duke University Press, 2003.

———. *Tendencies.* Durham: Duke University Press, 1993.

Sedgwick, Eve Kosofsky, and Adam Frank. "Shame in the Cybernetic Fold: Reading Silvan Tomkins." In *Touching Feeling: Affect, Pedagogy, Performativity*, edited by Eve Kosofsky Sedgwick, 93–122. Durham: Duke University Press, 2003.

Seiter, Ellen. *Television and New Media Audiences.* New York: Oxford University Press, 1999.

Sender, Katherine. *Business, Not Politics: The Making of the Gay Market.* New York: Columbia University Press, 2004.

———. "Queens for a Day: *Queer Eye for the Straight Guy* and the Neoliberal Project." *Critical Studies in Media Communication* 23, no. 2 (2006): 131–51.

Sender, Katherine, and Margaret Sullivan. "Epidemics of Will, Failures of Self-Esteem: Responding to Fat Bodies in *The Biggest Loser* and *What Not to Wear.*" *Continuum* 22, no. 4 (2008): 573–84.

Sennett, Richard. *The Culture of the New Capitalism.* New Haven: Yale University Press, 2006.

Skeggs, Beverley. "The Moral Economy of Person Production: The Class Relations of Self-Performance on 'Reality' Television." *Sociological Review* 57, no. 4 (2009): 626–44.

Skeggs, Beverley, Nancy Thumim, and Helen Wood. "'Oh Goodness, I *Am* Watching Reality TV': How Methods Make Class in Audience Research." *European Journal of Cultural Studies* 11, no. 1 (2008): 5–24.

Skeggs, Beverley, and Helen Wood. "The Labour of Transformation and Circuits of Value 'around' Reality Television." *Continuum* 22, no. 4 (2008): 559–72.

Smythe, Dallas. "Communications: Blindspots of Western Marxism." *Canadian Journal of Political and Social Theory* 1, no. 3 (1977): 1–27.

Snorton, Riley. "Trapped in the [Epistemological] Closet: Black Sexuality and the Popular Imagination." PhD diss., University of Pennsylvania, 2010.

Sontag, Susan. *Illness as Metaphor; and, AIDS and Its Metaphors.* New York: Picador, 2001.

Stearns, Peter N. *Fat History: Bodies and Beauty in the Modern West.* New York: New York University Press, 2002.

Taylor, Charles. *Sources of the Self: The Making of the Modern Identity.* Cambridge: Harvard University Press, 1989.

Thornton, Sarah. *Club Cultures: Music, Media, and Subcultural Capital.* Hanover: Wesleyan University Press, 1996.

Turner, Graeme. *Ordinary People and the Media: The Demotic Turn.* London: Sage, 2010.

Van Maanen, John. *Tales of the Field: On Writing Ethnography.* Chicago: University of Chicago Press, 1988.

Vanzant, Iyanla. *One Day My Soul Just Opened Up: 40 Days and 40 Nights toward Spiritual Strength and Personal Growth.* New York: Fireside, 1998.

Watts, Amber. "Queen for a Day: Remaking Consumer Culture, One Woman at a Time." In *The Great American Makeover: Television, History, Nation,* edited by Dana Heller, 141–58. New York: Palgrave, 2006.

Weber, Brenda R. *Makeover TV: Selfhood, Citizenship, and Celebrity.* Durham: Duke University Press, 2009.

White, Mimi. *Tele-advising: Therapeutic Discourses in American Television.* Chapel Hill: University of North Carolina Press, 1992.

Willett, John, ed. and trans. *Brecht on Theatre.* New York: Hill and Wang, 1957.

Wilson, Natalie. "Vilifying Former Fatties: Media Representations of Weight Loss Surgery." *Feminist Media Studies* 5, no. 2 (2005): 252–57.

Wood, Helen. *Talking with Television: Women, Talk Shows, and Modern Self-Reflexivity.* Urbana: University of Illinois Press, 2009.

Wood, Helen, and Beverley Skeggs. "Spectacular Morality: 'Reality' Television, Individualisation, and the Remaking of the Working Class." In *The Media and Social Theory,* edited by David Hesmondhalgh and Jason Toynbee, 177–93. London: Routledge, 2008.

Wood, Helen, Beverley Skeggs, and Nancy Thumim. "'It's Just Sad': Affect, Judgement, and Emotional Labor in 'Reality' Television Viewing." In *Feminism, Domesticity, and Popular Culture,* edited by Stacy Gillis and Joanne Hollows, 135–50. London: Routledge, 2008.

Woodstock, Louise. "Cure without Communication: Self-Help Books and Popular Notions of Self and Communication, 1860–2000." PhD diss., University of Pennsylvania, 2002.

candidates of, 94–95, 99; before-and-after comparisons in, 31–32; candidate publicness on, 86; candidates, 12; canonical narratives of confession on, 161; cosmetic surgery in, 95–97, 223n25; crisis of self precipitated by, 138–39; emotional expressiveness produced on, 129–34; entertainment compared to learning from, 55; expansion of, 5–6; expertise gained from, 168; fairy tale narrative of, 153–54, 166; formulaic rituals repeated in, 158–59; habitus in, 37; humiliation on, 80–81, 104; identifying problems as problems in, 162–63; intimate public produced by, 45–46; learning and instruction from, 56; narratives of experiences from, 154–55, 158; negative view of, 165–66; online social engagement from, 60–67; product consumption from, 43; product placement complaints of, 72–73; professional expertise from, 66; profits generated by, 194; promises of, 198; racial differences referenced in, 38–39; realism critiques of, 175; reflexive engagement with, 187–88; reflexive representation limits of, 112–13; reflexive self from, 4, 17; reflexive self produced in, 184–85; reflexivity making sense of, 189; representational routines of, 23; Romantic ideas about self from, 203; schadenfreude and, 97–100; self cared for through, 195; self-expression in, 167–68; self-reflexivity types in, 174; self-transformation through, 196; Seth's comments on, 3–4; shame represented in, 83–84, 104; social uses of, 56–60; surveillance used in, 81–83, 100; talk show conventions used in, 31; transformation experience from, 12; visualizing techniques used in, 82; women's complaints on, 43–44; women-targeted media and, 21. *See also* Candidates; *specific shows*
Male makeovers, 70–71
Manipulation, 113
Marketing model, 72
Marvin, Carolyn, 159–60
Masculinity, 27
Mask metaphor, 146–47
McRobbie, Angela, 36, 38, 41, 88

Media: engagement, 173–74, 184; literacy, 18; psy disciplines produced through, 16; self-recognition and construction through, 17; self-reflexivity in, 156; social, 156–57; social bonds through, 56–57; women's engagement with, 46; women-targeted, 21
Media reflexivity, 77–79, 180, 187; of audience, 176; audiences social interactions facilitating, 111; emotional realism reinforced by, 106, 134–35
Melodrama, 197–98
Men: *The Biggest Loser* dealing with emotions of, 125; crying of, 125–27; emotional expression of, 124–29, 155–56; homophobic, 78; intimate consumption and self-care of, 27–28; self-reflexivity mobilized by, 178; women passing on tips to, 57–58
Message boards: audience expertise offered on, 66–67; personal anonymity on, 63; *What Not to Wear* information shared on, 61–62
Michaels, Jillian, 53
Middle class, 36, 174–75
Middle-class women, 174–75, 183
Miles (*Queer Eye* candidate), 27–28
Miller, Toby, 156
Minority groups, 82
Modern self, 15–17
Money shot, 31, 68, 129
Moral person, 141
Moral value, 140–41, 149, 150
Motivation, 52–53, 75
Mulvey, Laura, 81
Murray, Susan, 84
Musicals, 198

Narratives, 153; *The Biggest Loser* creating, 109; canonical, 161; of experiences, 154–55, 158; fairy tale, 153–54, 166; personal, 166–67; reality television's construction of, 6; transparent, 118
Neoliberalism, 52
Nichols, Bill, 106, 123, 134
Nonnormative sexual pleasure, 161–62
Normative citizenship, 77
Normative self, 8–9
Norwood, Robin, 30